Pneumatology

Pneumatology

The Holy Spirit in Ecumenical, International, and Contextual Perspective

Veli-Matti Kärkkäinen

Baker Academic
Grand Rapids, Michigan

© 2002 by Veli-Matti Kärkkäinen

Published by Baker Academic
a division of Baker Publishing Group
P.O. Box 6287, Grand Rapids, MI 49516-6287
www.bakeracademic.com

Fourth printing, January 2008

Printed in the United States of America

Library of Congress Cataloging-in-Publication Data
Kärkkäinen, Veli-Matti.
    Pneumatology : the Holy Spirit in ecumenical, international, and contextual
    perspective / Veli-Matti Kärkkäinen.
        p.   cm.
    Includes bibliographical references and index.
    ISBN 10: 0-8010-2448-X (pbk.)
    ISBN 978-0-8010-2448-1 (pbk.)
        1. Holy Spirit. I. Title.
    BT121.3.K37 2002
    231′.3—dc21   2001058959

Contents

Abbreviations

Comm	*Communio*
Greg	*Gregorianum*
TDNT	*Theological Dictionary of the New Testament,* ed. G. Kittel and G. Friedrich, trans. G. W. Bromiley, 10 vols. (Grand Rapids: Eerdmans, 1964–76).
SC	*Sources chrétiennes* (Paris: Cerf. 1943–).
TS	*Theological Studies*
Pneuma	*Pneuma: Journal of the Society for Pentecostal Studies*
WA	Standard abbreviation for the German/Latin original of Martin Luther's *Weimarer Ausgabe.*

Vatican II Documents

AA	*Apostolican Actuositatem*
LG	*Lumen Gentium*
UR	*Unitatis Redintegratio*

Preface

Any talk about the Spirit of God in the contemporary world, in my opinion, should be guided by two overarching principles. On the one hand, pneumatological discourse can be meaningful only insofar as it takes into account the diverse and rich variety of approaches to the experience of the Spirit ecumenically. No church can claim a monopoly on the Spirit, and no tradition is a specifically "spirited" one. Only by carefully listening to and learning from the various, often even conflicting, testimonies concerning the Spirit can we come to any kind of comprehensive understanding. On the other hand, talk about the Spirit must always be contextual and therefore culture specific. The Spirit of God is no general spirit hovering above the cosmos but a Person of the Triune God who indwells believers and creation in specific and tangible ways. Listening to the voices from places once considered the margins of Christian theology, such as the voices of women, or liberationists, or Green theologians, sensitizes us to the necessary pluralism of pneumatologies. Attention to the emerging voices of the Third World provides correctives to classical theology, not only because the growth of the Christian church is taking place outside the West but also because the vivid spiritual life of these voices is a greenhouse of new insights into old doctrines. While it is left to the reader to assess to what extent these two guiding principles have been followed in the present text, it is only appropriate for me to reveal what my intentions have been.

Living as we are amidst a pneumatological renaissance, books on the Spirit abound, and rightly so. Theology, which simply means reflection on the spiritual life and experience, usually develops by responding to

9

themes that are acutely felt in the church and society. Most books on pneumatology, especially those that are by nature textbooks, tend to be topical, discussing various aspects of pneumatology. The approach of the present book is different and complementary. Rather than focusing on any single topic, the aim is to chart the various territories of writings and reflections in the area of pneumatology. Consequently, we will look at various theological and denominational approaches to the understanding of the Spirit, single out some leading theologians' views, and also inquire into several contextual approaches. The purpose of the book is to offer an up-to-date survey of the most noteworthy and theologically pregnant orientations to the Spirit in the worldwide ecumenical and intercultural situation at the beginning of the third millennium.

Textbooks usually grow out of teaching experience, and this book is no exception to that rule. I have been fortunate to live, study, and teach in three different continents: Europe, where I originally come from and where I currently teach as visiting professor of ecumenics; Asia, where for several happy years I had the privilege of teaching in a college in a native language; and North America, specifically the United States, where my current full-time teaching position is in the field of systematics. My students, past and present, in these three continents, have not only challenged my thinking but also taught me about the richness of the Spirit experience more than they probably acknowledge themselves. It is therefore in gratitude and joy that I devote this book to all of them and commit myself as a lifelong co-learner with them.

Three academic mentors have shaped my understanding of theology and ecumenics in general and pneumatology in particular, and to them also I wish to express my heartfelt thanks: Professor (Emeritus) of Ecumenics, University of Helsinki, Dr. Tuomo Mannermaa, my *Doktorvater;* Professor (Emeritus) of Mission, University of Birmingham, Dr. Walter Hollenweger, the academic opponent at my doctoral defense; and Professor (Emeritus) of Theology, St. John's University, and President of Ecumenical and Cultural Research, Collegeville, Minnesota, Kilian McDonnell, OSB, the academic reader. Representing three Christian traditions, Catholic, Reformed, and Lutheran, and four different linguistic-cultural areas, Scandinavian, German/Swiss, British, and American, they have provided direction for my own theological work.

Finally, I am grateful to Susan Carlson Wood at Fuller Theological Seminary, Pasadena, California, for editing my foreign English to give this book a more readable style.

1

Introduction to Pneumatology as a Theological Discipline

A Pneumatological Renaissance

In recent years, one of the most exciting developments in theology has been an unprecedented interest in the Holy Spirit. A pneumatological renaissance concerning the doctrine and spirituality of the Holy Spirit has in these days stirred much interest and even enthusiasm from all theological corners. The reverberations can be felt everywhere from new theological studies in the academy to publications of popular books to the emergence of new spiritual orientations and movements such as green pneumatology or liberation pneumatology. The Catholic theologian Elizabeth Dreyer vividly describes this renewed enthusiasm over pneumatology:

> Renewed interest in the Holy Spirit is visible in at least three contexts: individual Christians who hunger for a deeper connection with God that is inclusive of all of life as well as the needs of the world; the church that seeks to renew itself through life-giving disciplines and a return to sources; and the formal inquiry of academic philosophy and theology. In effect, one can hear the petition, "Come Creator Spirit" on many lips these days.[1]

1. Elizabeth A. Dreyer, "Resources for a Renewed Life in the Spirit and Pneumatology: Medieval Mystics and Saints," in *Advent of the Spirit: Orientations in Pneumatology*, Conference Papers from a Symposium at Marquette University, 17–19 April 1998 (unpublished), 1.

While there may be several reasons for the resurgence of pneumatology, two reasons in theology and spirituality seem to be of decisive importance.[2] First, the entrance of the Eastern Orthodox churches into the official ecumenical organization, the World Council of Churches (WCC), has made the rich pneumatological and spiritual tradition of this ancient church family more easily available to other churches. The doctrine of the Spirit has always played a more prominent role in Eastern Orthodox theology, with roots in the classical works of Athanasius, Cyril of Alexandria, and Basil the Great. According to many Orthodox theologians, the Eastern church gives priority to pneumatology, and the Western to Christology, although both profess the same Trinitarian faith.[3] The Eastern tradition pays more attention to the Holy Spirit both in the doctrine of salvation and in ecclesiology.

Second, the dramatic spread of the Pentecostal movement throughout the world has made other Christians wake up to the significance of the Holy Spirit in the lives of all Christians. "The rise of the charismatic movement within virtually every mainstream church has ensured that the Holy Spirit figures prominently on the theological agenda. A new experience of the reality and power of the Spirit has had a major impact upon the theological discussion of the person and work of the Holy Spirit," remarks Anglican Alister McGrath.[4]

The world's largest Christian family, the Roman Catholic Church, in preparation for the commencement of the third millennium, under the enthusiastic leadership of Pope John Paul II, assigned the year 1998 for special devotion to the Holy Spirit;[5] the previous year was assigned to the Son and 1999 to the Father. The issuing of publications, celebration of special services, and organizing of lectures and research programs took place as the largest church of Christendom desired to deepen her understanding of pneumatology.

In 1991, the General Assembly of the WCC, under the overall theme "Come Holy Spirit—Renew the Creation," focused theological reflection on various aspects of the doctrine of the Holy Spirit in

2. Bernd Jochen Hilberath, "Pneumatologie," in *Handbuch der Dogmatik*, ed. Theodor Schneider et al. (Düsseldorf: Patmos, 1992), 1:448–49.

3. See further Constantine N. Tsirpanlis, *Introduction to Eastern Patristic Thought and Orthodox Theology*, Theology and Life Series 30 (Collegeville, Minn.: Liturgical Press, 1991), chap. 4; and John Zizioulas, *Being as Communion: Studies in Personhood and the Church* (Crestwood, N.Y.: St. Vladimir's Seminary Press, 1985), chap. 3.

4. Alister McGrath, *Christian Theology* (Cambridge: Blackwell, 1994), 240.

5. Pope John Paul II, *Celebrate 2000! Reflections on the Holy Spirit: Weekly Readings for 1998*, sel. and arr. by Paul Thigpar (Ann Arbor, Mich.: Servant Publications, 1997), contains weekly reflections on the Holy Spirit through the entire year of 1998.

relation to the church, ecumenism, and creation. Two years later, the WCC-related Faith and Order meeting was held at Santiago de Compostela, Spain, and offered a groundbreaking theological understanding between the Spirit and *koinōnia*, the church communion. Similarly, the latest WCC General Assembly at Harare, Zimbabwe (1997), gave attention to pneumatological topics and founded a Joint Working Group between Pentecostal/Charismatic Christians and the WCC. One of the purposes of this team is to assess the meaning of the pneumatological renaissance for the Christian church worldwide.

These "signs of the Spirit" and many others are reverberations from a renewed theological reflection on the Spirit that had already begun during previous generations of contemporary theology. It was the "church father" of the twentieth century, Karl Barth, who wrote these often-quoted programmatic words toward the end of his life as he reflected on the starting point of Christian theology:

> Everything that one believes, reflects and says about God the Father and God the Son . . . would be demonstrated and clarified basically through God the Holy Spirit, the *vinculum pacis* between Father and Son. The work of God in behalf of creatures for, in, and with humanity would be made clear in a teleology which excludes all happenstance.[6]

In another instance, Barth called the theology of the Spirit "the future of Christian theology."[7] And the great Russian Orthodox theologian Nikolay Berdayev named pneumatology "the last unexplored theological frontier."[8]

The Experience of the Spirit

A distinctive feature of this new search for the Spirit and spiritual life is that rather than looking for generalizations and abstract defini-

6. Karl Barth, *Schleiermacher: Auswahl mit einem Nachwort von Karl Barth*, ed. Heinz Bolli (Munich: Siebenstern-Taschenbuch, 1968), 311; for a contemporary appropriation of Barth's desire to construct a pneumatological starting point for doing theology, see, e.g., Kilian McDonnell, "A Trinitarian Theology of the Holy Spirit?" *TS* 46 (1985): 193.

7. Quoted in Paul D. Lee, "Pneumatological Ecclesiology in Roman Catholic-Pentecostal Dialogue: A Catholic Reading of the Third Quinquennium (1985–1989)" (Dissertatio Ad Lauream in Facultate S. Theologiae Apud Pontificiam Universitatem S. Thomae in Urbe, Rome, 1994), 200. Cf. McDonnell, "A Trinitarian Theology," 191, 193.

8. Nikolay Berdayev, *Spirit and Reality* (London: G. Bles, 1964), 22.

tions, as too often has been the case in the past, people are experiencing a hunger for a concrete, lived experience of the life-giving Spirit:

> Many faithful desire to encounter a Holy Spirit who brings new life to their spirits in the concrete circumstances of their lives and who renews the face of the earth as we approach the third millennium. Not unlike earlier times of perceived crisis, Christians today attempt to reconnect with the well-springs of the faith, hoping these roots will bring stability, order and meaning to a postmodern world that is often felt to be hopelessly fragmented. In particular, many seek to retrieve a three-personed God who is related to the human community and to the entire universe in love, challenge, and care—a personal God who identifies with human joys and sorrows.[9]

Consequently, the challenge given to theology in its reflection on the Holy Spirit is to retrieve concrete, particular aspects of the pneumatological tradition. The task of theology is to reflect on these experiences. In the words of Jürgen Moltmann, one of the most widely acclaimed pneumatologists of our day, "Whatever we may say in general about ourselves and other people in the light of eternity, the Spirit of life is present only as the Spirit of this or that particular life."[10] Therefore, "the experience of the Holy Spirit is as specific as the living beings who experience the Spirit, and as varied as the living beings who experience the Spirit are varied."[11]

The Catholic theologian John R. Sachs, speaking at a recent academic conference on pneumatology, asked, "What is it that invites us, perhaps compels us, to think and to speak about the Spirit today?" He mentions several reasons, such as:

> an incredible interest today in the Spirit and spirituality. People are paying attention to the spiritual dimension of their lives and often seem to be experiencing the Spirit in ways and places that often challenge traditional theologies and Church structures and sometimes have little connection with traditional religious practice. The Spirit is present and active beyond the official structures and ordained ministries of the Church.[12]

Sachs then added a noteworthy comment: "Theologians from who[m] I have learned the most, both ancient and modern, all warn against try-

9. Dreyer, "Resources for a Renewed Life," 1.

10. Jürgen Moltmann, *The Spirit of Life: A Universal Affirmation*, trans. Margaret Kohl (Minneapolis: Fortress Press, 1992), 8.

11. Ibid., 8.

12. John R. Sachs, "'Do Not Stifle the Spirit': Karl Rahner, the Legacy of Vatican II, and Its Urgency for Theology Today," in *Catholic Theological Society Proceedings*, ed. E. Dreyer, 51 (1996): 15.

ing to comprehend the Spirit in a systematic way." He recommends the attitude of "honorable silence." Otherwise pneumatology cannot avoid useless speculation. Overly speculative study of the Spirit would also hinder us from becoming more acutely desirous of and sensitive to the Spirit.[13]

The most prominent contemporary Catholic theologian on the Spirit, Yves Congar, approaches the challenge of the Spirit experience by seeking a balance between what he calls a distrust of "personal principle" and an eclipse of an "institutional principle." The "personal principle" refers to the place accorded to the initiatives of individuals as persons and to what those persons have to say on the basis of personal convictions. The "institutional principle" sees the church as a communion of such persons led by the Spirit.[14] A healthy pneumatology requires balance between these two seemingly contradictory orientations. On the one hand, the Spirit's works are experienced in the individual lives of believers, but on the other hand, the only way for an individual believer to grasp the message of the Spirit is via the church communion through its worship and the Word of God.

It has been the task of the rapidly growing Pentecostal and Charismatic movements to remind the church catholic that in the devotion to God's Spirit, it is not theology that is primary but rather a revitalization of the experience of the Spirit. Even though experience of the Spirit always leads to theological reflection about its meaning, spirituality is the first contact point.[15] This is clearly evident in the biblical record: A powerful, often charismatic experience of the Spirit came first; only afterward, and in a slow tempo, came theological reflection.

Approaching the topic of the Spirit and pneumatology from the perspective of experience is the only way to do justice to the "object" of our study. It is one of the rules of scientific inquiry that the methodology has to fit the object, not vice versa. However, a word of warning is in order here: The Spirit is not an "object" of human study in the same way that, for instance, the objects of the physical sciences are. In fact, we can say that the Spirit, rather than being an object of our scrutiny, is the One who searches us. Paul was quite emphatic about that.

> The Spirit searches all things, even the deep things of God. For who among men knows the thoughts of a man except the man's spirit within

13. Ibid.

14. Yves Congar, *I Believe in the Holy Spirit* (New York: Crossroad Herder, 1997), 2:152–53.

15. See further Kilian McDonnell, "Theological Presuppositions in Our Preaching about the Spirit," *TS* 59 (1998): 219–35.

him? In the same way no one knows the thoughts of God except the Spirit
of God.

1 Corinthians 2:10b–11

Spirituality and Pneumatology

Even linguistically the Spirit, *pneuma*, and spirituality belong together. Early in church history, Augustine reflected on the relationship
between these two as he noticed that the main difficulty in speaking
about the Spirit is that "he withdraws from us into mystery even more
than Christ."[16] According to Augustine, there are three conditions for
speaking about the Spirit. First, talk about the Spirit cannot be based
on pure theory but must touch an experienced reality. But, second, experience alone does not suffice. It must be tested and tried so that
"'one's own spirit' does not take the place of the Holy Spirit."[17] This is
the critical task of theology as it attempts to discern this difference.
Third, the originality of an individual theologian has to be replaced by
the communal discernment of the whole church, which is guided by
the very same Spirit. Writes Augustine: "Suspicion will always arise
when someone speaks on his own account, 'from within.' . . . The Spirit
does not speak on his own (John 16:13)." In this respect, originality and
truth can easily lead to a paradox. Therefore, the importance of submitting one's experience of the Spirit to the control and testing of the
church cannot be overemphasized.[18]

The Holy Spirit as the "Cinderella of Theology"

The times are gone when it was commonplace to say that the Holy
Spirit is the Cinderella of the Trinity; when the other two "sisters" went
to the ball, Cinderella was left at home. Nowadays, it will not do to
speak about the Holy Spirit as the *theos agraptos*—the God about
whom no one writes—as did Gregory of Nazianzus in the fourth century,[19] or as "the forgotten God," as did Catholic theologians of the
nineteenth century.[20]

16. Joseph Ratzinger, "The Holy Spirit as *Communio:* Concerning the Relationship
of Pneumatology and Spirituality in Augustine," *Comm* 25 (1998): 325.
17. Ibid.
18. Ibid.
19. Donald J. Gelpi, "The Theological Challenge of Charismatic Spirituality," *Pneuma*
14, no. 2 (1992): 185.
20. Ibid.

But that was not always the case. Even before the division of the church in 1054, the theologians of the East accused their Western counterparts of "forgetfulness of the Spirit." The Greek Orthodox theologian and the WCC official Nikos Nissiotis, following Vladimir Lossky, most dramatically articulated the charge of "Christomonism" against Western theology.[21] According to Nissiotis, Christianity in the West was seen as unilaterally referring to Christ, the Spirit being an addition to the church, to its ministries and sacraments. Although Nissiotis's and Lossky's critiques were one-sided and may have been too harsh, a pneumatological deficiency certainly existed—and still does, in some quarters—in the Western church.[22]

Even though in recent years it has become commonplace to introduce pneumatological treatises with a lament of the Spirit's neglect,[23] it is probably inaccurate to claim that the church and theology in general had lost sight of the Holy Spirit until twenty years or so ago. Rather than speaking of a *Geistvergessenheit* (oblivion of the Spirit), we should speak of a pneumatological deficit. There is a subordinate, secondary role assigned to the Holy Spirit, who is thrust aside and controlled.[24] According to Kilian McDonnell, the criterion for a healthy pneumatology is not so much the number of references to the Spirit as the integrity of the theological vision. One can have a superabundance of references to the Spirit and still have a serious pneumatological deficit. Critical questions in this regard include, What is the role of the Spirit in the doctrine of the Trinity, or the church, or salvation? and What would change in the theological system if the Spirit were introduced?[25]

21. Nikos A. Nissiotis, "The Main Ecclesiological Problem of the Second Vatican Council and Position of the Non-Roman Churches Facing It," *Journal of Ecumenical Studies* 6 (1965): 31–62. For the views of Vladimir Lossky, see, e.g., John H. Erickson and Thomas E. Bird, eds., *In the Image and Likeness of God* (Crestwood, N.Y.: St. Vladimir's Seminary Press, 1985), especially chap. 4, "The Procession of the Holy Spirit in Orthodox Trinitarian Doctrine."

22. Lee ("Pneumatological Ecclesiology," 195) names as the most obvious deficiencies of the West (1) a weak regard for the *epiclēsis* in the past, (2) the absence of a developed synodality, and (3) a certain clerical autonomy vis-à-vis the Christian community as a whole.

23. Both Moltmann (*Spirit of Life*, 1) and Alister McGrath (*Christian Theology: An Introduction* [Oxford, U.K./Cambridge, Mass.: Blackwell, 1994], 240) use the striking illustration of Cinderella, who has been left home when the other two went to the divine ball, in regard to the Holy Spirit. Already in the 1960s, Hendrikus Berkhof (*The Doctrine of the Holy Spirit* [Atlanta: John Knox Press, 1964], 10) lamented that even in the Anglo-Saxon literature one could discover little of substance on the topic of pneumatology.

24. Hilberath, "Pneumatologie," 445–52.

25. See, e.g., Kilian McDonnell, "The Determinative Doctrine of the Holy Spirit," *TS* 39 (1982): 142–61.

According to Bernd Jochen Hilberath, there are several reasons for this deficit in most theologies:

> With regard to the doctrine of the Trinity, Augustine's "de-personalized" approach to the Spirit (with his idea of the Spirit as *vinculum amoris*, the bond of love between the Father and Son) laid not only the theological groundwork for *filioque*, the view that the Spirit proceeds both from the Father and Son, but also divested the Spirit of full personality.[26]

The other source of this deficit is theological. From the church fathers on, the Holy Spirit has often been introduced as "the Unknown Third." On the basis of biblical hints, it has been seen that the Spirit hides himself and retreats rather than stands in the forefront, so to speak. Eastern Orthodox leader J. Meyendorff speaks of the "kenosis"[27] of the Spirit: The Spirit never calls persons to himself but to the Son. Some theologians have also spoken of the "self-effacing" nature of the Spirit: The Spirit does not show us himself; rather, he shows us the face of the Father in the face of the Son.

Another reason for the subordinate role of the Spirit has been ecclesial. The church's ambiguous experience with charismatic and prophetic movements has often led the leadership of the church to try to control the work of the Spirit out of fear of chaos and lack of order. Some theologians wonder, for example, whether the church catholic, in its rejection of the second- and third-century charismatic-prophetic movement Montanism, lost an opportunity to integrate charismatic-pneumatological spirituality more fully into its life. What were the church's criteria for a "heretical pneumatology" in this case? Many erroneous arguments were advanced in the condemnation process.

Reflecting on the minor role assigned to the Spirit in the past, the general secretary of the WCC, Konrad Raiser, has noted that what is most characteristic of theology in general and ecumenical theology in particular is its *dialogical* nature; it has taken shape in response to challenges from both inside and outside the ecumenical movement. Genuine dialogue does not aim at comprehensiveness; it can leave things open or unsaid, to be taken up at a later stage. Dialogue is moved for-

---

26. Bernd Jochen Hilberath, "Identity through Self-Transcendence: The Holy Spirit and the Communio of Free Persons," in *Advent of the Spirit*, 2–4; see also Hilberath, "Pneumatologie," 446–47. Hilberath's analysis of Augustinian influence seems to be more adequate than the approach of textbooks that usually attribute the depersonalizing tendency to Augustine's use of psychological analogies.

27. For this, see D. Lyle Dabney, *Die Kenosis des Geistes: Kontinuität zwischen Schöpfung und Erlösung in Werk des Heiligen Geistes* (Neukirchen-Vluyn: Neukirchener Verlag, 1997).

ward by what the respective partners perceive to be the most pressing issues at a given time, allowing for later reformulation of earlier insights once a new challenge arises. The doctrine of the Holy Spirit is a case in point. Until the 1980s or so, the ecumenical movement did not seem to see the need to enter more fully into a discussion of pneumatology.[28] Now that the need has been felt and fresh impulses given, the result has been a flood of works on various aspects of the Spirit.

The Place of Pneumatology in (Systematic) Theology

Traditionally, pneumatology has not received a separate locus in Christian systematic theologies.[29] Unlike the doctrine of the Trinity or the church, the discussion of the Spirit has not stood on its own feet, so to speak. Most often pneumatological topics have been incorporated into the doctrine of salvation (soteriology). Pneumatology has also at times been connected with the doctrine of the church. This placement seems natural in view of the fact that already in the ancient creeds the Holy Spirit was connected with the church. In the creeds, the church is named in the clause following that of the Holy Spirit.[30] According to the *Traditio apostolica* of Hippolytus, the third baptismal question is, "Do you believe in the Holy Spirit in the Church?"

> From the [Nicene-Constantinopolitan] Creed itself it should be clear that ecclesiology can only be understood in connection with and as a consequence of Pneumatology. The Church cannot be grasped apart from the Holy Spirit, and can only be grasped as the work of the Holy Spirit. Only after Pentecost, that is, after the sending of the Spirit through the Risen One.[31]

Thomas Aquinas articulated the medieval tradition: "The phrase 'the holy catholic church' is to be understood to mean that our faith is in the

28. Konrad Raiser, "The Holy Spirit in Modern Ecumenical Thought," *The Ecumenical Review* 41, no. 3 (1989): 375.

29. Hilberath, "Pneumatologie," 449–50.

30. E.g., in the Creed of Constantinople and the (Western) Apostles' Creed, noted by Miguel M. Garijo-Guembe, *Communion of the Saints: Foundation, Nature, and Structure of the Church*, trans. Patrick Madigan (Collegeville, Minn.: Liturgical Press, 1994), 2.

31. Cited ibid., 1. Patristic author Faustus of Riez (d. before 500) concluded that the last clauses in the creed were connected with the Holy Spirit: "Whatever in the Creed follows the words 'the Holy Ghost' should be understood without reference to the preposition 'in,' so that our belief about the Holy Church, the communion of saints, etc., is said as part of our appeal to God. This means we believe that these things have been ordered by God and derive their existence from him" (*De Spiritu Sancto* 1.2, Corpus scriptorum ecclesiasticorum latinorum, 21:103–4).

Holy Spirit who sanctifies the church. The meaning is, therefore, I believe in the Holy Spirit sanctifying the church."[32]

Wolfhart Pannenberg, in his monumental three-volume *Systematic Theology*, in which his distinctive pneumatology plays a crucial role, connects the Spirit with each of the main loci of theology. His treatments of God, creation, human beings, Christology, soteriology, and eschatology are heavily imbued with pneumatological foundations. In this approach, the Holy Spirit, far more than serving as a "gap-filler," is part of the theological structure and discussion itself.

In more recent approaches to the discussion of the Spirit, such as that of Pannenberg, pneumatology bears obvious similarities with Christology. Although the discussion of Christ's person and work usually occupies a central role in any systematic theology, Christology also has integral connections with other systematic topics: How could the doctrines of revelation, God, salvation, church, or eschatology be construed without a christological foundation? The same question could be asked regarding pneumatology.

Various Contemporary Approaches to the Study of the Spirit

Although separate treatises on the Holy Spirit have been written during church history—one need only refer to classical works such as those of Athanasius, Cyril of Alexandria, and Basil—never before have so many pneumatological studies appeared as during the past two decades or so. Understandably, several approaches have been taken.

Jürgen Moltmann's *Spirit of Life*, while original in several topics and insights, follows more traditional patterns. It provides extensive interaction with the way the Spirit has been conceived in the history of theology and with traditional topics, such as the Trinity. Moltmann also devotes a long section to typical soteriological topics such as justification and sanctification. However, he also relates his discussion to pressing modern themes, such as the environment, justice, and equality. He is in search of a "holistic" pneumatology in which the doctrine of the Spirit encompasses areas that are often left behind in older pneumatologies, such as the human body and the earth.

Michael Welker's *God the Spirit*[33] presents a unique approach to the doctrine of the Spirit. Welker interacts with biblical materials, especially the Old Testament, and attempts to discern the patterns and leading themes that emerge from the biblical discussion of pneumatology.

32. *Summa Theologia* 2.1.1–2.1.9, questions 1–5.
33. Trans. John F. Hoffmeyer (Minneapolis: Fortress Press, 1994).

Rather than relying on general conceptions and philosophical general-ization, Welker, whose academic training is in both philosophy and theology, listens to "concrete," "realistic" voices in the canon and, rather than trying to reconcile them, freely allows the plurality its own wit-ness. In a qualified sense, Welker's study could be labeled a "biblical theology" of the Spirit.

Clark Pinnock, one of the leading evangelical theologians of our day, in his *Flame of Love,* subtitled *A Theology of the Holy Spirit,*[34] endeavors to construct a full-scale systematic theology from a pneumatological perspective. He discusses the topics of revelation, the Trinity, creation, Christology, the church, and theology of religions and connects them with pneumatological foundations. The result is an exciting mixture of theology, spirituality, and insights about the Spirit.

These three studies represent the main approaches to the Spirit in use today in addition to studies that approach the topic from a specific discipline, such as biblical or historical studies. Furthermore, a host of specialized studies on the Spirit is growing rapidly.

Joseph Comblin's *The Holy Spirit and Liberation*[35] finds its point of departure in the liberation theologies of Latin America and attempts to discern the work of the Spirit from the perspective of liberation, free-dom, and community development.

The feminist Elizabeth Johnson, from the Roman Catholic tradi-tion, in her book *She Who Is: The Mystery of God in Feminist Theolog-ical Discourse,*[36] attempts to discover a distinctively feminist perspec-tive on the doctrine of God in general and the doctrine of the Spirit in particular.

Blair Reynolds has written his study *Toward a Process Pneumatol-ogy*[37] in critical interaction with process philosophy and theology. His creative work inquires into potential commonalities between a process approach and some marginal Christian spiritualities, especially those that draw from the wells of mysticism.

Politically oriented theologians, such as Geiko Mueller-Fahrenholz in the study titled *God's Spirit: Transforming a World in Crisis*[38] and Miroslav Volf in his *Work in the Spirit,*[39] relate pneumatological dis-cussion to political realities and work. A distinctive feature of Volf's

34. Downers Grove, Ill.: InterVarsity Press, 1996.
35. Maryknoll, N.Y.: Orbis, 1989.
36. New York: Crossroad, 1992.
37. London: Associated University Presses, 1990.
38. New York: Continuum, 1995.
39. With the subtitle *Toward a Theology of Work* (New York/Oxford: Oxford Univer-sity Press, 1991).

work is that it also interacts with the Marxist understanding of work and society.

A new approach to the study of Christian theology and pneumatology is environmental. An example of an insightful "green" or ecological pneumatology is Mark Wallace's *Fragments of the Spirit: Nature, Violence, and the Renewal of Creation.*[40] Wallace takes careful note of biblical and historical resources in Christian theology and faces the environmental challenges with a full-blown pneumatological approach to creation, ecology, and environmental issues.

Having surveyed the theological landscape with regard to the place and role of pneumatology in current theology, the next task is to inquire into the varied biblical perspectives concerning the doctrine and spirituality of the Spirit.

40. New York: Continuum, 1996.

2

Biblical Perspectives on the Spirit

Images of the Spirit in the Bible

The Bible presents no systematized outline of the work of the Spirit, anymore than it does of any other systematic topic. It teaches about the Spirit through symbols and stories, and the accent is on the work of the Spirit, in other words, spirituality. This is no wonder when the nature of the Bible as a witness to the works of almighty God is taken into consideration. In this sense, we could perhaps describe biblical pneumatology as a sort of "lived" pneumatology rather than a schematized doctrine. To do justice to the biblical account, we need to look first at various images and terms used of the Spirit and his work. The images of the Spirit in the Bible are taken from the material, animal, and personal world.[1]

Life-Breath. Genesis 2:7 presents one of the earliest biblical conceptions of the Spirit: The Lord breathes into the nostrils of the man and the man becomes a living being. Although this passage uses the Hebrew word *neshamah,* the more familiar Hebrew word *ruach,* which means "breath," "wind," or "spirit," is also used in this sense of life-breath

1. The main source for this section is George T. Montague, "The Fire in the Word: The Holy Spirit in Scripture," in *Advent of the Spirit: Orientations in Pneumatology,* Conference Papers from a Symposium at Marquette University, 17–19 April 1998 (unpublished). A detailed study is that of George Montague, *The Holy Spirit: Growth of a Biblical Tradition* (Peabody, Mass.: Hendrickson, 1994).

(e.g., Gen. 6:17; Ezek. 37:5). The act of God breathing life into human beings at creation is an important forerunner of John 20:22, where Jesus breathes upon the disciples and says, "Receive the Holy Spirit."

In the Old Testament, the breath of all creatures belongs to God, who can recall it at his pleasure (Ps. 104:29–30). The Spirit, then, can stand for life itself as a gift of God. God is the source of human (and animal) life. In the Old Testament, the life-breath is shared with the animal kingdom (Ps. 104:29), but only with regard to the creation of human beings is it said that God breathed into his nostrils. Moreover, the human responsibility of naming the animals shows that human beings are given power over them.

Wind. Closely related to the idea of breath is that of wind (Gen. 8:1; Num. 11:31; Isa. 27:8; etc.). This dual meaning for the word *ruach* is evident, for example, in Exodus 15:8, 10: "At a breath *[ruach]* of your anger the waters piled up. . . . When your wind *[ruach]* blew, the sea covered them" (Montague's translation). John 3 more explicitly connects the image of wind with God's Spirit, speaking of the mysterious nature of wind and the Spirit's role in a believer's new birth.

Fire. This description of the Spirit is not as common as those of life-breath and wind. Still, Isaiah 4:4 speaks of the time "when the Lord . . . purges Jerusalem's blood from her midst with the spirit of judgment and with the spirit of fire," and 33:11 states, "my spirit shall consume you like fire" (Montague's translation). Undoubtedly, this text and similar ones form the background for John the Baptist's preaching about baptism with the Spirit and fire (Matt. 3:11–12; Luke 3:16–17). According to Luke Johnson, Luke's saying in 12:49, "I have come to bring fire on the earth," is intentionally obscure, having two meanings: (1) the coming judgment by the Son of Man and (2) the eschatological gift of the Holy Spirit (Acts 2:3).[2]

Water. Two passages from Isaiah foretell the coming salvation in terms of God's Spirit being "poured out." The impending devastation will last "till the Spirit is poured upon us from on high" (32:15). At that time, God says, "I will pour water on the thirsty land, and streams on the dry ground; I will pour my spirit upon your descendents, and my blessing on your offspring" (44:3 NRSV). This Old Testament usage creates the context for the passages in the Gospel of John in which water symbolizes the Spirit (4:10; 7:38–39). The water symbolism culminates with the vision of the Apocalypse of the blessed river of life-giving water springing from the throne of God and the Lamb (Rev. 22:1–2).

Cloud. In the Old Testament, the cloud serves as a frequent manifestation of God's presence and glory, as with Moses on Mount Sinai

2. Luke Johnson, *Gospel of Luke* (Collegeville, Minn.: Liturgical Press, 1991), 209.

(Exod. 24:15–18), at the tent of meeting (Exod. 33:9–10), in the desert (Exod. 40:36–38), and at the dedication of the Solomonic temple (1 Kings 8:10–12). While it is true that in the Old Testament the cloud is not explicitly associated with the Spirit, if God's presence is made possible only through the all-present Spirit, then this symbolism can legitimately be related to the Spirit. Some commentators remind us of a parallel usage at the beginning of Luke's Gospel: The Holy Spirit "overshadows" Mary as the cloud overshadowed the tent of meeting. The Greek word used in the Septuagint (LXX) in Exodus 40:35 *(episkiazō)* is the same word used in Luke 1:35.

Dove. It is noteworthy that Jesus' baptism in the Jordan is one of the events recorded by all four Gospels. In those narratives, the Holy Spirit in the form of a dove descends on Jesus. The Catholic pneumatologist Kilian McDonnell has posited that the dove over the Jordan gives the baptism of Jesus a truly cosmic significance: As the dove brought news of a new creation to the ark, so the Holy Spirit proclaims that the world will be made anew beginning with the baptism of Jesus.[3]

Paraclete. This is the first and only personal image; it points to the personality but does not demand that the Holy Spirit be a separate *hypostasis* (a Greek term used to refer to the three distinct Persons of the Trinity). If the Holy Spirit is the second Paraclete, "another Counselor" (John 14:16), Jesus Christ obviously is the first, as 1 John 2:1 says ("one who speaks . . . in our defense"=*paraklētos*).

The Spirit in the Old Testament

In the Septuagint (LXX), the Greek term *pneuma* is almost always the equivalent of the Hebrew *ruach*.[4] Of the 377 instances of *ruach*, 264 are translated *pneuma* (the next most frequent translation is *anemos*, "wind," 49 times).[5] The idea behind *ruach* is the extraordinary fact that air should move; the basic meaning of *ruach* is, therefore, "blowing." Both terms in the Bible, the Old Testament *ruach* and the New Testament *pneuma*, carry the same ambiguity of multiple meanings: "breath," "air," "wind," or "soul."[6]

3. Kilian McDonnell, *The Baptism of Jesus in the Jordan: The Trinitarian and Cosmic Order of Salvation* (Collegeville, Minn.: Liturgical Press, 1996); for a summary, see his "Jesus' Baptism in the Jordan," *TS* 56 (1995): 209–36.

4. The outline and basic material for this section is taken from E. Kamlah, "Spirit," in *Dictionary of New Testament Theology*, ed. Colin Brown (Grand Rapids: Zondervan, 1978), 3:690–92.

5. Ibid., 690.

6. Friedrich Baumgärtel, "πνεῦμα *[pneuma]*," *TDNT*, 6:360.

The Old Testament contains roughly one hundred instances of the term "Spirit of God" (Gen. 1:2) or "Spirit of the LORD" (Isa. 11:2). The most disputed passage is Genesis 1:2. The question is whether *ruach elohim* should be translated as "a mighty wind [that] swept over the waters" (NAB) or as "the Spirit of God [that] was moving over the face of the waters" (RSV). In some cases, *ruach* literally means "wind," and in other cases, it is more appropriate to translate it as "spirit." In addition to referring to God, *elohim* can also refer to an adjective such as "extraordinary," "magnificent," "tremendous," "powerful," or "divine." Consequently, several translations are possible with regard to the linguistic data, but the theological consensus is that the rendering of the Revised Standard Version (and most other translations similar to it) is the preferable one. The author was referring to God's Spirit in this passage. Elsewhere *ruach elohim* is always rendered "Spirit of God," why not here? Furthermore, why should we have to regard "Spirit" and "wind" as alternatives?[7]

Generally speaking, there are three major uses for the term *ruach:* (1) wind, or a breath of air; (2) the principle of life, in other words, the force that vivifies human beings; and (3) the life of God himself, both at the physical and the spiritual level. It is important to note that it is not opposed to the concepts of "body" or "bodily" anymore than is *pneuma* in the New Testament. In the words of Yves Congar, "It is a subtle corporeality rather than an incorporeal substance. The *ruach*-breath of the Old Testament is not disincarnate. It is rather what animates the body."[8]

When "spirit" is opposed to "flesh," it reminds us of the power of God vis-à-vis human beings as a purely earthly reality. Isaiah 31:3 illustrates this contrast: "The Egyptians are men and not God; their horses are flesh and not spirit." This is in consonance with the Old Testament usage, in which the impotence of flesh is contrasted with the "spirit" as the power of God, which is universally present in the world (Ps. 139:7).

God as life-giving spirit is the proper source of life and strength; in a derivative sense, *ruach* also denotes the life-force of the individual (Judg. 15:19) and of the group (Num. 16:22). That life-force is lacking in idols (Jer. 10:14), but it is in God (Ps. 33:6) and in the Messiah (Isa. 11:4). God is the only one who gives the life-force (Isa. 42:5) and protects it (Ps. 31:5).

7. Wolfhart Pannenberg, *Systematic Theology* (Grand Rapids: Eerdmans, 1994), 2:77–78. See also Gordon J. Wenham, *Genesis 1–15*, Word Biblical Commentary, ed. David A. Hubbard et al. (Waco: Word, 1987), 1:16–17.

8. Yves Congar, *I Believe in the Holy Spirit* (New York: Crossroad Herder, 1997), 1:3.

It is characteristic of Old Testament pneumatology that *ruach* is common to both humans and animals. It is not a specifically human endowment, and it denotes God as the source of life for both. Related to this concept as well in the Old Testament is the Spirit's cosmic function that goes far beyond the human sphere of life.[9]

Illustrative of the manifold usage in the Old Testament, *ruach* may also denote emotions of God (Exod. 15:8; Job 4:9: "the blast of his nostrils") and of humans. In people, for example, it refers to anxiety (Gen. 41:8) and to despair (Job 17:1).

As a charismatic power, *ruach* can come mightily upon a human being (Judg. 14:6; 1 Sam. 16:13) and "clothe" (equip) that person for powerful works (Judg. 6:34ff.). The very same Spirit also enables human beings to perform supernatural deeds, such as the physical salvation of Israel by the judges (Judg. 3:10; 6:34) or visions by the prophets (Ezek. 3:12; 8:3; 11:1). It can even denote the source of the craftsman's skill (Exod. 31:3) or of any outstanding ability (Dan. 6:3). The charismatic ministry of the Spirit comes into focus especially in the Book of Judges, which tells of several charismatic leaders or warriors:

- Othniel: "The Spirit of the LORD came upon him" (3:10).
- Gideon: "the Spirit of the LORD came upon Gideon" (6:34).
- Jephthah: "the Spirit of the LORD came upon Jephthah" (11:29).
- Samson: "and the Spirit of the LORD began to stir him" (13:25; see also 14:6, 19).

In the prophetic books, the figure of the Messiah and his anointing by the Spirit occupy a major role. The Book of Isaiah introduces the Messiah ordained and empowered by the Spirit (11:1–8). The missionary work of the Messiah, including the salvation of the Gentiles, will be accomplished through the Spirit (42:1–4; 49:1–6). The messianic pouring out of God's Spirit will effect both judgment and peace (32:15–20). God gives a new Spirit to heal and restore his people (Ezek. 11:19ff.; 18:31; 36:36ff.). The Old Testament often emphasizes the Spirit's role in establishing righteousness and justice.[10] In fact, the work of the Spirit is nothing less than resurrection, a new creation (Ezek. 37:1–14). The prophet Joel expresses this hope in dramatic terms (2:28–32). The Wisdom literature also makes numerous references to the Spirit: Wisdom can be identified with the Word/Logos or the Spirit (Prov. 8:22–31).

9. Erik Sjöberg, "πνεῦμα," *TDNT*, 6:386.
10. See further ibid., 383.

The Intertestamental Period

> In Judaism under the influence of its Hellenistic environment, the spirit
> was a vital force divinely breathed into man and forming a distinct part
> of his being: it was not distinguished from the "soul" as far as terminol-
> ogy was concerned, but was contrasted rather with the body: the body is
> of the earth, the spirit stems from heaven (Wis. 15:11).[11]

In contrast, in Palestinian Judaism, consonant with the Old Testament anthropology, the body was never the prison-house of the soul.
Palestinian Judaism also emphasized that the spirit is created by God
alone, and therefore, there is a distinction between the Creator and
the creature.

In the intertestamental literature, the expressions "Spirit of God,"
"divine spirit," and "holy spirit" sometimes mean the God-given spirit
of humans. In some cases, these terms may also refer to that spiritual
reality that performed God's work on earth (Sir. 48:12). Following the
Old Testament written prophetic traditions, this literature also places
special emphasis on Isaiah's promise of a Messiah of the Spirit (*Testament of Levi* 18.7, 11).[12]

The Spirit in the New Testament

Terminology

The term *pneuma*, like its Old Testament counterpart *ruach*, has the
basic meaning of "air" and "breathing."[13] This meaning is especially significant in view of the fact that in the ancient world, the air breathed
was considered the bearer of life. Roughly forty times in the New Testament, *pneuma* refers to the human spirit insofar as it belongs to the
spiritual realm. In other words, the spirit of a human being is that aspect of a man or a woman through which God most immediately encounters him or her (Rom. 8:16; Gal. 6:18; Phil. 4:23; Heb. 4:12; etc.),
that dimension wherein one is most immediately open to God (Matt.
5:3; Luke 1:47; Rom. 1:9; 1 Peter 3:4). It should be noted, though, that
in several instances it is not absolutely clear whether the word refers to
the human spirit or the divine Spirit (Mark 14:38; Rom. 8:15; 11:8;
1 Cor. 4:21; etc.).

11. Kamlah, "Spirit," 692.
12. Ibid., 693.
13. The outline and basic material in the section "The Spirit in the New Testament"
is from James D. G. Dunn, "Spirit," in *Dictionary of New Testament Theology*, 3:693–709.

The New Testament also speaks of spirits. It recognizes the reality of a battle between the kingdom of God and evil spirits, a perspective depicted especially in the Synoptic Gospels (e.g., Mark 3:23–27). Since there are both good spirits and bad, the church and individual Christians need to be able to discern the spirits (1 Cor. 12:10; 14:12; 2 Cor. 11:4).[14]

The Spirit in the Synoptic Gospels

The Q tradition presents John the Baptist as a prophet of judgment (Matt. 3:7–12). The coming Messiah would baptize "in holy spirit and fire" *(en pneumati hagiō kai pyri)*. But John's message was not only about judgment; it also offered a promise to those who accepted the baptism of repentance. The Baptist's background was, of course, apocalypticism: The new age could be inaugurated only after a period of affliction, the birth pangs of the Messiah. Thus, "fire" and *pneuma* could denote both judgment and purification. According to James D. G. Dunn:

> John's baptism in the Jordan . . . was therefore a very potent symbol of the end-time tribulation=baptism in Spirit and fire=God's fiery *pneuma* like a great stream through which all men must pass. Those who acknowledged their liability to judgment by submitting to the symbolized judgment of John's baptism would experience the messianic woes as a cleansing by a spirit of judgment and by a spirit of burning (Isa. 4:4). Those who denied their guilt and did not repent would experience the Coming One's baptism in the Spirit and fire as the bonfire which burned up the unfruitful branches and chaff.[15]

Jesus' own understanding of his mission in terms of the Spirit was different; this difference becomes clear especially in his role as an exorcist and in his consciousness of inspiration. According to the Synoptics, his success as an exorcist was undeniable. "But if I drive out demons by the Spirit of God, then the kingdom of God has come upon you" (Matt. 12:28). The presence of the kingdom is defined in terms of the effective power of the Spirit: The end-time power is at work through the Spirit. Also, Jesus' consciousness of inspiration established him as a prophet of the end-time. The Spirit was principally regarded as the Spirit of prophecy in the Judaism of that time, and it is well known that according to the rabbis, the Spirit had been withdrawn from Israel at the time of Malachi. Now Jesus was claiming to be the eschatological prophet (Deut.

---

14. See further Eduard Schweizer, "πνεῦμα," *TDNT*, 6:396–97.
15. Dunn, "Spirit," 695.

18:15ff.; Isa. 61:1ff.). Indeed, Jesus believed that Isaiah 61:1ff. was fulfilled in his own ministry, as Luke 4:18–19 clearly shows:

> The Spirit of the Lord is on me,
>   because he has anointed me
>   to preach good news to the poor.
> He has sent me to proclaim freedom for the prisoners
>   and recovery of sight for the blind,
> to release the oppressed,
>   to proclaim the year of the Lord's favor.

Rather than being a prophet of judgment, Jesus saw his ministry in the Spirit in terms of eschatological blessing: good news, freedom, healing. Indicative of this eschatological ministry of the Spirit is Jesus' role as the Baptizer in the Spirit.[16] Thus, the Gospels also depict him as the dispenser of the Spirit (Matt. 10:20; Mark 13:11). Luke especially emphasizes the charismatic ministry of Jesus (Luke 4:1, 14; 10:21).[17] Many commentators have also noticed a parallelism between the Spirit's ministry in Luke and Acts. In Acts, Luke compares the birth and ministry of the church by the power of the Spirit to that of Jesus. The church ministered to and healed people by the power of the Spirit just as Jesus had done.

Generally speaking, according to the Gospels, Jesus was the wholly unique Man of the Spirit. The Spirit effected his birth (Matt. 1:18–25; Luke 1:35). He was anointed with the Spirit at his baptism (Matt 3:16–17; Mark 1:10–11; Luke 3:22; John 1:33)[18] and led by the Spirit to the desert for his temptations (Matt. 4:1; Mark 1:12; Luke 4:1). His overall ministry was born of the Spirit.

The Spirit in Acts and in the Earliest Christian Communities

Perhaps the most characteristic feature of Luke's portrayal of the ministry of the Spirit is his stress on the Spirit's abiding with the community. Whether speaking of an individual or the community, Luke seeks to overcome the concept of the Spirit as a power that leaps on a human being and then leaves again.[19] In fact, the Spirit is a "feature of the age of the Church."[20] The fact that each of the baptized possesses the Spirit, and that this fact is often manifested in a visible and percep-

16. Cf. Dunn, "Spirit," 697.

17. See further Roger Stronstadt, *The Charismatic Theology of St. Luke* (Peabody, Mass.: Hendrickson, 1984).

18. Schweizer ("πνεῦμα," *TDNT*, 6:400) sees in the baptism of Jesus also a prophetic call.

19. Ibid., 6:406.

20. Ibid., 409.

tible way, is the emphasis of the Lukan story.[21] Dunn summarizes the role of the Spirit in the earliest Christian communities as follows:

> "Holy Spirit" denotes supernatural power, altering, working through, directing the believer. . . . This is nowhere more clearly evident than in Acts where the Spirit is presented as an almost tangible force, visible if not in itself, certainly in its effects.[22]

The transforming power of the Spirit is evident at the beginning of the history of the Christian church. Actually, the birth of Christianity at Pentecost is a dramatic work of the Spirit: Three thousand repent, and charismatic elements are visible. Jürgen Moltmann argues that the Christian church was born with the speaking in tongues.[23] And the same Holy Spirit empowered the church in its ministry and miracles. Reading the Book of Acts leads one to the conclusion that the reception of the Spirit often took place with visible signs (see 4:31; 8:15–19; 10:44–47; 19:6). Such signs were so essential that when they were missing, believers doubted the presence of the Spirit, as among the Samaritans (8:12ff.) and the group of disciples in Ephesus (19:11ff.). Often at pivotal moments in the life of an individual or the church, the Holy Spirit was seen as the source of an extraordinary power (9:17; 11:15–18; 15:8; 19:1–7).

As with Jesus, the Spirit was instrumental in prophecy with the early Christians.[24] Dunn even goes so far as to contend that "for the first Christians, the Spirit was most characteristically a divine power manifesting itself in inspired utterance" (see Acts 1:16; 3:18; 4:25; 28:25).[25] This evidence fulfills Moses' desire that all the Lord's people would be prophets and that the Lord would put his Spirit upon them (Num. 11:29). Furthermore, for the first Christians, the Spirit gave boldness of speech and inspiration even in crisis (Acts 4:8, 13, 29–31; 13:9) by enabling effective teaching and testimony (5:32; 6:10; 18:25).[26]

---

21. Ibid., 410.

22. Dunn, "Spirit," 698.

23. Jürgen Moltmann, "The Spirit Gives Life: Spirituality and Vitality," in *All Together in One Place: Theological Papers from the Brighton Conference on World Evangelization,* ed. Harold D. Hunter and Peter D. Hocken (Sheffield: Sheffield Academic Press, 1993), 26.

24. See further Schweizer, "πνεῦμα," *TDNT,* 6:398.

25. Dunn, "Spirit," 699. See further Max Turner, *Power from on High: The Spirit of Prophecy in Luke-Acts* (Sheffield: Sheffield Academic Press, 1996).

26. Of course, the expectation of the whole people of God acting as "prophets" does not contradict the existence of a special group of people depicted as prophets as is evident in the Book of Acts (11:27ff.; 13:1; 15:32; 20:23; 21:4, 9–11; also 6:3, 5; 7:55; 11:24). For the general prophethood of every Christian in Luke-Acts, see Roger Stronstadt, "Affirming Diversity: God's People as a Community of Prophets," *Pneuma* 17, no. 2 (1995): 145–57.

Another means by which the Spirit helped the early church in her mission was by giving special authority to the leadership of the community (4:31; 5:1–10; 6:10; 8:9–13; 13:9–11). The Spirit was also constantly directing missionaries to new areas (8:29, 39; 10:19; 11:12; 13:2, 4; 16:6–7; 19:21). In this guidance, ecstatic visions evidently played a significant role as well (9:10; 10:3, 7, 10–16; 16:9–10; 22:17–18).[27]

The Spirit in the Pauline Letters

Paul's pneumatology is christologically founded: The Spirit is the Spirit of Christ (Rom. 8:9; Gal. 4:6; Phil. 1:19).[28] Therefore, it is only through the Spirit that the believer is able to confess that "Jesus is Lord" (1 Cor. 12:1–3). The Spirit makes it possible for us to know and recognize Christ. Jesus' Abba prayer wells up from the Spirit of sonship in believers (Rom. 8:15). To be "in Christ" and "in Spirit" are virtually synonymous;[29] therefore, the Spirit cannot be experienced apart from Christ (1 Cor. 12:3). Paul even goes so far as to say that Christ became "a life-giving Spirit" (1 Cor. 15:45).

It is one of the canons of recent New Testament scholarship that there is a basic difference between the pneumatological orientations of Luke and Paul. While both of them know the Spirit's ministry as charismatic, certainly for Paul another major facet is the Spirit's soteriological dimension. Luke does not refer to the Spirit in relation to salvation. For Paul, however, the fundamental mark of belonging to Christ is the gift of the Spirit that makes one a Christian (Rom. 8:9) and a sharer in sonship (8:14–16; Gal. 4:6). Whatever disputes there are with regard to the difficult expression "baptized with/in the Spirit," it is safe to say that for Paul, "baptized with/in the Spirit" is the way to become a member of the body of Christ (1 Cor. 12:13). The difference between the old covenant and the new is that through the reception of the Spirit, immediate access to the Lord is provided (2 Cor. 3:3; 13:14; cf. Jer. 31:33). In this regard, the reception of the Spirit is another term for justification (1 Cor. 6:11; Gal. 3:14) and a virtual synonym for grace (Rom. 3:24; 1 Cor. 15:10; Gal. 1:15).

Along with the soteriological aspect of Paul's teaching on the Spirit, also crucial for Paul is the charismatic element—charismatic utterances and acts (1 Cor. 1:4–7; Gal. 3:5). For the charismatic church at Corinth, Paul offers quite extensive teaching and correction with re-

27. For the role of the Spirit in Acts with regard to mission, see further John M. Penney, *The Missionary Emphasis of Lukan Pneumatology* (Sheffield: Sheffield Academic Press, 1997).

28. We are now fortunate to have the magisterial work of Gordon Fee, *God's Empowering Presence: The Holy Spirit in the Letters of Paul* (Peabody, Mass.: Hendrickson, 1994). It provides both detailed exegesis of all the passages in the Pauline corpus (including the Pastorals) and an extended theological summary.

29. For a detailed discussion, see Congar, *I Believe in the Holy Spirit*, 1:37–38.

gard to the proper use of the *charismata*.[30] Another role of the Spirit is the experience of illumination and divine revelation in the face of affliction (1 Cor. 2:10–12; 2 Cor. 3:14–17; 1 Thess. 1:6).

While there is an eschatological side to the person of the Spirit for Luke, for Paul it is even more explicit: The Spirit of the new age has already broken into the old. Paul refers to the Spirit as an *arrabōn*, a down payment of the glory to come (2 Cor. 1:22; 5:5; Eph. 1:13–14), and as the first installment of the believer's inheritance in the kingdom of God (Rom. 8:15–17; 14:17; 1 Cor. 6:9–11; 15:42–50; Gal. 4:6–7).

In addition to charismatic, prophetic, and eschatological dimensions, a moral transformation by means of the Spirit is also to be expected (1 Cor. 6:9–11). It is the task of the Spirit to renounce the flesh.[31] Even though the new has come and the old has passed away, there is a constant struggle, even warfare, between "spirit" and "flesh" (Rom. 8:1ff.; Gal. 5:16ff.); therefore, the believer has a responsibility to live his or her life in the power of the Spirit, "walking in the Spirit," being led by the Spirit (Rom. 8:4–6, 14; Gal. 5:16, 18, 25). As far as there is advancement, the fruit of the Spirit will become evident (Gal. 5:18ff.).

Both Paul and Luke highlight the communal aspect of the Spirit's ministry. Paul speaks of the Spirit as a shared Spirit, the Spirit of *koinōnia* (1 Cor. 12:13; 2 Cor. 13:14; Eph. 4:3; Phil. 1:27; 2:1). Thus, the purpose of the *charismata* is to build up the community (Rom. 12:4–8; 1 Cor. 12:14–26; Eph. 4:11–16).[32] One of the related roles of the Spirit is to open the way to God in prayer, which often leads to an openness with one's neighbor.[33] For Paul, charisms play a crucial role both in the communal life and in an individual believer's life. *Charismata* may be spectacular Spirit-inspired utterances or acts (1 Cor. 12:8–11) or more regular ministries (Rom. 12:6–8; 1 Cor. 12:28; Eph. 4:11). Nevertheless, the preferred gift for Paul is prophecy, because it builds up the body (Rom. 12:6–8; 1 Cor. 14:1–5, 13–19). Paul seeks a balance between not restricting the exercise of the Spirit's gifts (1 Thess. 5:19–20) and not overemphasizing or abusing them (Rom. 12:3; 1 Cor. 2:12–14; 1 Thess. 5:19–22).

One of the most distinctive expressions in Paul's writings is the term *pneumatikos*. It is used as (1) an adjective meaning "spiritual";[34] (2) a

30. See further Fee, *God's Empowering Presence*, 886–95.

31. Schweizer, "πνεῦμα," *TDNT*, 6:428–29.

32. See further Ralph P. Martin, *The Spirit and the Congregation: Studies in 1 Corinthians 12–15* (Grand Rapids: Eerdmans, 1984).

33. See further Schweizer, "πνεῦμα," *TDNT*, 6:430–31.

34. E.g., spiritual gift (Rom. 1:11); spiritual law (deriving from the Spirit; Rom. 7:14); spiritual (resurrection) body (1 Cor. 15:44, 46); spiritual blessings (deriving from the Spirit; Eph. 1:3); spiritual understanding (Col. 1:9); and spiritual songs (Eph. 5:19).

masculine noun, "spiritual man;[35] and (3) a neuter noun, "the spiritual things."[36] At least sometimes in Paul's writings the ambiguity of the term is evident, as in 1 Corinthians 12:1.

Gordon Fee summarizes Paul's theology of the Spirit as follows:[37]

1. The Spirit plays an absolutely crucial role in Paul's Christian experience and his understanding of the gospel.
2. Crucial to the Spirit's central role is the thoroughly eschatological framework within which Paul both experienced and understood the Spirit.
3. Equally crucial to the Pauline perspective is the dynamically experienced nature of the coming of the Spirit in the life of the individual and community.
4. The coming of the eschatological Spirit meant the return of God's own personal presence to dwell in and among God's people.
5. Trinitarian presuppositions are absolutely fundamental to the Pauline theology of the Spirit.
6. Paul's trinitarian pneumatology is foundational to the "heart of his theological enterprise," namely, salvation in Christ.
7. The Spirit is the essential component of the whole of Christian life, from beginning to end.
8. Finally, the Spirit is the key to all truly Christian spirituality, including prayer in the Spirit.

The Spirit in John's Gospel and Letters

John draws heavily on the Old Testament imagery of the Spirit related to the life-giving power of water and breath, as is evident in his metaphors of rebirth (John 3:5–8), spring of life (John 4:14; 6:63; 7:38–39), and reception of the Spirit as new life (John 20:22; cf. Gen. 2:7; Ezek. 37:9). He is also fond of another Old Testament metaphor with regard to the Spirit, that of anointing (1 John 2:20, 27).

With Paul, John shares a vested interest in the integral relationship between Christ and the Spirit, but he depicts this in a different way. Although John presents a high Christology, meaning he regards Jesus as divine and equal to God, he gives a firm place to Jesus' being anointed with the Spirit at the Jordan (John 1:32). Jesus has been given the Spirit "without measure" (3:34). And John also ties Jesus' gift of the Spirit

35. As in 1 Cor. 2:13, 15; 3:1; 14:37; Gal. 6:1 as over against those who are not.

36. Rom. 15:27; 1 Cor. 9:11, "the things of the Spirit"; *pneumatika* in 1 Cor. 12:1; 14:1 (probably also 2:13) refers to spiritual gifts, more or less equivalent to *charismata*.

37. Fee, *God's Empowering Presence*, 896–99.

more closely to Jesus' death (John 6:53, 62–63). The Catholic commentators especially have also seen in the ambiguous words from the cross, "[Jesus] gave up his spirit" (John 19:30), a reference to the divine Spirit.[38]

One of the most distinctive features of Johannine pneumatology is the introduction of the Spirit as the "other Paraclete" (John 14:16), obviously implying that Jesus is the first (1 John 2:1). The term *paraklētos* (from *para* + *kalein*) in its elementary sense means "one called alongside to help," thus an advocate or defense attorney.[39] While the Paraclete acts as a defender of the disciples, his role is also that of a prosecuting attorney proving the world guilty. It has to be noted, though, that in addition to the forensic meaning, the term *paraklētos* also carries several other meanings, such as "comforter," "intercessor," and "the one who exhorts and encourages." No single translation captures the complexity of the functions assigned to the Paraclete in John.[40] This becomes evident as one looks at the various roles assigned to him: witness, revealer, interpreter, and leader into the truth.[41]

John also connects eschatology to the Spirit. Paul, of course, teaches that the Spirit is the foretaste of the things to come, but John focuses more on the present experience of the salvation already come in Christ through the Spirit.[42]

Other New Testament Writings

The Pastorals.[43] The Pastoral Letters show far less consciousness of the Spirit as a present reality; the Spirit's manifestations have become more formalized and institutionalized in that they are associated with ordination for ministry and the laying on of hands (1 Tim. 4:14; 2 Tim. 1:6). Nevertheless, for the writer of the Pastorals, the Spirit's role in the inspiration of prophecy and prophetic Scriptures is one of the main themes (2 Tim. 1:7; 3:16). In addition, 1 Timothy 3:16, an important christological passage, speaks of Jesus as "vindicated by the Spirit." Titus 3:5 connects the Holy Spirit with regeneration.

Hebrews. The writer obviously knows about the charismatic vitality evident in earlier times. God confirmed the gospel with signs and won-

---

38. Raymond E. Brown, *The Gospel according to John 13–21: A New Translation with Introduction and Commentary*, The Anchor Bible 29A (Garden City, N.Y.: Doubleday, 1970), 931.

39. See further Schweizer, "πνεῦμα," *TDNT*, 6:442–44.

40. See further Brown, *The Gospel according to John 13–21*, 1135–43, especially 1136–37.

41. For a detailed analysis, see Congar, *I Believe in the Holy Spirit*, 1:54–56.

42. See further Schweizer, "πνεῦμα," *TDNT*, 6:437–38.

43. See further Fee, *God's Empowering Presence*, 755–95.

ders and gifts of the Holy Spirit (Heb. 2:4). Commensurate with the Pastorals, Hebrews also connects the Spirit with the inspiration of Scripture (3:7; 9:8; 10:15) and with Christology, namely Christ's self-offering through the Spirit (9:14).

James. James has almost nothing to say about the Spirit. The only mention, 4:5, contains an ambiguous reference either to the human spirit as the breath of God (cf. Gen. 6:3; Job 33:4) or to the divine Spirit given in conversion, an interpretation drawing on a common understanding in the New Testament.

The Letters of Peter. As is typical of the New Testament, 1 Peter 1:11 mentions the Spirit as the source of prophecy and the inspirer of mission and the power of the gospel (1:12). Another passage (4:14) speaks of the Spirit as the source of blessing and strength in the midst of suffering. The only mention in 2 Peter relates to the inspiration of Scripture (1:21).

Jude. Jude's only reference, verses 19–20, sounds Pauline in character: Believers are those who have the Spirit.

Revelation.[44] In consonance with the overall theme of the last book of the Christian canon, the Spirit plays a crucial role in inspiration and vision (1:10; 4:2; 14:13; 17:3; 21:10; 22:17). For the seer of the Apocalypse, "the testimony of Jesus" is "the Spirit of prophecy" (19:10). In addition, the Apocalypse mentions "seven spirits" (1:4; 4:5) or the spirits of Jesus (3:1; 5:6), phrases that are typical of apocalyptic literature.

The Bible offers a variety of approaches to and perspectives on the Spirit. Even though there is no one "doctrine" of the Spirit in the Bible, there is a common core. In the Old Testament, the Spirit is the principle and source of life. The New Testament builds on this foundation, highlighting the Spirit's role in Jesus' life and the charismatic power that Jesus passed on to his disciples. The rich historical traditions to which we now turn show how these and other biblical orientations came to be understood doctrinally and appropriated for spirituality.

---

44. See further Schweizer, "πνεῦμα," *TDNT*, 6:449–51.

3

The Historical Unfolding of the Experience of the Spirit

In Search of a Doctrinal Understanding of the Spirit

> The Old Testament preached the Father openly and the Son more obscurely, while the New revealed the Son and hinted at the deity of the Spirit. Now the Spirit dwells in us and reveals himself more clearly to us. For it was not right, while the deity of the Father had still not been confessed, to preach the Son openly and, before the deity of the Son had been acknowledged, to force us to accept the Holy Spirit.[1]

In this way, Gregory of Nazianzus—one of the Cappadocian fathers, who were theologians of the Trinity and the Spirit—explained the process by which the church came step by step to a fuller understanding of the Spirit. It is characteristic of the development of Christian theology that in various epochs different questions come under the scrutiny of theologians and church leaders. The growth of the Christian tradition began with a proper doctrine of God. The doctrine of the Trinity was developed during the first centuries. Then christological questions had to be settled before the church was ready to focus on the doctrine of the Spirit. The driving question in this regard was the divinity of the Spirit.

---

1. Gregory of Nazianzus, *Orationes theologicae* 31, 5.26.

"Long before the Spirit was a theme of doctrine, He was a fact in the experience of the community."[2] This remark of Eduard Schweizer with regard to the unfolding of the doctrine of the Spirit in the New Testament applies as well to its unfolding in church history. Even though different Christian traditions experienced the Spirit in vivid ways, they did not immediately feel a need for a more precise concept of the Spirit's person and work. The doctrine of the Spirit grew gradually on the basis of the Old and New Testaments, along with the life of the church, its ministry, and its liturgy.

Informative histories of pneumatology abound,[3] and there is no need to attempt any kind of systematic history here. The purpose of the present chapter is rather to look more closely at the ways the church and Christian theology appropriated the Spirit's person and work during history and to investigate the main challenges that drove the church toward a fuller understanding. Therefore, in order to pay tribute to the richness of the pneumatological tradition and spirituality, we will discuss several different orientations to the Spirit. The way Augustine understood the Spirit complements, say, the vivid experience of the Spirit of some medieval mystics. Or the way Hegel attempts to define the Spirit philosophically in relation to his overarching world theory is certainly distinctive when compared to the enthusiasm of Anabaptist traditions.

Throughout history, powerful Spirit movements have challenged the conventional doctrine and practice of the church catholic.[4] One such movement was that of the Montanists. Not only did they question the pneumatological understanding of the church but also its ecclesiology and view of revelation. To these varied, complementary, and to some extent contradictory experiences of the Spirit we now turn.

2. Eduard Schweizer, "πνεῦμα," *TDNT*, 6:396.
3. For the history of pneumatology, see the following recent works: Yves Congar, *I Believe in the Holy Spirit* (New York: Crossroad Herder, 1997), 1:65–166, 3:19–216; Stanley M. Burgess, *The Holy Spirit: Ancient Christian Traditions* (Peabody, Mass.: Hendrickson, 1984); idem, *The Holy Spirit: Eastern Christian Traditions* (Peabody, Mass.: Hendrickson, 1989); and idem, *The Holy Spirit: Medieval Roman Catholic and Reformation Traditions* (Peabody, Mass.: Hendrickson, 1997). For older works, see Howard Watkin-Jones, *The Holy Spirit from Arminius to Wesley* (London: Epworth, 1929); idem, *The Holy Spirit in the Medieaval Church* (London: Epworth, 1922); and Charles Williams, *The Descent of the Dove: A Short History of the Holy Spirit in the Church* (Grand Rapids: Eerdmans, 1939).
4. The term *church catholic* is used to indicate the catholic—meaning "universal"—church, as distinguished from the Roman Catholic Church. Church catholic also designates the mainstream church or the general theological consensus in the first four centuries A.D.

The Charismatic Experience

The New Testament theologian James D. G. Dunn has argued that, from the beginning of Christianity, strands of charismatic, enthusiastic Christian expressions emerged that differed from the more conventional, traditional church catholic. These enthusiastic groups wanted to keep alive the flame of vivid charismatic experience that was characteristic of and central to early Christianity.[5] It might well be the case that, in the first two centuries, charismatic, "enthusiastic" spiritual life was a norm rather than a barely tolerated minority voice in the church.

Yves Congar contends that in the beginning the church saw itself subject to the activity of the Spirit and filled with his gifts. As an example he mentions Clement of Rome, who said that the apostles "set out, filled with the assurance of the Holy Spirit, to proclaim the good news of the coming of the kingdom of heaven."[6] Toward the end of the first century, Clement was also obliged to provide rules for the church at Corinth as to the right use of charisms, implying that spiritual gifts were active at that time. This assumption is confirmed by the witness of Justin Martyr in the middle of the second century, when he claimed that prophecy and charismatic gifts still existed; in fact, it was believed that the charisms should accompany the church until the end.[7] In the early centuries, prophecy was held to be the most important charism. *The Didache* gave an important place to the ministry of prophets and provided criteria for determining their authenticity.[8]

According to Congar, no opposition yet existed between "hierarchical" and "charismatic" ministries in the church. By definition, ministry as well as the whole church itself was considered charismatic.[9] Those who questioned the charismatic nature of the church were seen as sectarians. The emerging role of bishops was not regarded as a means of quenching the Spirit since bishops were charismatics. Montanus, the initiator of one of the first "charismatic"

---

5. See, e.g., James D. G. Dunn, *Unity and Diversity in the New Testament: An Inquiry into the Character of Earliest Christianity* (London: SCM Press; Philadelphia: Trinity Press International, 1991), chap. 9.

6. Clement of Rome, *Cor* XIII, 3.

7. Congar, *I Believe in the Holy Spirit*, 1:65. A substantial part of this section is drawn from Congar, 1:65–72.

8. See *Didache* 9.8–12 and chap. 13.

9. Very soon, however, there arose what Schweizer ("πνεῦμα," *TDNT*, 6:451) calls "the official strand," an understanding and practice of the ministry in which the one who is rightly instituted into office is now guaranteed the Spirit of God, rather than the other way around, i.e., the one whom God appoints by endowment with the Spirit is ordained to the ministry. See also Bernd Jochen Hilberath, "Pneumatologie," in *Handbuch der Dogmatik*, ed. Theodor Schneider et al. (Düsseldorf: Patmos, 1992), 1:491–92.

movements, was the first to make the distinction between the church of the Spirit and the church of the bishops, indicating a lack of opposition up to that point. Furthermore, there was no opposition yet between the growth of tradition (doctrinal development) and charisms, such as visions and warnings from the Spirit. Cyprian said of the Council of Carthage (252) that it had made decisions "under the inspiration of the Holy Spirit and according to the warnings given by the Lord in many visions." Cyprian himself (d. 258) is claimed to have had various kinds of visions from the Spirit.[10] Irenaeus (c. 130–c. 200) said of the Spirit: "Faith is received from the Church and kept by us; it always makes us young again and, under the influence of the Spirit, like a costly drink contained in a precious vase, even renews the vase that holds it."[11]

Christological and pneumatological orientations were regarded as both complementary and in some tension with each other. Ignatius (c. 35–c. 107) suggested that the ecclesiality of the church—what makes the church the church—could be ascertained by Christ's presence: "Wherever Jesus Christ is, there is the universal church."[12] According to Irenaeus, what is decisive is the presence of the Spirit of God: "Wherever the Spirit of God is, there is the church, and all grace."[13]

For Hippolytus (c. 170–c. 236), the Holy Spirit ensured that the tradition of the apostles would be preserved. The Spirit was believed to refute heresies. One can also speak of a kind of succession of transmission of the Spirit in the church.[14] A description written in 251 by Novatian gives a vivid picture of the charismatic vitality of the church in the first centuries:

> (That Spirit, who enabled the disciples not to fear, in the name of the Lord, either the powers of the world or its torments) gives similar gifts, like jewels, to the Bride of Christ, the Church. He causes prophets to appear in the Church, instructs the Church's teachers, encourages tongues, obtains power and health, works wonders in the Church, brings about the discernment of spirits, helps those who govern the Church, inspires the Church's councils and dispenses the other gifts of grace. In this way, he perfects and completes the Church of Christ everywhere and in all things.[15]

10. Congar, *I Believe in the Holy Spirit,* 1:65–66, 68.
11. Irenaeus, *Adversus haereses* 3.11.9.
12. Ignatius, *Smyrn.* 8.2.
13. Irenaeus, *Adversus haereses* 3.24.1.
14. See the prologue in Hippolytus, *Apostolic Tradition.*
15. Novatian, *De Trin. Lib.* 29.

One of the first major challenges to the catholic church came from a group of Christians who believed that the charismatic vitality of the church was waning and prophetic activity was no longer held in honor.

The Montanist Challenge: Who Is the Real Paraclete?

How can the catholic church discern a real move of the Spirit? What is the role of written Scripture in discerning authentic and false spirits? Who are real prophets? Who is a spiritual person? These kinds of questions came to the fore along with the emergence of the first major "charismatic movement" in church history, namely, Montanism.[16] If the Montanist prophets were mouthpieces of God, opposing their oracles, which were delivered in the Spirit, was a very bold spiritual decision. Prophetic charismatic movements also usually touch theological loci other than pneumatology. In this case, Didymus reported that Montanists (re)baptized even those who were baptized. Was then their baptism valid, if they themselves were heretical?

The Montanist movement emerged in roughly A.D. 160–170 around the Phrygian Pentapolis area, in what is modern Turkey. The Christian church in Hierapolis, for example, was vulnerable to it.[17] There are various, even contradictory, assessments of Montanism. The overall evaluation is that it arose from a false spirit and held an erroneous pneumatology. Apollonius of Ephesus alluded to the evil lifestyle of their prophets and believed them in need of exorcism. He also criticized them for "revelational novelty" and for undermining the authority of the apostles, which in fact meant opposing the Lord himself.[18]

A much more positive evaluation comes from Tertullian (c. 160–c. 230), the Carthaginian church's most prominent early lay theologian.

16. The main source here is William Tabbernee, "'Will the Real Paraclete Please Speak Forth!': The Catholic-Montanist Conflict over Pneumatology," in *Advent of the Spirit: Orientations in Pneumatology*, Conference Papers from a Symposium at Marquette University, 17–19 April 1998 (unpublished). The most recent study on Montanism in English is Christine Trevett, *Montanism: Gender, Authority, and the New Prophecy* (Cambridge: Cambridge University Press, 1996). For a brief survey, see also Tabbernee, "Remnants of the New Prophecy: Literary and Epigraphical Sources of the Montanist Movement," *Studia Patristica* 21 (1989): 193–201.

17. Little valid historical information is available; we know about the Montanists mostly through other people. Avircius Marcellus, the bishop of Hierapolis, consulted another bishop, an expert on Montanism, who was an opposer. A now anonymous writer sent a response to Marcellus, a response known to us through Eusebius's *Ecclesiastical History*. Apollonius, (probably) another catholic bishop, also wrote a lengthy treatise against the Montanists. Tabbernee, "'Will the Real Paraclete Please Speak Forth!'" 2–3.

18. Tabbernee, "'Will the Real Paraclete Please Speak Forth!'" 3–5.

According to Jerome (c. 347–419/20), Tertullian wrote a treatise on ecstasy originally consisting of six books, to which a seventh was added, refuting the charges of Apollonius. Tertullian became attracted to Montanism but most probably did not leave the catholic church. What makes his case even more interesting is that even though he was sympathetic to Montanism, he remained an authority in catholic theology in North Africa. Unfortunately, this writing, *De Ecstasi*, has not survived.[19]

Tertullian's definition of "ecstasy" is the ability of the soul "to stand out of itself." Just as in dreaming the body is asleep but the soul remains active, so the human spirit is overshadowed by the Spirit of God. But for Tertullian, the prophet is not mad or demon-possessed. Proof that a dreamer is still of sound mind is the ability to recall dreams.[20] Thus, according to Tertullian, Montanists did not introduce any novelties: The Paraclete is not an "institutor" (of anything new) but rather a "restitutor" (of what Christ said and taught). Even when the Paraclete reveals something new, it is not actually new but rather a return to the underlying principles of the message of Christ. The Paraclete's final revelation was postponed to the time of Montanism because the church was not yet ready. William Tabbernee is correct when he insists that Tertullian championed the view of progressive revelation, but only with regard to matters of practice: There is a distinction between *regula fidei* (the completed body of doctrine and truth) and *disciplina* (the as-yet-incomplete teaching regarding conduct of life).[21]

Tertullian firmly believed that the Holy Spirit, operative in the church for all ages, cannot contradict himself. He also attempted to correct the charge (about which we have no evidence one way or another) that Montanists distinguished between the Holy Spirit who was in the apostles and the Paraclete who was only in the Montanist prophets.

So the question remains: Were Montanists heretical?

An anonymous writer noted that the Montanists held the same view of the Triune God as the catholic church, but their emphasis on "spiritual gifts" had caused them to devote themselves to demonic spirits. He thought that the true Holy Spirit does not create ecstasy, a loss of possession of one's faculties. He also stated that their prophecies did not come to fulfillment; the end did not come as they had prophesied.

19. For Tertullian's relationship with Montanism and its potential influence on his theology, see Kilian McDonnell, "Communion Ecclesiology and Baptism in the Spirit: Tertullian and the Early Church," *TS* 49 (1988): 671–93.

20. Tabbernee, "'Will the Real Paraclete Please Speak Forth!'" 6.

21. Ibid., 7–8.

Other charges were also leveled against the Montanists. Well known is the criticism of Basil the Great (c. 330–379), according to whom Montanus identified himself with the Paraclete. But we do not have convincing evidence for this charge. Neither is there any longer legitimate grounds for the charge of modalistic monarchianism—an equating of the three persons of the Trinity.[22]

The conclusion by Tabbernee is balanced. He first acknowledges that historically speaking many of the pneumatological charges leveled against the Montanists are blatantly erroneous. But then he points to the lasting contribution, the theological challenge, that Montanism and similar charismatic movements pose to the church and theology:

> Is ecstatic utterance proof of the presence of the Holy Spirit or is it a sign of demonic possession? To what extent may the fullness of the Holy Spirit be said to have been completed at Pentecost? Is there such a thing as progressive revelation, even if limited to matters of Christian practice rather than doctrine? Does heresy with regard to one dimension of Christian theology affect detrimentally all other components of that theology? What is required of rank and file Christians to live as "spiritual persons"?[23]

The Eastern Fathers: The Deifying Spirit

The Eastern fathers were impressed by the grace that deifies humans and makes them sharers of divine life.[24] They believed that through the incarnation the mortal had been changed into immortal and from passible into impassible. The great Eastern teachers, Athanasius, Gregory of Nyssa, Gregory of Nazianzus, and Cyril of Alexandria, insisted that it was by the incarnation of the Logos that humanity was anointed by the Holy Spirit. According to Cyril, "Christ filled his whole body with the life-giving power of the Spirit. . . . It was not the flesh that gave life to the Spirit, but the power of the Spirit that gave life to the flesh."[25]

Quite early in the history of the church, the Eastern fathers combated a serious pneumatological heresy, that of Macedonius (d. c. 362) and the Pneumatomachoi ("enemies of the Spirit"). The Pneumatomachoi believed that the Spirit was a power or an instrument of God that had been

22. Ibid., 10–11.
23. Ibid., 21.
24. For the main sources, see Congar, *I Believe in the Holy Spirit*, especially 1:73–77 and 3:29–35. For a more detailed exposition, see C. N. Tsirpanlis, *Introduction to Eastern Patristic Thought and Orthodox Theology*, Theology and Life Series 30 (Collegeville, Minn.: Liturgical Press, 1991); and Burgess, *The Holy Spirit*.
25. Quoted in Congar, *I Believe in the Holy Spirit*, 1:73.

created in order to act in us and the world. According to their understanding, the Spirit remained solely at the level of "economy" (referring
to God's dealings with the world, in contrast to God's intra-trinitarian relations).[26] As usual, threatening views also helped consolidate and refine
the orthodox views. The struggle against the Pneumatomachoi influ-
enced two liturgical developments. First, during the fourth century, it
helped shape the *epiclēsis*, the invocation of the Holy Spirit over the
bread and wine. Second, Pentecost came to be regarded not only as the
feast of the Holy Spirit but also of the Father and the Son: The Spirit was
"co-adored and co-glorified with the Father and the Son."[27]

The main Eastern treatise on the Holy Spirit is *Treatise on the Holy
Spirit* (374–75), written by Basil of Caesarea. It was partly a response to the
criticism of his newly formulated doxology: "Glory to the Father, with the
Son, with the Holy Spirit" (instead of the standard: "Glory to the Father,
through the Son, in the Holy Spirit"). He justified the new doxology with
Scripture and tradition. However, Basil, as well as Athanasius (c. 293–
373), was hesitant to call the Holy Spirit "God," since that is not the language of the Bible. Even though the Cappadocians were keenly interested
in a more conceptual understanding of the Spirit and the Trinity, they
wanted to preserve the biblical, "economic" language at any cost.

Even with these reservations, the Cappadocians helped convince the
church that the Spirit belonged, both in equality and in dignity, to the holy
Trinity. For Athanasius, the trinitarian baptismal formula showed that the
Spirit shares the same divinity as the Father and the Son. Furthermore,
deification requires it: If the Spirit is not consubstantial with the Father
and the Son, the Spirit cannot make us conform to the Son and therefore
cannot save us. For Athanasius and Basil, the Spirit has a relationship with
the Son similar to that which the Son has with the Father.[28]

Basil's brother, Gregory of Nyssa (c. 330–c. 395), further developed
the doctrine of the divinity of the Spirit. Building on his brother's and
Athanasius's formulations, he argued that the formation *(morphōsis)* of
the Christian and his perfection *(teleiōsis)* according to Christ's model
are the work of the sanctifying Spirit; the Spirit therefore is consubstantial with the Son and the Father. In other words, there is a unity of
nature but a distinction between *hypostases*. However, the *monarchy* of
the Father is always maintained here as in the rest of Eastern theology.
As illustrations, Gregory spoke of a lamp that communicates its light to
another lamp and through that lamp to a third one.[29]

26. Hilberath, "Pneumatologie," 495–96.
27. Congar, *I Believe in the Holy Spirit*, 3:76.
28. Ibid., 30.
29. Ibid., 31–32.

Another Gregory, that of Nazianzus (329–389), the "Theologian" of the East, was probably the first Eastern father who dared to call the Holy Spirit "God." In addition, his gateway to a more precise understanding of the Spirit was the Trinity: "The name of the one who is without beginning is Father; the name of the beginning is Son; the name of the one who is with the beginning is Holy Spirit." Illustrations such as source, stream, and river, or sun, ray, and light were provided to make this relationship more easily understandable.[30]

The first decisive step in the doctrinal understanding of the church concerning the Spirit was reached at the Council of Constantinople, which drafted the Nicene-Constantinopolitan Creed in 381. According to the creed, the Spirit is neither "God" nor "consubstantial" with the Father and the Son but is rather the "Lord and life-giver, proceeding from the Father, object of the same worship and the same glory with the Father and the Son."[31] The following year the same 150 bishops met again and offered further refinement of the doctrine by speaking of "one substance, the uncreated Trinity, consubstantial and eternal."[32]

Stanley Burgess summarizes the main Eastern patristic orientations in pneumatology as follows:[33]

1. The Eastern view of the Trinity emphasizes the unity as opposed to the individuality within the Godhead, while at the same time it recognizes the reciprocal nature of trinitarian persons *(perichōrēsis)*.
2. Eastern anthropology, while not operating in guilt concepts (the need for salvation is understood from the perspective of guilt and needed satisfaction) as its Western counterpart does, looks forward to the renewing of the image of God.
3. Since the divine Spirit is the giver of life, his main soteriological operation is the divinization of human beings *(theōsis)*.
4. Even though among the Eastern fathers there have been differing understandings of the exact nature of the experience of the Spirit, they have always emphasized the experiential nature of the divine Spirit.
5. One of the reasons why pneumatology has been so central to theology and liturgy in the East is the array of rich symbolic vocabulary and imagery of the Spirit of God. "Symbols are not merely pointers to understanding the reality of that which is

30. Ibid., 32–33.
31. Hilberath, "Pneumatologie," 499.
32. Congar, *I Believe in the Holy Spirit*, 1:75.
33. Burgess, *The Holy Spirit*, 1–9.

hidden. They also are within themselves the actual presence of what they symbolize."[34]

Augustine: The Spirit as the Bond of Love

In the Western wing of the church, Augustine (354–430) laid the groundwork for the view of the Holy Spirit. His comment on the pneumatological lacuna has not yet lost its relevance:

> Many books have been written by scholarly and spiritual men on the Father and the Son. . . . The Holy Spirit has, on the other hand, not yet been studied with as much care and by so many great and learned commentators on the scriptures that it is easy to understand his special character and know why we cannot call him either Son or Father, but only Holy Spirit.[35]

Augustine had a lifelong interest in the Holy Spirit. He discussed the topic in several of his works, the most comprehensive being *De Trinitate* (399–419). But he was conscious of the difficulty of the matter and struggled with objectivity. Rather than attempting to introduce anything novel, he wanted to elaborate the common understanding of the church.[36] The starting point for Augustine's understanding is that some attributes are common both to the Father and the Son without any contrast or distinction. The main biblical passage is John 16:13, which for him reveals the foundational truth that the Father is only the Father of the Son and the Son is only the Son of the Father, but the Spirit is the Spirit of both![37] Therefore, although the Spirit is quite distinct, he is also that which is common to both; he is their shared holiness and their love.[38]

The traditional names given to the Holy Spirit indicate his unique character. For Augustine, the following three are most indicative of the Spirit's nature: Holy Spirit, Love, and Gift. With regard to the name Holy Spirit, Augustine finds a problem: The name does not reflect his

34. Ibid., 4.
35. Augustine, *De fide et symbolo* 9.18–19.
36. The main source here is Joseph Ratzinger, "The Holy Spirit as *Communio:* Concerning the Relationship of Pneumatology and Spirituality in Augustine," *Comm* 25 (1998): 324–39. See also Marc Quellet, "The Spirit in the Life of the Trinity," *Comm* 25 (1998): 199–213; and Congar, *I Believe in the Holy Spirit*, 3:80–95.
37. Augustine also alludes to several passages that talk about the Spirit as the Spirit of the Father (Matt. 10:20; Rom. 8:11) and others that speak about the Spirit as the Spirit of the Son (Rom. 8:9; Gal. 4:6).
38. Congar, *I Believe in the Holy Spirit*, 1:78.

uniqueness, since the Father and Son could also be so named.[39] But this provides an important clue to who the Holy Spirit is. The particularity is that the Spirit shares what the Father and the Son have in common; in other words, the Spirit is the *communio* between them. This idea of the Holy Spirit as *communio* also relates to ecclesiology. The Spirit is the *communio* between Christians and God and among Christians. In Joseph Ratzinger's words, "The Spirit is person as unity, unity as person."[40]

Love is another biblical term for the Spirit. Here the central text is 1 John 4:16: "God is love." It applies both to the undivided divinity and specifically to the Holy Spirit. The proof for the latter is found in 1 John 4:7–16. Here Augustine drew an ingenious conclusion:

- v. 12   If we love one another, God abides in us.
- v. 16b   God is love, and he who abides in love, God abides in him.
- v. 13   We recognize that we abide in him and he in us because he has given us of his Spirit.

In the first two instances, love gives abiding; in the third, the Holy Spirit. Augustine also alludes to Romans 5:5, which speaks of God pouring out his love in our hearts through the Holy Spirit, and 1 John 4:7, 12, 13, and 16, in which "love is from God" and "love is God"; therefore, love is "God from God," or the Holy Spirit. The Spirit is the gift of love.[41]

From this Augustine drew an all-important conclusion: The primary presence of the Holy Spirit is love, not knowledge. It is love that creates abiding, constancy, and unity. This line of reasoning led Augustine to crucial ecclesiological implications. The church is the temple of the Holy Spirit. Every division and strife opposes the Spirit's very nature as the Spirit of unity. Augustine notes the eschatological role of love as judge, both in Jesus' (Matthew 25) and Paul's (1 Corinthians 13) teaching. The lack or the presence of love is the final criterion. This principle applies to the Donatists, a schismatic group refuted by Augustine: They have right sacraments and doctrines, but they have broken love. Without love everything else is empty. Augustine even goes so far as to say that the church is love![42]

39. John 4:24 states that "God is spirit," and God's being spirit and holy could allow us to call him Holy Spirit.
40. Ratzinger, "The Holy Spirit as *Communio*," 327.
41. Ibid., 328–29.
42. Congar, *I Believe in the Holy Spirit*, 1:80.

The third basic name for the Spirit, the Gift, is based on a New Testament teaching, with John 4:7–14 serving as the basic text.[43] The *donum* spoken of here, the "water," is the promise given in John 7:37 (and explained in 7:39). Another passage is 1 Corinthians 12:13: "We were all given the one Spirit to drink." This name of the Holy Spirit establishes the close connection between Christology and pneumatology. Christ is the well of the living water, the crucified Christ of John 19. This name also explains for Augustine the difference between the Son and the Holy Spirit: "He [the Holy Spirit] comes from God not as born but as given *(non quomodo natus, sed quomodo datus)*. Therefore he is not called son because he is neither 'born' like the 'first-born' nor 'created' as we are *(neque natus . . . neque factus)*."[44] For Augustine, this name makes a theology/pneumatology of "giving" possible. The Holy Spirit is always in his essence the gift of God, God as the self-giving God. Herein also lies the ground for creation: God giving himself to the world.[45] This idea of the Spirit as Gift was later embraced enthusiastically by Martin Luther.

In this discussion, Augustine introduced the much debated *filioque:* Since the Spirit is the Spirit and Love of the first two Persons, he must be said to proceed from those Persons. In the first place, the Spirit proceeds from the Father, since the Son derives his being from the Father. But the Son, along with the Father, is also the origin of the Spirit.[46] According to Scripture, this Holy Spirit is neither only the Spirit of the Father nor only the Spirit of the Son; he is the Spirit of both. Because of this, he is able to teach us that charity that is common to both the Father and the Son and through which they love each other.[47]

Augustine's work was formative for Western theology, even through the Middle Ages. Neither Anselm of Canterbury (1033/34–1109)[48] nor Thomas Aquinas (1224/25–1274)[49] produced anything unique with regard to pneumatology; rather, they concentrated their efforts on a more precise understanding of the Augustinian outline. What was distinctive and spiritually refreshing was the approach of several medieval mystics.

43. See further Hilberath, "Pneumatologie," 503–4.
44. Augustine, *De Trinitate* 5.14.15. Augustine distinguishes three modes of origin from God: being born, being given, and being created *(natus, datus, factus)*.
45. Ratzinger, "The Holy Spirit as *Communio*," 330–33.
46. Hilberath, "Pneumatologie," 506–11.
47. Augustine, *De Trinitate* 15.17.27.
48. See further Congar, *I Believe in the Holy Spirit*, 3:96–102.
49. See ibid., 1:118–21, 3:116–27.

Medieval Mystics on the Spirit Experience

It has become commonplace to claim that in the footsteps of Augustine, Western theology in general and pneumatology in particular, in contrast to their Eastern counterparts, fell out of living touch with creation and redemption and became occupied with philosophical distinctions often removed from real life and spirituality. The Catholic Catherine Mowry LaCugna's comment is representative:

> Even if Augustine himself intended nothing of the sort, his legacy to Western theology was an approach to the Trinity largely cut off from the economy of salvation. . . . When the *De Trinitate* is read in parts, or read apart from its overall context and in light of Augustine's full career, it is both possible and common to see no real connection between the self-enclosed Trinity of divine persons and the sphere of creation and redemption.[50]

While there is no denying this one-sided orientation of much of Western theology, some resources can help us retrieve a fuller view of the Spirit. The rich spirituality of medieval mystics and saints "corrects the common perception that doctrines of the Holy Spirit were divorced from the original, polyvalent and enlivening experiences that were its source."[51] These "narratives of the Spirit" are full of life, vigor, and enthusiasm about the life in the Spirit. As such they give a powerful testimony to the varied and manifold experience of the Spirit through church history. The following four medieval authors, two women and two men, provide distinctive testimony to the spirituality of the Spirit: Hildegard of Bingen, Bernard of Clairvaux, Bonaventure, and Catherine of Siena.

Hildegard of Bingen: "The Greening of the Spirit"

The year 1998 was the nine hundredth birthday of the twelfth-century Benedictine Hildegard (1098–1179). This multitalented woman was a theologian, herbalist, medical theorist, composer, visionary, prophet, and preacher. She authored no less than four hundred letters and *Scivias,* a "Summa," a doctrinal work with a trinitarian structure.[52]

---

50. Catherine Mowry LaCugna, *God for Us: The Trinity and Christian Life* (San Francisco: HarperCollins, 1991), 102–3.

51. Elizabeth Dreyer, "Resources for a Renewed Life in the Spirit and Pneumatology: Medieval Mystics and Saints," in *Advent of the Spirit,* 2–3. My exposition in this section is heavily indebted to that article. I have also benefited from Elizabeth Dreyer, "Narratives of the Spirit: Recovering a Medieval Resource," in *Catholic Theological Society Proceedings,* ed. E. Dreyer, 51 (1996): 45–90.

52. Her other two main works are *Liber vitae meritorum,* on virtues and vices, and *De operatione Dei,* on cosmology, history, and eschatology. Dreyer, "Narratives of the Spirit," 55.

Hildegard called the church back to poverty and humility and acted as a prophetic critic.

Hildegard was often addressed by God:

> O you who are wretched earth, and, as a woman, untaught in all learning of earthly teachers and unable to read literature with philosophical understanding, you are nonetheless touched by My light, which kindles in you an inner fire like a burning sun; cry out and relate and write these My mysteries that you see and hear in mystical visions. So do not be timid, but say those things you understand in the Spirit as I speak them through you.[53]

Toward the end of her life, she recalled an oracle she received at the age of sixty-one:

> From infancy you have been taught, not bodily, but spiritually, by true vision through the Spirit of the Lord. Speak these things that you now see and hear. . . . Speak and write, therefore, now according to me and not according to yourself.[54]

While employing tender images and sweet pictures, Hildegard obviously claimed a profound spiritual authority for herself. In a letter to Pope Eugenius III, she described her own vocation through the image of a small feather, touched in such a way that it flew miraculously, sustained by the wind of the Spirit so that it would not fall. Her friend and secretary, Guilbert of Gembloux, wrote on this:

> The Apostle does not permit a woman to teach in the Church. But this woman is exempt from this condition because she has received the Spirit, and with a heart instructed in wisdom by his teaching, she has learned through her own experience what is written: "Blessed is the one whom you have instructed, O Lord, and out of your law you have taught him" (Ps. 94:12). . . . But although the anointing of the Spirit, like a school-mistress, teaches her all things inwardly and bids her . . . to offer confidently in public what it has taught her in secret so as to instruct her hearers, she is nonetheless mindful of her own sex and condition. . . . Yes she obeys the Spirit, not him whom the Spirit sends.[55]

53. Hildegard of Bingen, *Scivias,* trans. Columba Hart and Jane Bishop (New York/Mahwah, N. J.: Paulist Press, 1990), 2.1.

54. Hildegard of Bingen, *Liber vitae meritorum,* trans. Bruce W. Hozeski (New York: Garland Publishing, 1994), 9–10.

55. Quoted in Dreyer, "Resources for a Renewed Life in the Spirit," 12.

Hildegard's sustained reflections on the Pentecost event reveal her love of the wondrous works of the Spirit and her sensitivity toward spiritual movings. On the day of Pentecost, the Spirit "bathed" the disciples in the fire, gave them the ability to speak in tongues, and made them proclaimers of God's truth, so much so that "the whole world was shaken by their voices." The same Spirit also expelled all fear and timidity.[56]

What is most distinctive of Hildegard's thinking is that she links the Holy Spirit with the term *viriditas,* or "greening." She imagined the outpouring of the Spirit in natural rather than cultural metaphors. She combined images of planting, watering, and greening to speak of the presence of the Spirit. Hildegard linked the flow of water on the crops with the love of God that renews the face of the earth and by extension the souls of believers.[57] For this spiritual mystic, *viriditas* was a key concept that expressed and connected the bounty of God, the fertility of nature, and the enlivening, fresh presence of the Spirit. Furthermore, the *viriditas* of the Spirit pointed to a life of virtue, the active fruit of the Spirit's gift. In a masterful way, Hildegard applied this imagery to the role of the Spirit in the Trinity:

> And so these three Persons are in the unity of inseparable substance; but They are not indistinct among themselves. How? He Who begets is the Father; He Who is born is the Son; and He who in eager freshness proceeds from the Father and the Son, and sanctified the waters by moving over their face in the likeness of an innocent bird, and streamed with ardent heat over the apostles, is the Holy Spirit.[58]

Bernard of Clairvaux: "The Spirit as Kiss of the Beloved"

Hildegard's contemporary Bernard of Clairvaux (1090–1153) played a key role in the renewal of twelfth-century Cistercian monasticism. His most well-known work is the collection of eighty-six sermons on the Song of Songs. In this highly allegorical exposition, the main theme is union with Christ expressed in sexual images of human lovers.

Bernard was a theologian of the experience.[59] He often invited believers to consult their own experiences in order to test what he was saying about the spiritual life. For Bernard, experience yielded several truths. It conveyed the understanding of sinfulness and also taught spiritual

56. Hildegard of Bingen, *Scivias* 3.7.7; Dreyer, "Narratives of the Spirit," 72.
57. Quoted in Dreyer, "Resources for a Renewed Life in the Spirit," 13–14.
58. Hildegard of Bingen, *Scivias* 3.7.9; Dreyer, "Narratives of the Spirit," 56.
59. See further Kilian McDonnell, "Spirit and Experience in Bernard of Clairvaux," *TS* 58 (1997): 3–18.

aliveness and growth, when the Spirit is bearing witness that we are
children of God:

> You do not need any speech of mine to comment this to you. The Spirit
> reveals it himself (1 Cor. 2:10). You do not need to look it up in the pages
> of a book. Look to experience instead. Man does not know the price of
> wisdom. It comes from hidden places and it has a sweetness with which
> no sweetness known to living men can compare. It is the sweetness of the
> Lord, and you will not recognize it unless you taste it. "Taste and see," he
> says, "how sweet the Lord is" (Ps. 33:9).[60]

There is no separate treatise on the Spirit in Bernard's writings.[61]
Doctrinally, he held the traditional orthodox position in the footsteps
of Augustine. The Spirit is the mutual love between the Father and the
Son. However, Bernard's characterization of the Trinity is vivid: The
Spirit is "the imperturbable peace of the Father and the Son; their un-
shakable bond, their undivided love, their indivisible unity . . . the love
and the benign goodness of them both."[62]

In his *On the Song of Songs*, Bernard linked the Spirit with the truth
that the Spirit will try to communicate and that his listeners should try
to receive: As one advances in the spiritual life, the Spirit provides nour-
ishment through Ecclesiastes, Proverbs, and the Canticles. These are the
"loaves of bread." Their text was composed by the artistry of the Spirit,
and they arise out of Solomon's experience of exulting in the Spirit.[63]

Peculiar to Bernard's characterization of the Spirit is the Spirit's role
as the "kiss." As such he has two functions. The Spirit makes the knowledge of revelation possible and represents the intimacy of love within
the Trinity and between God and the believer. When the bride seeks her
beloved, she does not trust her external senses but asks for a kiss. When
the bride receives the Spirit's kiss, she understands with love and loves
with understanding. The way of contemplation leads one from the kiss
that is the Holy Spirit to participation in the life of the Trinity, since the
Spirit is the very kiss of the Father and the Son.[64]

---

60. Bernard of Clairvaux, *On Conversion* 13.25; Dreyer, "Resources for a Renewed
Life in the Spirit," 16.

61. One of my graduate students at Fuller Theological Seminary wanted to write a
term paper on the pneumatology of Bernard of Clairvaux. His first disappointment was
that he had trouble finding sections in Bernard's sermons on the Song of Songs that deal
explicitly with the Spirit, even though that work and even others, more doctrinal, are imbued with spirituality and the presence of the Spirit.

62. Bernard of Clairvaux, *On the Song of Songs* 8.2.4.6; Dreyer, "Resources for a Renewed Life in the Spirit," 16.

63. Dreyer, "Resources for a Renewed Life in the Spirit," 17.

64. Ibid., 17–18.

Bonaventure: "The Spirit as Magnanimous God"

As background to Bonaventure's discussion of the Spirit is the intense interest among some medieval Franciscans in the pneumatology of Joachim of Fiore (1132–1202). Bonaventure (c. 1217–1274) both condemned and embraced Joachim's speculative approach to history, which was based on the "three ages of the Trinity." The age of the Father was the Old Testament dispensation, that of the Son was the New Testament aeon, including the church, and the age of the Spirit was about to be launched in Joachim's time. It was signaled by the rise of new religious movements, leading to the reform and renewal of the church, and the final establishment of peace and unity on earth. In line with other apocalyptists of history, the theologian of Fiore offered precise dating: Each age consisted of forty-two generations of thirty years each; the age of the Son was due to end in 1260.[65] This intensive eschatological outlook in particular may have made Bonaventure quite reserved when it came to talk about the Holy Spirit and the Joachimite eschatology.[66]

One of Bonaventure's images of the Spirit builds on Pseudo-Dionysius's concept of God as self-diffusive goodness *(bonum diffusivum sui)*.[67] Bonaventure emphasized God's generosity manifested in the incarnation, in the sending of the Spirit, and in endless gifts, virtues, fruits, and beatitudes. God's generosity was expressed especially in the cross, the familiar Franciscan emphasis.[68] Distinctive of this theologian of Bagnoreggio was his sensitivity to the overflowing fullness of God's love, which resulted in narratives about the Holy Spirit that emphasize God's overflowing (self-)giving, an idea that was later embraced and elaborated by Martin Luther, among others.

For Bonaventure, the First Person of the Trinity is the fountain of all fullness, the fecund source from which all goodness flows. But in a distinctive way, he related the generous gifts of God to the Third Person, to whom was given the name Gift, according to the Augustinian tradition. The Spirit who came in fire at Pentecost bestowed a host of charisms on the church.[69] In a Pentecost sermon, Bonaventure invited

65. The major recent study on Joachim is Christopher Walsh, *The Calabrian Abbot: Joachim of Fiore in the History of Western Thought* (New York: Macmillan, 1985). See also Bernard McGinn, "The Abbot and the Doctors: Scholastic Reactions to the Radical Eschatology of Joachim of Fiore," *Church History* 40 (1971): 30–47. For the relationship between Bonaventure and Joachimite views, see David Burr, "Bonaventure, Olivi and Franciscan Eschatology," *Collectana Franciscana* 53 (1983): 23–40.

66. Dreyer, "Resources for a Renewed Life in the Spirit," 20.

67. Surprisingly, this expression occurs no less than 240 times in Bonaventure's writings!

68. Dreyer, "Narratives of the Spirit," 57–58.

69. Ibid., 17.

his Franciscan brothers "to gather in, ruminate on, and embrace with affection the unparalleled event of Pentecost, since it revealed so clearly the divine mysteries."[70]

An ethical dimension appears in his pneumatology as well. The Holy Spirit is also given to believers to assist in the proper living of the vows, in holding the community together, and in decision making. One of the roles of the Spirit is to help cultivate the virtue of humility.[71]

Not unlike Hildegard, Bonaventure also employed the imagery of nature to describe the Holy Spirit's work in the believer. He was especially fond of water imagery and fluid images: flowing, gushing, bubbling, and so on. The church is like a watered garden that will not fail because of the influence of the Spirit in her sacraments and members.[72]

Catherine of Siena: "The Spirit as Servant"

Following Augustinian teaching, Catherine's theology is explicitly trinitarian.[73] Catherine (1347–1380) also adopted the Augustinian view of the Holy Spirit as the mutual love between the Father and the Son; by extension, the Spirit is also the mutual love between humans and God. One of her prayers, again reflecting Augustinian influence, depicts Catherine's trinitarian faith:

> You made us in your image and likeness so that, with our three powers   .
> in one soul, we might image your trinity and your unity. And as we image,
> so we may find union: through our memory, image and be united with
> the Father . . . through our understanding, image and be united to the
> Son . . . through our will, image and be united with the Holy Spirit, to
> whom is attributed mercy, and who, is the love of the Father and the
> Son.[74]

In Catherine's holistic theology, the entire Trinity works together in both creation and redemption. God is saying, "For the Holy Spirit did not come alone, but with the power from me the Father

70. Quoted in ibid., 58.

71. Ibid., 59.

72. Dreyer, "Resources for a Renewed Life in the Spirit," 23. As a keen student of the Bible, Bonaventure found, of course, strong biblical attestation to his water imagery: Gen. 2:10; Ezek. 36:25; Zech. 12:10; 13:1; Rev. 22:1; and so on.

73. According to the judgment of Marie Walter Flood ("St. Thomas's Thought in the Dialogue of St. Catherine," *Spirituality Today* 32, no. 1 [1980]: 27), the Trinity is the centerpiece of Catherine's theology.

74. Catherine of Siena, *The Prayers of Catherine of Siena*, ed. Suzanne Noffke (New York: Paulist Press, 1983), #4, 42.

with the wisdom of the Son and with his own mercy. So you see, he returned, not in the flesh but in his power, to firm up the road of his teaching."[75]

As a vivid poet, she employed unusually rich imagery. One of the most striking speaks of the Father as the table, the Son as the food, and the Holy Spirit as the servant, offering enlightenment and charity for souls and blazing desires for the church's reform.

> This waiter carries to me [God the Father] their tender loving desires, and carries back to them the reward for their labors, the sweetness of my charity for their enjoyment and nourishment. So you see, I am their table, my Son is their food, and the Holy Spirit, who proceeds from the Father and from the Son, waits on them.[76]

Obviously, this unique imagery stems from her own life experience as a maid while she was a young woman. A related image, applied to the Eucharist, is the "hand of the Holy Spirit . . . dispensing this food, sweetly serving those who relished it."[77] Sometimes she also used the image of cellarer—the person in the monastery who managed the cellar of food and wine—for the Spirit![78]

"Left-Wing" Pneumatology: The Anabaptist Vision of the Spirit

The Spirit and the Word

Histories and theologies frequently contend that the Anabaptists and other groups of the "left wing" of the Reformation devalued Scripture and put in its place a reliance on the Holy Spirit.[79] While there is undeniably some truth to this claim, it is also clear that this impression more often comes from the less than fair judgments of their opponents. As is well known, the mainline Reformers, especially Martin Luther, had difficulty tolerating these "rebels," let alone listening to their distinctive testimony. The irony of the Reformation debates lies not only in the impasse between the Reformers and the Catholic Counter-Reformation representatives but also in the less than honor-

---

75. Catherine of Siena, *The Dialogue*, ed. Suzanne Naffke (New York: Paulist Press, 1980), #29, 70; #63, 119; Dreyer, "Resources for a Renewed Life in the Spirit," 26.

76. Quoted in Dreyer, "Resources for a Renewed Life in the Spirit," 27.

77. Ibid.

78. Ibid.

79. See, e.g., Gary D. Badcock, *Light of Truth and Fire of Love: A Theology of the Holy Spirit* (Grand Rapids: Eerdmans, 1997).

able silencing of those left-wing Christians who drew from the very same wells of reformation.[80]

It is more correct to say that rather than devaluing the written Word, the Anabaptists had a distinctive view of the relationship between the Spirit and the Word. Even though they emphasized the Holy Spirit, they were also rigorously obedient to the Bible. Scripture was the supreme authority for Anabaptists. In fact, the point of their often quite narrow and even exclusivist view of the church and matters relating to society was their insistence on obedience and the most literal interpretation of Scripture.

The Anabaptists saw an integral relationship between the Spirit and the Word. God's Spirit, which the Anabaptists believed they possessed, was the ultimate authority that first gave authority to the written Word of the Bible. They made a distinction between the "outer" Word (mere hearing and reading of the Word) and the "inner" Word (personal appropriation of the Word) to emphasize the importance of this appropriation. Hans Denck, one of the early leaders, even compiled a list of contradictory Scripture passages, not to lessen the authority of the Word but to show that to reconcile these there had to be a deep personal penetration of the texts' meaning. And this happens only with the help of the Spirit.[81]

Anabaptists share many more similarities than differences with Lutherans and those of the Reformed tradition. The similarities include views on the authority of the Bible, the insistence that interpretation be free from church authority, and the importance of obedience.

When it comes to differences, the pneumatological orientations come into focus. The Anabaptists insisted that whoever has made the commitment to obedience and has the Spirit can read with understanding. Furthermore, far from being individualistic, they emphasized the importance of the community for the right understanding of revelation. In short, they claimed that the Spirit was operative in the church even though their opponents highly doubted it. This, of course, made the common people supreme Bible interpreters in an even more concrete way than in the mainline Reformation. Finally, the Anabaptists did not eschew speaking of the "inner" Word in the face of Luther's harsh critique. They believed the Word of God can come directly to the heart without an intermediary, for example, through prophecy. In that sense, the Word is broader than the Bible,

80. For Luther's harsh judgment against the Enthusiasts *(Schwärmerei)*, see further Congar, *I Believe in the Holy Spirit*, 1:139–40.

81. Donald K. McKim, *The Bible in Theology and Preaching* (Nashville: Abingdon Press, 1985), 37.

the written Word, a view that hardly can be considered contradictory to the biblical view of revelation.[82]

The Spirit and the Church

The Anabaptist free church ecclesiology was appropriated and distinctively developed by several free church traditions. While the baptistic version is currently the most well known, the Quakers, descendants of the left-wing Reformation, provide a prime case study in pneumatological ecclesiology.[83] The basic idea centers around a direct, unmediated access to God and to salvation. There is, therefore, no need for sacraments or formal worship. In an important sense, the Holy Spirit is the rule of the true worship. In many cases, no human worship leadership was assigned in favor of letting the Spirit be the "Master of Ceremonies." For Quakers and others, God continued to speak through history. Each person is capable of a personal, direct relationship with God.

There is no denying the heavy accent on individualism and the Quakers' ambiguous view of the meaning of community. What makes the category of community ambiguous is that, on the one hand, these groups of Christians held everything in common. On the other hand, no human community, and certainly no church hierarchy, was allowed to make spiritual decisions.

Yves Congar's appraisal of Quakers' pneumatological ecclesiology raises some questions. He contends that there is little distinction between the inner light of the human conscience and the Holy Spirit. He also claims that there is in fact no Quaker theology of the Holy Spirit as the Third Person.[84] While the second statement is accurate, one cannot label the Quakers' view of the Spirit a classical-liberalism type of "immanent pneumatology" with any validity. They shared with mainline Reformers a sharply dichotomic view of grace and nature vis-à-vis the classic Catholic view, which emphasizes continuity between God's grace/Spirit and human nature/spirit. It is more accurate to think that while the left-wing Reformers maintained a clear demarcation line between the Spirit and spirit, Anabaptists and Quakers in particular allowed much more intimate and unmediated influence of the Spirit of God on the human spirit. The same holds true with regard to the Spirit's direction of the community.

82. Ibid., 38.
83. See further Congar, *I Believe in the Holy Spirit*, 1:141–43.
84. Ibid., 142–43.

The Philosophical Pneumatology of Hegel

If pressed to name the most definitive influence on contemporary theology, it would be the Enlightenment and the subsequent liberal theology. Even though the theological agenda long ago moved beyond classical liberalism, the reverberations of this view are still felt in theology in general and pneumatology in particular. To help gain some perspective, we will look briefly at the intellectual giant G. W. F. Hegel (1770–1831), whose "idealistic" philosophy and pneumatology laid the groundwork and also became the object of criticism for the emerging liberalism.

Immanuel Kant (1724–1804), another major shaper of modern philosophy and theology, pointed his critique at cheap metaphysical talk about God. In his *Critique of Pure Reason* (1781), he did not allow any kind of legitimate talk about God. However, he found God-talk possible in another context, which he defined as the realm of "practical reason." In his subsequent work, *The Critique of Practical Reason* (1788), Kant located metaphysics in the area of ethics and morality. Of course, he had to split reality into two spheres: the factual and the ethical. Kant chose to locate faith in the moral experience. In addition, he claimed that we do not have knowledge of "things in themselves," only of their "appearance" or effects toward us. God comes into the picture in that our moral nature presupposes certain transcendent beliefs in order to postulate a moral order: (1) human freedom, (2) the immortality of the soul, and subsequently, (3) the existence of God.

For Hegel, denying metaphysics was far too high a price to pay for meaningful God-talk. He was convinced that religion belongs to the realm of reason. By joining theology with philosophy, Hegel wanted to give speculative reason a crucial role in religion. His understanding of truth as process and dialectic favors a dynamic view of reality. Truth, rather than being a static concept, is the process of reasoning itself. Furthermore, as the major philosopher of history, Hegel introduced the category of history as an integral part of the process moving toward the truth. Actually, for Hegel, truth is history.[85]

Hegel's philosophy is usually called "idealistic," which means his outlook presumes the primacy of the spirit/spiritual/Spirit (as over against, for example, materialism). In fact, one of his main works is titled *The Philosophy of the Spirit* (1830; originally, *Philosophie des Geistes*). The name of another important work of Hegel concerning pneumatology gives further insight about his purposes: *The Phenome-*

---

85. See further W. H. Walsh, *An Introduction to the Philosophy of History* (London: Hutchinson's University Library, 1951), 137ff.

nology of the Spirit (1807; originally, *Phänomenologie des Geistes*). Despite the difficulty in defining what he means by the ambiguous term *phenomenology,* what is clear is that he focuses his intellectual capacities on attempting to grasp the essence of the Spirit as clearly as possible.[86]

The basic term *Spirit* in its original German form *(Geist)* is more comprehensive a term than the English equivalent. It means both "spirit" and "mind." And it has to be noted that at least in young Hegel, the "spirit" in fact substituted for "life," making it thus a dynamic, living concept.[87] Hegel's pneumatology and philosophy are also highly rationalistic, as already mentioned. The rationalism becomes even more understandable when we remember that "Spirit" also denotes "mind." "Reality for Hegel is Spirit: The universe is, in a sense, the product of mind and therefore intelligible to mind."[88] Whether the Spirit is understood as "spirit" or "mind," it is important to note that it is an active subject, an activity. In fact, the whole world process is the activity of the Spirit: "Through that process Spirit takes on objective form and comes to full awareness of itself."[89] All processes in nature and history form a unified whole and are the manifestation of an underlying spiritual principle.

For Hegel, God is not a transcendent creator of the world but rather a Spirit permeating everything.[90] God and world are not two separate entities but belong together.[91] In fact, even God as Spirit is in the process of becoming. Hegel had

the vision of a God, present in all of history, becoming who God is, realizing God's own potentialities of being, through all the changes and contradictions. He viewed the world as God in God's development, as God externalizing God's own self in history and leading the world onward and

86. For recent studies on Hegel's philosophical pneumatology, see Alan Olson, *Hegel and the Spirit: Philosophy as Pneumatology* (Princeton: Princeton University Press, 1992); and Steven G. Smith, *The Concept of the Spiritual: An Essay in First Philosophy* (Philadelphia: Temple University Press, 1988).

87. Hilberath, "Pneumatologie," 523; and Bernhard Taureck, "Geist/Heiliger Geist/ Geistesgaben VII," in *Theologische Realenzyklopädie,* ed. Horst Robert Balz et al. (Berlin/ New York: Walter de Gruyter, 1984), 12:250–53.

88. Walsh, *Introduction to the Philosophy of History,* 137.

89. Stanley J. Grenz and Roger E. Olsen, *Twentieth-Century Theology: God and the World in a Transitional Age* (Downers Grove, Ill.: InterVarsity Press, 1992), 33.

90. Even though Hegel rarely uses the term "God," it is clear that for him "Spirit" is equivalent to the divine/God. See further Robert C. Solomon, *From Rationalism to Existentialism: The Existentialists and Their Nineteenth-Century Backgrounds* (Lanham, Md.: Littlefield Adams, 1992), 52.

91. Hegel represents a kind of pantheism in which a clear line of demarcation between God/God's Spirit and the world/world spirit cannot be drawn.

upward in stages to God's own divine fullness. Reality itself is the history of God, God going out from and returning to God's own self.[92]

This concept of God leads us to the distinctive "trinitarian" view of Hegel.[93] Hegel gave the doctrine of the Trinity a new central significance by deriving the Trinity from the concept of God as Spirit.[94] In the Godhead, there are three moments of divine reality, which approach the classic trinitarian persons. The Essential Being, pure, abstract being, resembles the role of the "Father." The Explicit Self-Existence refers to the entrance of the abstract Spirit into existence through the creation of the world ("Son"). God moves outside himself, entering into relationship with that which is other than himself. The Self-Knowledge is the Spirit passing into self-consciousness. The final goal of all historical happening and the process of the Spirit is God returning to himself in humanity. This takes place in the religious life in which humanity comes to know God as God knows himself. This is the final reconciliation within reality. In the incarnation of Christ, the idea of the unity of God and humankind has been made explicit in history. The universal philosophical truth of the divine-human unity has been actualized in a particular historical individual.[95]

It was Christianity that discovered this vision and was the first to introduce it to the world. According to Hegel, this makes Christianity the highest religion. Hegel came to this conclusion by reflecting on the incarnation of the Son. Even though incarnation is a concept known to many other religions, Christianity renders explicit what is only implicit in other religions. How is this so? It is because the Infinite Spirit (God) and the finite spirit (human being) are brought together. For Hegel, unlike most of his predecessors, these two are not radically different or mutually incompatible. The incarnation of Jesus was the perfect manifestation of the Infinite Spirit:

92. Clark H. Pinnock, *Tracking the Maze: Finding Our Way through Modern Theology from an Evangelical Perspective* (Dallas: ICI University Press, 1996), 103.

93. For the purposes of this short presentation of Hegel's pneumatology, there is neither need nor space to delve into the problem of Hegel's Trinitarian view. It has been debated whether Hegel even had a Trinitarian understanding. Jürgen Werbick, "Trinitätslehre," in *Handbuch*, 2:560.

94. Hegel had a strong Trinitarian influence on one of the most significant theologians and pneumatologists of our time, Wolfhart Pannenberg, even though he is also critical of several aspects of Hegel's views. See further Stanley J. Grenz, *Reason for Hope: The Systematic Theology of Wolfhart Pannenberg* (New York/Oxford: Oxford University Press, 1990), especially 48–52.

95. See further, Grenz and Olsen, *Twentieth-Century Theology*, 37.

The Idea . . . when it was ripe and the time was fulfilled, was able to attach itself only to Christ, and to realize itself only in him. The nature of Spirit is still imperfectly realized in the heroic deeds of Hercules. The history of Christ, however, belongs to the community, since it is absolutely adequate in relation to the Idea. . . . It is the Spirit, the indwelling idea, which has witness to Christ's mission, and this is the verification from those who have believed and for us who possess the developed concept.[96]

The Spirit and spirit in Classical Liberalism

The opponents of classical liberalism rarely give favorable descriptions of its pneumatology. Certainly Karl Barth's critique of classical liberalism and its view of the Spirit was quite harsh:

To speak about God meant to speak about humanity, no doubt in elevated tone, but . . . about human faith and works. Without doubt human beings were magnified at the expense of God—the God who is sovereign Other standing over against humanity. . . . This God who is the free partner in a history which he himself inaugurated and in a dialogue ruled by him—this divine God was in danger of being reduced to a pious notion: the mythical expression and symbol of human excitation oscillating between its own psychic heights or depths, whose truth could only be that of a monologue and its own graspable content.[97]

Here Barth (1886–1968) condemns liberal theology, claiming it is left without God and thus replaces the traditional starting point of theology "from above" with an approach "from below." Barth's less than justified critique suggests that in their doctrine of the Holy Spirit, the liberals confused the Spirit of God with the human spirit, since their intention was to speak of God only from the standpoint of human religious sensibility.[98] It has become cliché to claim that the liberal tradition identified the Holy Spirit with the religious and ethical aspects of the human mind, thus treating the Spirit as merely "a cipher for the realm of moral and spiritual values."[99]

In fact, liberalism attempted both a reaction to earlier approaches and a post-Enlightenment proposal for a more immanent doctrine of

96. Quotation in Alister McGrath, *The Making of Modern German Christology* (Oxford: Basil Blackwell, 1986), 34.

97. Karl Barth, "The Humanity of God," in *Karl Barth: Theologian of Freedom*, ed. Clifford Green (London: Collins, 1979), 48.

98. See further Badcock, *Light of Truth and Fire of Love*, 108–12.

99. Alasdair I. C. Heron, *The Holy Spirit* (Philadelphia: Westminster, 1983), 113. I am indebted to Badcock (*Light of Truth and Fire of Love*, 29) for this reference.

the Spirit. What liberalism found highly problematic in the earlier pneumatologies was that the doctrine of the Spirit had been connected with the doctrine of the Trinity, which in liberals' minds was both a misleading and unnecessary addition to the teaching of Jesus. The liberals were also dissatisfied with the radical discontinuity between the divine and human spirit.

Classical liberalism's relation to Hegel's idealistic pneumatology is ambiguous. Its adherents learned from Hegel not to confine the Spirit to soteriological or ecclesiological havens; in his (almost) pantheistic pneumatology, Hegel discarded the demarcation line between the Spirit and the spirit. But liberalism also found problems with Hegel—not only with his highly speculative approach to the study of the Spirit but also with his insistence on the rationality of faith.

To do justice to liberalism, it has to be said that the doctrine of the Holy Spirit was not its primary concern. It did not set out to be a theology of the Holy Spirit. Indirectly, however, because of its concern with experience, liberalism dealt with pneumatological themes, for its "concern is with the experiential arena within which the doctrine of the Spirit is located in Christian theology."[100] The "father of liberalism," Friedrich Schleiermacher (1768–1834), set the tone for the liberal agenda.[101] Whereas Kant had located religion in the ethical realm and Hegel had insisted on the rational nature of religion, Schleiermacher located religion in human experience and "feelings" (it should be noted that the German term *Gefuhl* is a broader term than "feeling"; it denotes "intuitive," "pre-reflexive," and has to do with piety). Here one can see the pervasive influence that pietism—the renewal movement that sought to revitalize Christian life and save it from "dry head knowledge"—exerted on Schleiermacher.

For Schleiermacher, the central component in theology and religion is our experience of "God-consciousness," or the "feeling of absolute dependence."[102] Thus, while pneumatology is by no means the structuring principle of Schleiermacher's *Christian Faith*, because of the centrality of the category of experience, the Spirit is introduced as a crucial theme. The Spirit for Schleiermacher is effectively the spiritual influ-

100. Badcock, *Light of Truth and Fire of Love*, 112. In this section I am indebted to Badcock's elusive exposition of Schleiermacher's pneumatology.

101. By saying this, I am not denying the fact that, on the other hand, Schleiermacher was also deeply in debt to Kant. He shared with Kant the refusal to connect religion with speculative reason and science and rather to connect it with the practical realm. For this, see Schleiermacher's opening comments in his *Christian Faith*, ed. H. R. Mackintosh (Edinburgh: T & T Clark, 1928), §2.

102. Schleiermacher, *The Christian Faith*, §4.

ence left behind by Jesus that gives coherence to the life of the church as a spiritual entity, and therefore, to the life of Christian faith.[103]

The Holy Spirit in Schleiermacher's theology needs to be understood in relation to God, to Jesus Christ, and to the religious dimension of the human being. One way of understanding the church is to see it as based on the religious impulse as an essential element in human nature, for every such essential element is the basis for some sort of fellowship or communion.[104] Redemption for Schleiermacher involves the development of God-consciousness, the feeling of absolute dependence, and its "pervading the whole life, so that one's entire being is directed through the God-consciousness to the Kingdom of God."[105] In Jesus Christ, this God-consciousness reached its zenith.[106] This insight brings pneumatology once again into focus. The religious consciousness, both in Christ and in us, is a function of the presence of God, in other words, God's Spirit.

According to Gary Badcock, this provides the clue needed to see how Schleiermacher understood the person and work of the Holy Spirit.[107] First of all, the metaphysical definitions of older Trinitarian theology are ruled out in favor of "ethical" and "experiential" ones. Since even in Jesus' life the absolute God-consciousness was mediated by the Spirit of God, the Holy Spirit is the union of the "divine essence" with human nature in the form of the common Spirit that exists among believers, or among those who have been regenerated by Christ.[108] Schleiermacher had no interest whatsoever in metaphysical questions concerning the Spirit, since the decisive focus was the Spirit's role with regard to human beings and Jesus' relationship with the Father.

> What this means, however, is that the Holy Spirit is the presence of God in the Christian community in awakening and animating the life of faith, discipleship of Christ, and therefore devotion to the kingdom of God. The same God present in Christ is present in the church, in other words, the only difference being that in the one case his presence was particular, while in the other case it is general and corporate in the ecclesial sense.[109]

Against this background we have to conclude that, even though Barth was correct in that there is continuity between God's Spirit and

---

103. Ibid., §§121–25.
104. Ibid., §6; Badcock, *Light of Truth and Fire of Love,* 114.
105. Badcock, *Light of Truth and Fire of Love,* 115.
106. Schleiermacher, *The Christian Faith,* §94.
107. Badcock, *Light of Truth and Fire of Love,* 116–17.
108. Schleiermacher, *The Christian Faith,* §123.
109. Badcock, *Light of Truth and Fire of Love,* 116.

the human spirit in classical liberalism, his judgment that their doctrine of the Spirit is merely humanistic and ethical is not true.[110] For Schleiermacher, the Spirit is truly God present here and now in the church, which is itself the product of God's presence in Jesus Christ. The Spirit, in other words, cannot be studied alone but only in relation to Christ and Christ's church.[111]

Basically the same holds true for the theology of Albrecht Ritschl (1822–1889), perhaps the most significant liberal theologian. Ritschl connected the treatment of the Spirit even more closely with Christian life than did Schleiermacher. The only way to speak of the Spirit in any meaningful way is to do so on the basis of his activity in history. Anything else amounts to a spurious metaphysics. In line with neo-Kantian insistence that nothing can be known of God directly, only of his effects, Ritschl's pneumatology was exclusively the doctrine of the work of the Holy Spirit rather than of the Spirit's person.[112]

A recent example of the continuing direct influence of liberalism comes from the pneumatological program of Geoffrey Lampe. In his *God as Spirit*,[113] Lampe seeks to set aside the metaphysical questions, since the Spirit he is speaking of, in line with Schleiermacher, is the personal presence of God, first and foremost in Christ and then in his followers:

> We are speaking of God disclosed and experienced as Spirit: that is, in his personal outreach. The use of this concept allows us to say that God indwelt and motivated the human spirit of Jesus in such a way that in him, uniquely, the relationship for which man was intended by his Creator was fully realized; that through Jesus God acted decisively to cause men to share in his relationship to God, and that the same God, the Spirit who was in Jesus, brings believers into that relationship of "sonship" towards himself and forms them into a human community in which, albeit partially and imperfectly, the Christlike character which is the fruit of their relationship is re-presented.[114]

In other words, the particular significance of Jesus resided in his being the bearer of the Spirit of God, and thus an example of a spirit-filled Christian existence.

110. For Barth's own pneumatology, see Philip J. Rosato, *The Spirit as Lord: The Pneumatology of Karl Barth* (Edinburgh: T & T Clark, 1981).

111. See further Badcock, *Light of Truth and Fire of Love*, 116–17.

112. Ibid., 117.

113. Oxford: Clarendon Press, 1977.

114. Lampe, *God as Spirit*, 11.

The pervasive influence of liberal pneumatology can also easily be discerned in the work of Paul Tillich, whose third volume of *Systematic Theology* (1963) is one of the first modern pneumatologies to attempt to transcend the dividing line between the Spirit and spirit.[115] For Tillich, the Spirit of God is the life-giving principle that makes human life and the life of the entire creation meaningful and specific. He titles one of the major sections of his theology "Life and the Spirit."

Now that we have surveyed the various and sometimes conflicting ways in which Christian theology and spirituality have lived out and attempted to make sense of the Spirit and spiritual experience, it is time to survey the major Christian traditions concerning the Holy Spirit as they are represented by various churches today.

115. Paul Tillich, *Systematic Theology* (Chicago: University of Chicago Press, 1963), 3:11–294.

4

Ecclesiastical Perspectives on the Spirit

A Feast of the Spirit

One of the most exciting features of pneumatology is the variety of ways Christian churches have approached the Spirit's ministry. Even though there is only one Spirit of God, the differing emphases and needs of particular churches and traditions have created a rich treasure of spiritual experiences. Of course, the mystical tradition of the Eastern Orthodox Church sees the ministry of the Spirit differently than does the Lutheran Church. And it is to be expected that the new enthusiastic Pentecostal experience contrasts with the ancient tradition of Roman Catholic piety.

This chapter briefly surveys the main Christian traditions beginning with the oldest, the Eastern Church, and concluding with the youngest, the Pentecostal/Charismatic movements. The next chapter supplements the discussion of the various traditions by viewing each one through the lens of a particular theologian. For example, John Zizioulas represents a distinctive modern Eastern tradition, while Karl Rahner provides an example of modern Catholic thought on the Spirit.

The Spirit in the Eastern Orthodox Tradition

"Spirit-Sensitive" Theology[1]

The title given to Simeon, the Byzantine mystic and spiritual writer (949–1022), tells us something crucial about the nature of theology in

1. The phrase is taken from Robert Imbelli's endorsement on the cover of Yves Congar's book, *I Believe in the Holy Spirit* (New York: Crossroad Herder, 1997).

the East: Though he was not by any standard a great theologian but rather a great mystic, visionary, a person captured by the Spirit of God, he was given the title "New Theologian." He was not a theologian but a thoroughly spiritual man.[2]

Eastern Orthodox theology draws heavily from the early sources, namely, the writings of the church fathers of the East. Therefore, any inquiry into Eastern thought should incorporate the experiences and theological developments of the early centuries surveyed briefly in the previous chapter. A fine introduction to modern appropriations of ancient patristic thought is offered by Constantine N. Tsirpanlis in his *Introduction to Eastern Patristic Thought and Orthodox Theology*.[3]

Generally speaking, Eastern theology has been more "spirit-sensitive" than its Western counterparts. Eastern Orthodox theology is heavily imbued by pneumatology; Western theology in the main is built on christological concepts rather than on pneumatological ones. The pneumatological orientation of the East does not mean, however, that Eastern theology has neglected either Christ[4] or the Trinity.[5] Eastern thought is protected from a one-sided concentration on the Spirit by its focus on the primacy of the Father in the doctrine of the Trinity. Also, a good case can be made for the claim that Eastern pneumatology is anchored in Christology rather than operating as an independent theological locus.[6] Tsirpanlis illustrates the Eastern mind-set:

> Those who speak of an Orthodox "Pneumatocentrism" opposed to the so-called "Christocentrism" of the Roman Church, may express their own personal theology, but they speak a language alien to the Fathers and to the saints of the Eastern Orthodox Church. The three Persons, in the Holy Trinity, share in activity of each of them. The Father and the Son are included in every action of the Spirit.[7]

The mystical theology of the Eastern wing of the church is often more experience-based and concrete than Latin theology. "As he who grasps one end of a chain pulls along with it the other end to himself, so he who draws the Spirit draws both the Son and the Father along

2. See further Stanley M. Burgess, *The Holy Spirit: Eastern Christian Traditions* (Peabody, Mass.: Hendrickson, 1989), 53–65.

3. Theology and Life Series 30 (Collegeville, Minn.: Liturgical Press, 1991).

4. See, e.g., Nikos A. Nissiotis, "Pneumatological Christology as a Presupposition of Ecclesiology," in *Oecumenica: An Annual Symposium of Ecumenical Research* (Minneapolis: Augsburg, 1967), 235–52.

5. See, e.g., Vladimir Lossky, *In the Image and Likeness of God*, ed. John H. Erickson and Thomas E. Bird (Crestwood, N.Y.: St. Vladimir's Seminary Press, 1985), chap. 4.

6. See Tsirpanlis, *Introduction to Eastern Patristic Thought*, 83ff.

7. Ibid., 85.

with it," wrote Basil.[8] The role of the Spirit according to this understanding is to make the "first contact," which is followed by the revelation of the Son and, through him, the Father.[9] There is a genuine trinitarian outlook in the Eastern view: "The Father does all things by the Word in the Holy Spirit."[10]

The doctrine of salvation and the doctrine of the church are the two theological loci in which the distinctive Eastern orientation to the Spirit especially comes to the fore. To these two topics we now turn.

The Spirit and Salvation

As is well known, there is a pronounced difference in orientation between the East and the West in regard to Christology and soteriology. According to Eastern theology, Latin traditions have been dominated by legal, juridical, and forensic categories. Eastern theology, on the contrary, understands the need of salvation in terms of deliverance from mortality and corruption. Union with God is the goal of the Christian life, even becoming "in-godded." The underlying anthropology of the East,[11] in contrast with that of the West, seems to deal less with guilt and more with looking upward, so to speak, to the image of God to be fulfilled in mortal human beings.[12] The idea of divine-human cooperation in salvation is not only accepted but is enthusiastically championed, although it is not understood as nullifying the role of grace.

Many Eastern fathers' texts—from Simeon the New Theologian, whose view is always toward a pneumatological orientation, to Maximus the Confessor and the Cappadocian fathers—highlight the necessary connection between the Spirit and salvation. Basil attributes the experience of *theōsis* (deification) to the Holy Spirit, who "being God by nature . . . deifies by grace those who still belong to a nature subject to change."[13] St. Macarius likewise accentuates the role of the Spirit in *theōsis* when he says that persons to be deified, though they retain their own identity (i.e., do not overstep the distinction between God and human), "are all filled with the Holy Spirit."[14]

8. Basil, Letter 38, 4.

9. See John Meyendorff, *Byzantine Theology: Historical Trends and Doctrinal Themes* (New York: Fordham University Press, 1974), especially 168.

10. Athanasius, *Epistula ad Serapionum de more Arii* 1.31.

11. See Meyendorff, *Byzantine Theology*, chap. 11.

12. See, e.g., ibid., 161ff.

13. Basil, *On the Holy Spirit* 1.2.

14. Cited in Daniel B. Clendenin, "Partakers of Divinity: The Orthodox Doctrine of Theosis," *Journal of the Evangelical Theological Society* 37 (1994): 374. Cf. T. Ware, *The Orthodox Way* (Crestwood, N.Y.: St. Vladimir's Seminary Press, 1990), 168.

Interestingly, the Eastern fathers attribute to the Spirit all the multiplicity of effects of God's grace,[15] as is evident, for example, in the theologies of Gregory Nazianzus and Basil. The Eastern fathers freely speak about the Holy Spirit as effecting deification, perfection, adoption, and sanctification.[16] Eastern Christians sing, "The Holy Spirit giveth life to souls; he exalteth them in purity; He causeth the sole nature of the Trinity to shine in them mysteriously."[17]

The Eastern Church teaches that what is common to the Father and the Son is the divinity that the Holy Spirit communicates (cf. *perichōrēsis*) to humans within the church, in making them partakers of the divine nature.[18] According to Gregory Nazianzus, deification is the highest gift and blessing of the Holy Spirit.[19] In this sense, as St. Seraphim of Sarov said, "The true aim of the Christian life is the acquisition of the Holy Spirit of God."[20]

The role of the Holy Spirit in Eastern soteriology is highlighted by the ultimate goal of salvation. The immediate aim of redemption is salvation from sin, but salvation will have its ultimate realization in the age to come in our union with God, the deification of the created beings whom Christ ransomed. But this final realization involves the dispensation of the Holy Spirit. The work of the Spirit is, of course, inseparable from that of the Son, described in the words of Athanasius as "God bearing flesh," and as "bearing the Spirit."[21]

Prayer, asceticism, meditation, humble service, and similar exercises are recommended for the attainment of the noble goal of deification. The notion of merit, though, is foreign to those of the Eastern tradition. In general, their attitude toward grace and free will is less reserved than that of their Western partners. In the East, the question of free will has never had the urgency that it assumed in the West from the time of Augustine onward. The Eastern tradition never separates grace and human freedom. Therefore, the charge of Pelagianism (that grace is a reward for the merit of the human will) is not fair.

15. For a careful analysis of the relationship between grace and the Holy Spirit in Latin theology, see Wolfhart Pannenberg, *Systematic Theology* (Grand Rapids: Eerdmans, 1997), 3:197–200.

16. For a sample of representative texts, see Vladimir Lossky, *The Mystical Theology of the Eastern Church* (Crestwood, N.Y.: St. Vladimir's Seminary Press, 1976), 163ff.

17. Antiphon in the fourth tone from the Sunday Office.

18. Lossky, *Mystical Theology*, 162. See also Pannenberg, *Systematic Theology* (Grand Rapids: Eerdmans, 1991), 1:266ff.

19. See Tsirpanlis, *Introduction to Eastern Patristic Thought*, 168ff.

20. Cited in T. Ware, *The Orthodox Church* (London: Penguin Books, 1993), 230; see also Lossky, *Mystical Theology*, 196.

21. Athanasius, *De incarnatione et contra Arianos* 8; see also Lossky, *In the Image*, 103ff.

It is not a question of merit but of cooperation, of a synergy of the two wills, divine and human. Grace is a presence of God within us that demands constant effort on our part.[22] In the nineteenth century, Bishop Theophanes, a great Russian ascetic writer, asserted that "the Holy Ghost, acting within us, accomplishes with us our salvation" and that "being assisted by grace, man accomplished the work of his salvation."[23]

In fact, the idea of deification cannot be expressed on a christological basis alone; it demands pneumatological development as well. The mystical tradition of Eastern Christendom, Pentecost, which confers the presence of the Holy Spirit and the firstfruits of sanctification, signifies both the end and the final goal of the spiritual life. It is important to note that in the Eastern rite of confirmation,[24] chrism, "anointing" with the Spirit, follows immediately upon baptism. The Holy Spirit is operative in both confirmation and baptism. The Spirit recreates human nature by purifying it and uniting it with the body of Christ. The Spirit also bestows deity upon human persons.[25] Eastern theology even speaks about Christians as "christs," anointed ones: The Spirit who rests like a royal unction upon the humanity of the Son communicates himself to each member of Christ's body.[26]

The Spirit and the Church

Traditionally, it has been the legacy of Eastern Orthodox theology to highlight the mutuality of Christology and pneumatology in the doctrine of the church.[27] The church is founded on a twofold divine economy: the work of Christ and the work of the Holy Spirit.[28] Eastern theologians speak about the church as the body of Christ and the fullness of the Holy Spirit.[29] Significantly, Basil contended that "Christ comes, the Spirit goes before. He is present in the flesh, and the Spirit is insepara-

---

22. See, e.g., Lossky, *Mystical Theology*, 196ff.

23. Cited in ibid., 199.

24. For a fine exposition of confirmation-chrism in the Eastern tradition, see Tsirpanlis, *Introduction to Eastern Patristic Thought*, 111–15.

25. See Lossky, *Mystical Theology*, 170ff.

26. Ibid., 174.

27. For a recent discussion, see Grigorios Larentzakis, "Die Teilnahme am trinitarischen Leben: Die Bedeutung der Pneumatologie für die Ökumene heute," in *Der Heilige Geist: ökumenische und reformatorische Untersuchungen* (Veröffentlichungen der Luther-Akademie Ratzeburg; Erlangen: Martin Luther Verlag, 1995), 225–44.

28. Vladimir Lossky, "Concerning the Third Mark of the Church: Catholicity," in *In the Image*, 177–78.

29. Lossky, *Mystical Theology*, 157, 174.

ble from him."[30] This theological statement anchors Christ's work in the church in the economy of the Spirit.

Eastern theology also emphasizes the mutual relationship between the Son and the Spirit: Just as the Son comes down to earth and accomplishes his work through the Spirit, so the Spirit comes into the world, being sent by the Son (John 15:26). The work of the Spirit is not subordinate to the work of the Son, nor is Pentecost a "continuation" of the incarnation but rather its sequel, its result.[31]

As a result of the mutual work of the Son and the Spirit, the catholicity[32] of the church has two aspects: unity (as a result of the church's being the body of Christ) and diversity (as a result of the church's being the fullness of the Spirit).[33] The christological aspect creates the objective and unchangeable features of the church, while the pneumatological aspect shapes the subjective side of the church. In other words, the christological aspect guarantees stability while the pneumatological aspect gives the church a dynamic character.[34]

The Holy Spirit, who rests on Christ, the "Anointed One," communicates himself to each member of this body, creating, so to speak, many christs, or anointed ones.[35] Thus, in Eastern pneumatological ecclesiology, there is ideally a balance between hierarchy (the structures of the church) and charisms:

> But the Church is not only hierarchical, it is charismatic and Pentecostal. "Quench not the Spirit. Despise not prophesying" (1 Thess. 5:19–20). The Holy Spirit is poured out upon all God's people. . . . In the Apostolic Church, besides the institutional ministry conferred by the laying on of hands, there were other *charismata* or gifts conferred directly by the Spirit: Paul mentions "gifts of healing," the working of miracles, "speaking with tongues," and the like (1 Cor. 12:28–30). In the Church of later days, these charismatic ministries have been less in evidence, but they have never been wholly extinguished.[36]

30. Basil, *De Spiritu Sancto* 19, 49.

31. Lossky, *Mystical Theology*, 158–59.

32. For the understanding of catholicity in the Eastern tradition, see Lossky, "Concerning the Third Mark of the Church," 169–80.

33. Ibid., 178–79; Meyendorff, *Byzantine Theology*, 174–75; Lossky, *Mystical Theology*, 176: "This is the unfathomable mystery of the Church, the work of Christ and of the Holy Spirit; one in Christ, multiple through the Spirit, a single human nature in the hypostasis of Christ, many human hypostases in the grace of the Holy Spirit" (183). The classical biblical locus of this twofold nature of the church according to Eastern theology is Ephesians 1:22–23: "the church, which is his body, the fullness of him who fills everything in every way"; see 183–84.

34. Lossky, *Mystical Theology*, 190–92.

35. Ibid., 174; see also 166.

36. Ware, *The Orthodox Church*, 249–50; see also 240, 243.

The Spirit in the Roman Catholic Tradition

Developments in Catholic Pneumatology

The decisive turn in Roman Catholic theology in general and in pneumatology in particular came with the Second Vatican Council (1962–65), which was not only the single most important council of the Roman Catholic Church but also a historic watershed for the entire Christian church. However, many theological developments anticipated the full-blown pneumatology of Vatican II.[37] J. Adams Möhler of the nineteenth century, who is better known as the originator of the highly influential idea of "the Church as continued incarnation," wrote *Unity in the Church or the Principle of Catholicism* (1825), which clearly opted for a Spirit-centered ecclesiology.[38] Although in his later writings, the Spirit's role was marginal, Möhler's ideas were not forgotten. According to B. E. Hinze, the "twentieth-century renewal of Pneumatology in Catholic ecclesiology could be constructed in part as an attempt to reaffirm Möhler's early Spirit-centered approach and to reintegrate it with his later incarnational ecclesiology within a fully developed trinitarian framework."[39]

M. J. Scheeben (d. 1888), a younger contemporary of Möhler, wanted to develop Möhler's neglected pneumatological dimension of the church and spoke about the church as a "kind of incarnation of the Holy Spirit." Even though the intention of this endeavor should be welcomed, it was a problematic way of describing the Spirit: The phrase is foreign to the New Testament, and its content is unclear. The New Testament never calls the church the body of the Spirit but rather the body of Christ.

Characteristic of the earlier Catholic pneumatology is the papal encyclical *Divinum illud munus* by Leo XIII (1897), according to which Christ is the Head and the Holy Spirit is the soul of the church. The problem with this approach is that it makes the church and its struc-

37. See further Congar, *I Believe in the Holy Spirit*, 1:154–57; and Bernd Jochen Hilberath, "Pneumatologie," in *Handbuch der Dogmatik*, ed. von Theodor Schneider et al. (Düsseldorf: Patmos, 1992), 1:522.

38. For an extended treatment of Möhler's position, see B. E. Hinze, "The Holy Spirit and the Catholic Tradition: The Legacy of Johann Adam Möller," in *The Legacy of the Tübingen School: The Relevance of Nineteenth-Century Theology for the Twenty-First Century*, ed. Donald J. Dietrich and Michael J. Himes (New York: Crossroad Herder, 1997), 75–94; and Michael Himes, *Ongoing Incarnation: Johann Adam Möhler and the Beginning of Modern Ecclesiology* (New York: Crossroad Herder, 1997).

39. B. E. Hinze, "Releasing the Power of the Spirit in Trinitarian Ecclesiology," in *An Advent of the Spirit: Orientations in Pneumatology*, Conference Papers from a Symposium at Marquette University, 17–19 April 1998 (unpublished), 3.

tures absolute, divine in their origin, while the only task of the Spirit is to "animate" the already existing ecclesiastical apparatus. Not much better pneumatologically was the message of another encyclical, *Mystici Corporis*, in 1943. Though it basically reaffirmed the teaching of its predecessor, it rehabilitated the role of the Spirit in ecclesiology, creating one of the most significant theologies of the Spirit for the twentieth-century Catholic Church. Yves Congar criticized it for viewing the church in institutional terms.[40] He also argued that Catholic theology to some extent created substitutes for the Holy Spirit, such as the Eucharist, the pope, and Mary.[41]

Three theologians played a crucial role in initiating a fuller recovery of the doctrine of the Holy Spirit on the eve of Vatican II and afterward: Congar, Heribert Muehlen,[42] and Karl Rahner. Muehlen, while criticizing the view of the church as a continued incarnation, argued that the church should be seen as a continuation of Jesus' anointing with the Holy Spirit at his baptism. In Muehlen's estimation, attention to the identity of the Holy Spirit in the anointing of Jesus and in the anointing of Christians helps to avoid hierarchical (in Muehlen's terminology, "naturalistic") tendencies (tying the Spirit to the structures of the church) and mystical tendencies (having to do with personal piety), both represented in pre-council ecclesiologies.

The Pneumatology of Vatican Council II

Vatican II was instrumental in the new Catholic pneumatological renaissance.[43] Pope John XXIII, when formally announcing the council, wrote, "This getting together of all the bishops of the Church should be like a new Pentecost."[44] This council could be called the "Council of the Holy Spirit," for as Pope Paul VI pointed out, the pages of the council documents contain 258 references to the Holy

40. Congar, *I Believe in the Holy Spirit*, 1:154.

41. Ibid., 160–64.

42. Muehlen's pneumatological ecclesiology is developed in his two earlier works: *Una Mystica Persona: Die Kirche als das Mysterium der Heilsgeschichtlichen Identität des heiligen Geistes in Christus und den Christen: Eine Person in Vielen Personen*, 3d ed. (Munich, Paderborn, Wien: Ferdinand Schöningh, 1968); and *Der Heilige Geist as Person: In der Trinität bei der Inkarnation und im Gnadenbund: Ich-Du-Wir*, 3d ed. (Münster: Verlag Aschendorff, 1969).

43. Two basic sources that summarize neatly the pneumatological perspectives of Vatican II are Hans Urs von Balthasar, *Explorations in Theology*, vol. 3, *Creator Spirit* (San Francisco: Ignatius Press, 1993), 245–67; and Congar, *I Believe in the Holy Spirit*, 1:167–73.

44. Germain Marc'hadour, "The Holy Spirit over the New World: II," *The Clergy Review* 59, no. 4 (1974): 247.

Spirit.[45] And since the council, the popes have urged theologians and laypeople alike to revive their interest in the Spirit.[46]

A new pneumatological awareness characterizes many of the major documents of Vatican II, even though it did not present a systematically developed pneumatology. The most significant document, that on the church, *Lumen Gentium,* opens with a Trinitarian outlook in which pneumatology has its own secure place in ecclesiology. This approach widens the earlier christological concentration of traditional doctrines of the church. The church is the work of the Spirit, who makes believers one in the unity of the Triune God.[47] The document insists that the Holy Spirit sanctifies and leads the people of God not only through the sacraments and church ministries but also through special charisms bestowed freely on all the faithful in a variety of ways. Believers have "the right and duty to use them in the Church and in the world for the good of humankind and for the upbuilding of the Church."[48]

The explicit emphasis on the pneumatic nature of the church, including the gifts and graces of the Holy Spirit, was secured in the council by Leon Joseph Cardinal Suenens, who played a critical role in assuring the college of bishops of the importance of the Holy Spirit and of spiritual gifts to the future of the Roman Church.[49] The Catholic systematician Michael Fahey stated that "another way that the church is described in the perspective of the Second Vatican Council is as a community of charisms."[50] According to this understanding, the church is the body of Christ "created, ordered, and sustained by the charismatic

---

45. Ibid., 248. See also E. E. O'Connor, *The Pentecostal Movement in the Catholic Church* (Notre Dame: Ave Maria, 1971), 184.

46. For papal documents and evaluations of their significance, see Kilian McDonnell, *Open the Windows: The Popes and Charismatic Renewal* (South Bend, Ind.: Greenlawn Press, 1989).

47. *LG* 4 (Note that citations from Vatican II documents give paragraph numbers.). See also John R. Sachs, "'Do Not Stifle the Spirit': Karl Rahner, the Legacy of Vatican II, and Its Urgency for Theology Today," in *Catholic Theological Society Proceedings,* ed. E. Dreyer, 51 (1996): 17–18.

48. *AA* 3.

49. Jerry L. Sandidge, *Roman Catholic-Pentecostal Dialogue (1977–1982): A Study in Developing Ecumenism,* Studien zur interkulturellen Geschichte des Christentums 44 (Frankfurt: Peter Lang, 1978), 1:25.

50. Michael Fahey, "Church," in *Systematic Theology: Roman Catholic Perspectives,* ed. Francis Schussler Fiorenza and John P. Galvin (Minneapolis: Fortress Press, 1991), 2:39. He goes on to say, "In the Catholic community, as in the Christian community in general except possibly for Pentecostal Christians, there had been a general neglect of the term charism. It was almost as though while charisms were important in the early church, the age of charism was dead." He defines the charism as "a gift of ability conveyed to an individual within the Christian community enabling the person to fulfill a specific service, either over a long period of time or in a relatively short period of time."

inspirations of the Breath of the risen Jesus."[51] Since the Holy Spirit pervades the church and accomplishes a profound communion among the believers, every member of the church is meant to be permeated with Christ.[52] "Not only clergy but also laypeople are urged to live every dimension of their existence, including married and family life, their daily tasks and recreation in the anointing and power of the Holy Spirit."[53]

Several Vatican II documents (especially *Lumen Gentium* but also others[54]) established the existence and contribution of charisms under the supervision of the shepherds of the church. Vatican II emphasized repeatedly the Spirit's sovereign freedom in dispensing the charisms,[55] and the council insisted on the universal availability of the charisms: The Spirit calls all Christians, ordained and lay alike, to some form of charismatic ministry.[56] *Lumen Gentium* freely accepted both kinds of gifts, ordinary and extraordinary, but added a helpful corrective:

> Whether these charisms be very remarkable or more simple and widely diffused, they are to be received with thanksgiving and consolation since they are fitting and useful for the needs of the Church. Extraordinary gifts are not to be rashly desired, nor is it from them that the fruits of apostolic labors are to be presumptuously expected.[57]

In addition to changes in ecclesiology, since Vatican II, sacramental theology has taken a pneumatological course, with the idea of the church as the sacrament of the Spirit, and sacraments consequently integrated with *epiclēsis*, the prayer for the Spirit. The Constitution on the Sacred Liturgy in a special way emphasizes the role of the Spirit. Since the liturgy is the "summit" and source of the church's life, believers can grow most deeply in the life of the Spirit precisely through sacramental celebrations.[58]

> By means of the invocation of the Spirit on the sacramental elements, earthly realities such as water and oil, bread and wine are transformed to

51. Donald L. Gelpi, "The Theological Challenge of Charismatic Spirituality," *Pneuma* 14, no. 2 (1992): 187. He refers to the following Vatican II documents: *LG* 6, 32, 48, 50; *UR* 3; *AA* 3.

52. *LG* 12; see also Mary Ann Fatula, *The Holy Spirit: Unbounded Gift of Joy* (Collegeville, Minn.: Liturgical Press, 1998), 89.

53. *LG* 34; Fatula, *The Holy Spirit*, 89–90.

54. *LG* 12, 30; *AA* 3; *Presbyterorium Ordinis* 9.

55. *AA* 3; *Ad Gentes* 23; *LG* 7.

56. *AA* 3, 28, 30; *LG* 4.

57. *LG* 12.

58. *Sacrosanctum Concilium* 10.

mediate the Holy Spirit's presence and power. But the renewed liturgical rites stress, too, that the Holy Spirit is invoked also upon the Church community celebrating the sacraments, so that our own hearts and lives may be transformed as well.[59]

Other areas in which the pneumatological outlook has affected contemporary Catholic theology are the doctrines of salvation and revelation. In contrast to the earlier understanding of revelation as divine truths about God, the Vatican II document the Dogmatic Constitution on Divine Revelation, *Dei Verbum*, views revelation in its most basic sense as God's own self-communication to human beings through Jesus Christ in the Holy Spirit, through whom humanity "comes to share in the divine nature."[60] In other words, revelation is primarily the personal communication of the Spirit, that is, God's own life, not the disclosure of divinely privileged information about God.[61] Thus, Vatican II pneumatology also includes a firm faith that the "body of the faithful as a whole, anointed as they are by the Holy One, cannot err in matters of belief."[62]

In soteriology, the work of the leading modern Catholic theologian, Karl Rahner, has been decisive. For Rahner, grace is first and foremost God's self-communication to and presence through his Spirit with humans.[63] In opposition to the Neo-scholastic position, according to which grace cannot be experienced (because it is supernatural), he holds that people do experience grace. Rahner is, of course, not the first theologian to identify God's Spirit as the quintessence of the experience of salvation, but his impact on the modern Catholic theology of grace has been unsurpassed. Following Rahner, several leading theologians of the Catholic Church have described the essence of grace and salvation in pneumatological terms, where the experience of salvation is "captured by the symbol of God as Spirit being poured out anew in the world through the mediation of Jesus."[64]

59. Fatula, *The Holy Spirit*, 90.

60. *Dei Verbum* 2.

61. Sachs, "'Do Not Stifle the Spirit,'" 18. See further Veli-Matti Kärkkäinen, "'Reading in the Spirit in Which It Was Written': Pentecostal Bible Reading in Dialogue with Catholic Interpretation," *One in Christ* 4 (1998): 338–410; and idem, "Authority, Revelation, and Interpretation in the Roman Catholic-Pentecostal Dialogue," *Pneuma* 21, no. 2 (1999): 90–92.

62. *LG* 12.

63. Karl Rahner, *Foundations of Christian Faith: An Introduction to the Idea of Christianity* (New York: Seabury Press, 1978), especially 116–26, but also the entire chapter on salvation. See also Roger Haight, "Sin and Grace," in *Systematic Theology: Roman Catholic Perspectives*, ed. F. S. Fiorenza and J. P. Galvin (Minneapolis: Fortress Press, 1991), 2:109–10.

64. Haight, "Sin and Grace," 113.

Jesuit theologian Donald Gelpi, though, criticizes his own church for not taking seriously the charismatic and pneumatological teaching of the Second Vatican Council. He thinks it is not the responsibility of the so-called Catholic Charismatic Movement to renew the church; it is precisely the burden of the entire church with her theologians and teachers to implement what was rediscovered in the council.[65] He argues that the charisms play an indispensable role in the life of the church, and they therefore cannot be confined to the first generation of Christians, as most Catholics before Vatican II were taught to believe.[66] Kilian McDonnell said that "the charisms of the Spirit play an indispensable role in the life of the Church because they create the shared faith consciousness of the Christian community."[67]

Along with the resurgence of the pneumatological view of the church came an openness on the part of the Catholic Church with regard to other churches. The Catholic theologian Paul D. Lee, taking up the Johannine image of the Spirit as the *paraclete*, speaks about a true ecumenical theology as a healer, a consoler, an advocate.[68] Here the role of the Spirit is seen as "the go-between God,"[69] the bond of love, uniting men and women to God and to each other.

Papal Leadership in the Pneumatological Focus

The Roman Catholic Church worldwide, in preparation for crossing into the third millennium, made 1998 a year of special devotion to the Holy Spirit.[70] (The year 1997 was devoted to the Son and 1999 to the

65. Gelpi, "Theological Challenge," 188–89. When evaluating the role of the Catholic Charismatic Movement after twenty-five years of existence in 1982, Gelpi is not happy with the way the church theologians responded to it and to the pneumatic-charismatic teaching of Vatican II: "Theologians, however, tended at first to look somewhat aghast upon this rag-tag collection of enthusiastic, Catholic tongue-speakers. With time, of course, the theological community did come to take the renewal more seriously; but their failure to respond with clarity to the challenge this movement posed to the Church as a whole created a doctrinal vacuum into which others rushed, many of them spokespersons for the Classical Pentecostal tradition" (188).

66. See Donald J. Gelpi, *Charism and Sacrament* (New York: Paulist Press; London: SPCK, 1976), especially 97–110; idem, *The Divine Mother: A Trinitarian Theology of the Holy Spirit* (Lanham, Md.: University Press of America, 1984), 103ff.

67. Kilian McDonnell, "Communion Ecclesiology and Baptism in the Spirit: Tertullian and the Early Church," *TS* 49 (1988): 671ff.

68. Paul D. Lee, "Pneumatological Ecclesiology in Roman Catholic-Pentecostal Dialogue: A Catholic Reading of the Third Quinquennium (1985–1989)" (Dissertatio Ad Lauream in Facultate S. Theologiae Apud Pontificiam Universitatem S. Thomae in Urbe, Rome, 1994), 33–34.

69. John V. Taylor, *The Go-Between God: The Holy Spirit and the Christian Mission* (London: SCM, 1972), 43–44.

70. Pope John Paul II, *Celebrate 2000! Reflections on the Holy Spirit: Weekly Readings for 1998*, sel. and arr. by Paul Thigpar (Ann Arbor, Mich.: Servant Publications, 1997).

Father.) Publications were issued, special services were held, and lectures and research programs took place as the largest church of Christendom sought to deepen her understanding of pneumatology. When Pope Paul VI had been asked, "What is the greatest need of the church today?" his response had been "the Holy Spirit." On Pentecost 1986, Pope John Paul II, recalling the words of Paul VI, issued the encyclical *Dominum et Vivificantem* ("Lord and Giver of Life"). In doing so, the pope made his own the call of his predecessor, that the Christology and ecclesiology of Vatican II be followed by a "new study of and devotion to the Holy Spirit, precisely as the indispensable complement of the teaching of the Council."[71] In this encyclical, Pope John Paul II placed the church under the guidance of the Holy Spirit. "The disciples were filled with joy and with the Holy Spirit" (Acts 13:52). The pope stressed that the incarnation itself was accomplished through the Holy Spirit's power. So too the great "Jubilee of the Incarnation" had impelled the church to turn its "mind and heart" to the Holy Spirit.[72] In 1996, the Catholic Theological Society of America meeting was devoted to pneumatology: "Toward a Spirited Theology: Challenges of the Holy Spirit to Theological Disciplines."[73]

The Spirit in the Lutheran Tradition

The Context of Luther's View of the Spirit

In a general sense, whereas the Eastern church has more consciously built its theology on pneumatological foundations, the whole of Western theology has emphasized Christology. Reformation theology, especially in its Lutheran form, fits into this Western category. (Nevertheless, both Eastern and Lutheran theologies have been trinitarian in their own distinct ways).

A classic study of Martin Luther's pneumatology is Reginald Prenter's *Spiritus Creator: Studies in Luther's Theology.*[74] While still helpful, both its methodology and contents are outdated. The book is especially troubling in that Prenter sets Luther's doctrine over against Catholic doctrine and therefore, for example, makes the doctrine of the Trinity a foreign speculation for Luther. Furthermore, Prenter sets God and the

71. Pope John Paul II, *Dominum et Vivificantem*, Encyclical on the Holy Spirit in the Life of the Church and the World, 30 May 1986 (Washington, D.C.: United States Catholic Conference, 1986), #49.

72. Ibid., #2. See also Fatula, *The Holy Spirit*, xiii.

73. *Proceedings of the Fifty-First Annual Convention*, San Diego, 6–9 June 1996, vol. 51, ed. Judith A. Dweyer (Chicago: Catholic Theological Society of America, 1996).

74. Trans. John M. Jensen (Philadelphia: Muhlenberg, 1953).

world almost in opposition to each other, a view foreign to Luther. This and other older studies often implied that pneumatology had a meager role to play in Luther's thinking.[75] This is partly true in view of the fact that the Spirit is not the focus in Luther's writings; he focuses instead on Christ and the Trinity. But it is still inaccurate to relegate pneumatology to the margins of Luther's theology. Fortunately, in recent years, a renaissance of Luther studies has taken place in Scandinavia at the University of Helsinki under professor Tuomo Mannermaa, and scholars have taken a fresh look at Luther.[76]

Luther did not write a separate study on pneumatology. Rather, his study of the Holy Spirit is part of his theological corpus, which includes more than twenty Pentecost day sermons that were based on various texts supplied by the lectionary. One way to approach Luther's pneumatology is to analyze his exposition of the third article of the Nicene-Constantinopolitan Creed,[77] in which he relates everything to the Spirit: the church, forgiveness of sins, and so on. A lack of sufficient material in the creed, however, limits this method. A more helpful way is to set Luther's pneumatology in the context of his trinitarian teaching, since the doctrine of the Trinity was formative for Luther.[78]

To understand Luther's views of the Holy Spirit, one has to take note of the fact that "he had to fight on two fronts: on the one hand, against the Catholic position, which, according to Luther's interpretation, regarded the church/hierarchy as absolute, and on the other hand, against the Enthusiasts, who appealed to the Spirit in their claim that they were the true Reformers."[79]

The Spirit in the Trinity

Luther often followed Augustine in his theology. His Augustinian heritage, later disseminated by Peter Lombard in the West, made a distinction between the Holy Spirit as *persona*, "person," and *donum*,

75. This was the view of, e.g., Rudolf Otto, *Die Anschauung vom Hl. Geiste bei Luther: Eine systematisch-dogmatische Untersuchung* (Göttingen: Vandenhoeck & Ruprecht, 1898).

76. In my exposition of Luther's theology, I will basically follow the outline of Pekka Kärkkäinen's doctoral dissertation on Luther's pneumatology. The main results of the forthcoming dissertation written in German are to be found in Pekka Kärkkäinen, "Pyha Henki Lutherin teologiassa" (unpublished paper read at the symposium on Luther's theology at the University of Helsinki, 2–5 May 2000).

77. This is the approach of Eilert Helms, *Luthers Auslegung des Dritten Artikels* (Tübingen: Mohr, 1987); and also of Rolf Schäfer, "Der Heilige Geist: Eine Betrachtung zu Luthers Erklärung des Dritten Artikels," *Luther* 61 (1990): 135–48.

78. See further Bernhard Lohse, *Martin Luther's Theology: Its Historical and Systematic Development* (Edinburgh: T & T Clark, 1999), 232.

79. *Wider die himmlischen Propheten*, 1525. For Luther's harsh judgment against the Enthusiasts *(Schwärmerei)*, see further Congar, *I Believe in the Holy Spirit*, 1:139–40.

"gift." Actually, Lombard identified the Spirit with the divine *caritas*, "grace," and so established the integral connection between soteriology and pneumatology.[80] Luther, of course, knew of this distinction between the Spirit as person and as gift and at times adopted it. In a late disputation, he stated: "So we distinguish the Holy Spirit as God in his divine nature and essence from the Holy Spirit as he is given to us."[81] On the whole, however, he accented the Spirit's Godhead and personhood.

Luther had several approaches to the distinct character of the Holy Spirit. The most famous is the statement in the Large Catechism according to which the Holy Spirit is the spirit of sanctification, distinct from the Father of creation and the Son of redemption. There is a very interesting formulation in "Three Symbols or the Confessions of Christ's Faith" (1538): Just as the second person, the Son, was born in flesh unlike the Father and the Spirit, so also the Holy Spirit proceeded in a *material/bodily* way; both the Son and the Holy Spirit "have an image corresponding to their inner essence."[82] Here Luther joins with traditional dogma in stating that the Spirit proceeds from the Father and the Son but is not born like the Son. In Luther's writings, "proceeding" refers to intra-trinitarian relations, whereas the "material/bodily" sending refers to his relationship to creation.

Furthermore, Luther closely interrelated the inward and outward works of the Spirit. Consequently, there is an "incarnational" side to the work of the Spirit. In that sense, the work of the Holy Spirit in the world has many parallels to that of the Son. Luther describes in his Pentecost sermons the sending of the Spirit as a "visible coming to the world." The Spirit's sending differs from that of the Son, though, in that only in Jesus did God become human. The Son enfleshed himself with a human nature and retained his nature as God-man even after the resurrection and ascension. The Holy Spirit, on the other hand, acts through material signs at given points in time.

Luther further discusses the role of the Holy Spirit in the indivisible work of the Trinity. According to the classical canon of Augustine, the works of the Trinity *ad extra* are indivisible. Even though indivisible, the three Persons have their own specific roles to play. Thus, even in creation, the Holy Spirit was not inactive: He made creation live. Luther also describes beautifully the task of the Spirit in creation as God's satisfaction with his creation, or God's love without which the

80. It has to be noted, though, that not all medieval theologians identified the Spirit with grace.

81. *WA* 39 I, 370, 12–13. See also Lohse, *Martin Luther's Theology*, 233.

82. *WA* 50, 275.

creation could not have sustained itself. In his Genesis exposition, Luther compares the Spirit with a chicken who sits on the eggs to make them hatch.

Depending on his particular role, the Holy Spirit has various names within the Trinity. The most common, of course, is the Holy Spirit. As holy, the Spirit effects sanctification, making holy; this is the basis for differentiating between the Holy Spirit and other spirits in the cosmos. As Spirit, he is like wind or breath, which refers to movement and the bringing forth of life. When the Spirit is poured on us with manifestations of tongues and spiritual gifts, he is called Gift. With regard to creation, he is the Giver of life. Following Augustine, Luther also occasionally calls the Spirit Love, both in intra-trinitarian relations and in relation to human beings (Rom. 5:5). Another ancient name, Paraclete, has a close connection with love. Other fitting names for the Spirit include Goodness and Benevolence.

The Spirit and Christ

Luther's theology is Christocentric; so also is his pneumatology, although always in a healthy trinitarian context. What led Luther to link Christology with pneumatology were the various controversies, especially the controversy over the Lord's Supper: The bodily gift of the Supper is also "spiritual." The Spirit, as the Supper and naturally also the incarnate Word of God make clear, is not to be viewed in opposition to the body. Of course, for Luther the connection between pneumatology and Christology had a significance far beyond the complexities of theological disputes.[83] The task of the Holy Spirit is to point to Christ: "If Christ is not God, then neither the Father nor the Holy Spirit is God, because our article reads that Christ is God. When I therefore hear Christ speak, then I believe the undivided Godhead is speaking."[84] Whatever the Spirit does, his main purpose is to glorify Christ or mediate the work of Christ to us. Often Luther refers to John's Gospel, which speaks of the Spirit as sent by Christ to do his work and to remind us of his words.

Bernhard Lohse makes the bold statement that "with this constant reference to Christ the Holy Spirit assumed an extraordinarily important place in Luther's theology."[85] The accuracy of this statement also has a wider context, namely, that for Luther there was not a single doctrine in all theology in which the activity of the Spirit was not funda-

83. Lohse, *Martin Luther's Theology,* 234.
84. Quoted in ibid., 234.
85. Ibid., 235.

mental.[86] The Spirit's work and activity cannot be limited to the spheres of faith and church alone.[87]

The Spirit and the Law

Luther held an interesting view of the role of the Holy Spirit in giving and fulfilling the law. Luther always emphasized the indivisibility of the Trinity: "The Father does not have any divinity, wisdom, power or authority, which the Holy Spirit, who proceeds from Him and the Son, does not have."[88] One reason for this emphasis were the "antinomist" (literally, "opponents of the law") movements of the time. In his response to the antinomists in the 1530s, Luther argued that the Holy Spirit also played a role in giving the law and eliciting the sense of man's/woman's sinfulness. It is impossible for the law to accuse of sin and move hearts without the Holy Spirit, "who is God and Creator and who wrote the law with his own finger on stone tablets as the Second Book of Moses says."[89] The Spirit reminds us of our sins and makes us fear the judgment.

As the love of God, the Spirit fulfills the requirements of the law. In line with ancient teaching, Luther sees a parallel between the Jewish and Christian Pentecosts: The Jewish Pentecost was a festival commemorating the giving of the Decalogue, whereas the Christian Pentecost signified the giving of the spiritual law. In the pouring out of the Spirit at Pentecost, the requirement of the law is fulfilled: The Spirit does not nullify the law, but in agreement with Augustine's *Spirit and Letter,* Luther contends that the Holy Spirit fulfills the requirements of the law in a way that affirms the demands of the law. The law says, "You have to have Christ and his Spirit," whereas the gospel says, "Behold, here is Christ and his Spirit."

The Spirit, the Word, and the Sacraments

According to Luther's view, the Spirit works in the preached Word and the sacraments. This is perhaps the most characteristic of Luther's ideas of the work of the Holy Spirit. The Spirit is indispensable for preparation for faith: "I believe that I cannot believe in Jesus Christ my

---

86. See further Joachim Heubach, ed., *Der Heilige Geist im Verständnis Luthers und der lutherischen Theologie,* Veröffentlichungen der Luther-Akademie Ratzeberg 17 (Erlangen: Martin Luther Verlag, 1990).

87. This is made clear in Prenter, *Spiritus Creator.* It is also evident in a more recent study: Peter Albrecht, *Kommentar zu Luthers Katechismen,* ed. Gottfried Seebass (Göttingen: Vandenhoeck & Ruprecht, 1990–94), 2:175–250.

88. *WA* 31, 275.

89. Lauri Koskenniemi, *Laki ja evankeliumi* (Helsinki: Otara, 1954), 49ff.

Lord, or come to him, of my own reason or power but the Holy Spirit has called me by the gospel, enlightened me with his gifts, sanctified and upheld me in true faith."[90]

In his insistence on the integral relationship between the Spirit and the Word, Luther limits the phenomena of Pentecost (tongues, fire, wind) to the apostolic era. He understands the proper instruments of the Holy Spirit given to the church to be the Word and the sacraments, which are the visible Word. According to Luther, while the phenomena of Pentecost have ceased as such, they continue to operate through the ministry of the Holy Spirit in regard to the Bible and the sacraments. The wind and fire symbolize the encouragement and zeal given to the apostles, and speaking in tongues symbolizes the gospel itself, preached in every tongue.[91]

In other words, the work of the Holy Spirit is "clothed" in the Word and sacraments. This was Luther's insistence against the spiritualists, who in his view sought immediate access to grace apart from the Word and sacraments. According to Luther, this is the order set up by God himself with regard to the work of the Spirit. In opposition to the "Heavenly Prophets," or the spiritualists, he differentiates two ways God approaches us: (1) the "outer" way: through the preached Word and sacraments, and (2) the "inner" way: through the Holy Spirit and his gifts. Both ways are needed, but the outer is primary; the inner is a function of the outer, not vice versa. God does not give his Spirit apart from the preparing work of the Word and sacraments.

Luther argues that in the Bible nobody is given the Spirit without mediation. In this sense, the outer Word for him has a sacramental nature. However, this does not mean that the work of the Spirit is relegated exclusively to the outer Word. The Spirit lives inside believers. Luther also mentions a special kind of prayer wrought by the Spirit that causes human words to cease. Furthermore, some spiritual gifts such as healing were a normal part of spiritual life in Luther's time.

Justification and Deification: Convergences between Lutheran and Orthodox Views

Even though, generally speaking, Reformation theology viewed faith as the decisive work of the Holy Spirit,[92] the later development of Ref-

90. *WA* 30, 1367–68.

91. Here one should note the decisive role Luther played in the translation of the Bible to make it available to every Christian in his or her own language.

92. See further Wolfhart Pannenberg, *Systematic Theology* (Grand Rapids: Eerdmans, 1997), 3:2.

ormation soteriology, especially in the Lutheran tradition, was expressed more in christological than in pneumatological terms.[93]

It is a general consensus of the most recent Luther scholarship that the commonly held forensic doctrine of justification by faith, as articulated by later confessional writings under the leadership of Philipp Melanchthon, is a one-sided understanding of Luther's theology;[94] Luther himself spoke of the real presence of God in Christ and the Holy Spirit in the believer.[95] Not until the latest renaissance of Luther studies, especially in Scandinavia under the tutelage of the so-called Mannermaa School, has the pneumatological potential of Luther's writings been recovered.[96] An important impetus to the recovery of a pneumatological outlook in the doctrine of salvation came from an unexpected source. When the Lutheran churches started theological talks with the Eastern churches in the 1970s, they looked back to original Lutheran sources to uncover rich pneumatological resources.

Before the emergence of the Mannermaa School in the 1970s, it was thought that the idea of *theōsis* was completely foreign to Reformation—and certainly Lutheran—thought. Historically, the Lutheran doctrine of justification and the Eastern doctrine of deification have been considered to be diametrically opposed to each other. But the most recent Lutheran ecumenical theologizing has discovered an unexpected motif of deification and a pneumatological concept of grace within Luther's writings. The Mannermaa School has provided a most promising and to some extent controversial claim that *theōsis* was one of the images Luther used to describe salvation.

93. In Calvin's theology in general and soteriology in particular, the pneumatological orientation was preserved more carefully.

94. The term "Lutheran" has two meanings: It can denote either Martin Luther's theology as it is expressed in his own writings, or the theology/theologies of Lutheran confessions and subsequent Lutheran formulations. During the course of the discussion, I will show that these two have to be distinguished from one another since they not only have some differing emphases but can also end up in contradictory orientations, especially in regard to the cardinal doctrine of justification.

95. Cf. Kenneth L. Bakken, "Holy Spirit and Theosis: Toward a Lutheran Theology of Healing," *St. Vladimir's Theological Quarterly* 38, no. 4 (1994): 409.

96. For basic ideas, see the following: Carl E. Braaten and Robert Jenson, eds., *Union with Christ: The New Finnish Interpretation of Luther* (Grand Rapids: Eerdmans, 1998); Tuomo Mannermaa, "Theosis as a Subject of Finnish Lutheran Research," *Pro Ecclesia* 44 (1995): 37–48; Risto Saarinen, "Salvation in the Lutheran-Orthodox Dialogue: A Comparative Perspective," *Pro Ecclesia* 5 (1996): 202–13; Veli-Matti Kärkkäinen, "The Ecumenical Potential of Theosis: Emerging Convergences between Eastern Orthodox, Protestant, and Pentecostal Soteriologies," *Eastern Churches Journal* (forthcoming); and idem, "'The Holy Spirit Has Called Me': The Pneumatological Potential of Luther's Doctrine of Salvation," *Pneuma* (forthcoming).

The Finnish-Lutheran dialogue produced a highly influential soteriological document in Kiev in 1977 titled "Salvation as Justification and Deification." The preamble to the common affirmations claims that "until recently, there has been a predominant opinion that the Lutheran and Orthodox doctrines of salvation greatly differ from each other. In the conversations, however, it has become evident that both these important aspects of salvation discussed in the conversations have a strong New Testament basis and there is great unanimity with regard to them both."[97]

Since deification is a pneumatologically loaded image of salvation, it makes possible an approach to soteriology from the perspective of the Spirit. This was acknowledged in the Orthodox-Lutheran dialogue. Defining the "the new road leading to deification" as a "process of growing in holiness," the joint document cites two important Pauline texts: "We, who with unveiled faces all reflect the Lord's glory, are being transformed into his likeness with ever-increasing glory, which comes from the Lord, who is the Spirit" (2 Cor. 3:18). Deification takes place under the influence of the grace of the Holy Spirit by a deep and sincere faith, together with hope and permeated by love (1 Cor. 13:13).[98]

In Luther's theology, the core of the doctrine of deification is the idea of real participation in the divine life in Christ. We receive the salvatory gifts through participation in Christ.[99] The Lutheran tradition holds to the idea of God living in the believer (inhabitatio Dei). This for Mannermaa is analogous with the doctrine of theōsis. According to Luther, Christ and thus his person and work are present in the faith itself.[100] Although the term deification is not frequent in Luther's writings, the core idea is integral to his thought; he usually prefers terms such as "presence of Christ in faith," "the participation in God," "union with God," perichōrēsis, the famous Eastern term, and others.

Pneumatological implications of this new approach of Luther scholarship are obvious. The main idea, Christ present through faith, can be expressed pneumatically: It is through the Spirit of Christ that salvatory gifts are mediated. Participation in God is possible only through the Spirit of Christ, the Spirit of adoption.[101] "There is not justification

97. Hannu Kamppuri, ed., *Dialogue between Neighbours: The Theological Conversations between the Evangelical-Lutheran Church of Finland and the Russian Orthodox Church 1970–1986* (Helsinki: Luther-Agricola Society, 1986), 73.

98. Ibid., 75.

99. So also, e.g., Pannenberg, *Systematic Theology*, 3:215ff.

100. Mannermaa, "Theosis," 42–44; idem, "Luther ja Theosis," in *Pastor et Episcopus Animarum, Studia in Honorem Episcopi Pauli Verschuren*, ed. Pentti Laukama (Vammala, Finland: Vammalan Kirjapaino, 1985), 15–29.

101. For a brief summary of the idea of adoption in Luther, see Risto Saarinen, "The Presence of God in Luther's Theology," *Lutheran Quarterly* 3, no. 1 (1994): 9–10.

by faith without the Holy Spirit. Justifying faith is itself the experience that the love of God has been poured into our hearts 'through the Holy Spirit' (Rom. 5:5)."[102]

The Spirit in the Pentecostal/Charismatic Movements

The Emergence and Spread of the Pentecostal/Charismatic Phenomenon

The twentieth century witnessed dramatic developments in the Christian church with the emergence and rapid growth of Pentecostalism[103] and later Charismatic movements,[104] which have touched Christianity worldwide. The most popular history writings on Pentecostalism usually trace the origins in the American context to a revival that began on January 1, 1901, at Charles F. Parham's Bethel Bible School in Topeka, Kansas. There students began speaking in (unknown) tongues after spending concentrated time studying the accounts of tongues in the Book of Acts. Several years later this revival gained more publicity through a Holiness preacher, William J. Seymour, who preached the new message of Pentecost at the Azusa Street Mission in Los Angeles, California. From 1906 onward, the news of the "outpouring" of the Holy Spirit spread across the nation and around the world. Before long, Pentecostal revivals could be found in Canada, England, Scandinavia, Germany, and parts of Asia, Africa, and Latin America.

Although the story of the birth of Pentecostalism at the turn of the twentieth century is well known, there is not yet a consensus among researchers of Pentecostalism as to the exact origins of the movement.[105] Four main proposals have been set forth. (1) Some desire to connect the origins of the modern Pentecostal movement with the work of

102. Bakken, "Holy Spirit and Theosis," 410.

103. A short statement of the emergence of Pentecostalism and basic definitions can be found in the editorial article, "The Pentecostal and Charismatic Movements," in *Dictionary of Pentecostal and Charismatic Movements*, ed. Stanley M. Burgess and Gary B. McGee (Grand Rapids: Zondervan, 1988), 1–6. Still today, the most prominent presentation of the history and theologies of worldwide Pentecostalism is Walter J. Hollenweger, *Pentecostals* (London: SCM Press, 1972, and subsequent editions) and its sequel, *Pentecostalism: Origins and Developments Worldwide* (Peabody, Mass.: Hendrickson, 1997).

104. Perhaps the easiest introduction to the origins and history of major Charismatic movements is Peter Hocken, "The Charismatic Movement," in *The Dictionary of Pentecostal and Charismatic Movements*, 130–60. See also two recent issues of *Pneuma*: 16, no. 2 (1994) and 18, no. 1 (1996).

105. See Cecil M. Robeck, "Pentecostal Origins from a Global Perspective," in *All Together in One Place: Theological Papers from the Brighton Conference on World Evangelization*, ed. Harold D. Hunter and Peter D. Hocken (Sheffield: Sheffield Academic Press, 1993), 166–80.

Charles F. Parham and his students at Topeka, Kansas. (2) Non-white historians and theologians of the movement often emphasize the primary role of the black Holiness preacher William J. Seymour and the Apostolic Faith Mission that arose in Los Angeles, California, in April 1906.[106] (3) Some churches believe they constitute the earliest Pentecostal denominations and claim that their leaders or members spoke in tongues prior to either Parham or Seymour. (4) Finally, some view the origins of Pentecostalism as a sovereign work of God that cannot be traced to any single leader or group but should rather be attributed to a spontaneous and simultaneous outpouring of the Holy Spirit around the world.

A related question, that of the roots of the movement—theological, historical, and spiritual—is also disputed among scholars. The basic consensus, though, is that the nineteenth-century Wesleyan-Holiness heritage lies behind the movement. In addition to the formative influence of Wesleyan-Holiness movements, there was also, according to Walter Hollenweger, a strong influence from Catholic spirituality, which was mediated through Wesley and his writings.[107] From Wesley the Pentecostals received an emphasis on holiness and sanctification, sometimes called the "second blessing" or "baptism of the Spirit"; from Catholics they received the mystical-charismatic spiritual tradition; and from African American believers they received the enthusiastic, corporeal worship style.

Roughly fifty years after the emergence of Pentecostalism, the renewal began to enter older churches. News about this renewal in the United States—what was to be called the "Charismatic renewal/movement"[108]—began to surface on the national level in 1960 with the publicity accorded to remarkable happenings in the ministry of Dennis Bennett, an Episcopal rector in Van Nuys, California. As the movement grew, it spread to other Protestant churches, the Roman Catholic Church, and finally to the Orthodox Churches. It brought to many churches an experience of a revitalization of spiritual life.

106. See the article by the African American Pentecostalist James S. Tinney, "William J. Seymour: Father of Modern Day Pentecostalism," *Spirit: A Journal of Issues Incident to Black Pentecostalism* 1, no. 1 (1976): 33–34.

107. W. J. Hollenweger, "From Azusa Street to the Toronto Phenomenon: Historical Roots of the Pentecostal Movement," *Concilium* 3 (1996): 3–14.

108. Henry I. Lederle, *Treasures Old and New: Interpretation of "Spirit Baptism" in the Charismatic Renewal Movement* (Peabody, Mass.: Hendrickson, 1988), xiii, gives us a handy way to see the difference, mostly in terms of origins: "The most useful distinction between Pentecostal and charismatic is whether they have their roots, as it were, in 1906, or 1960."

The formation of a Charismatic prayer group among faculty members and students at Duquesne University (Pittsburgh) in 1967 is generally looked upon as the beginning of the Charismatic renewal in the Roman Catholic Church. A Pentecostal-type revival in the Lutheran Church of America under Larry Christenson in St. Paul, Minnesota, was the entrance of the Charismatic movement into Lutheranism.

During the twentieth century, the Pentecostal/Charismatic movement became the largest single category in Protestantism.[109] "Its growth from zero to 400 million in ninety years is unprecedented in the whole of church history," states Hollenweger.[110] If, currently, Roman Catholics are the largest Christian group, then classical Pentecostals are now the second largest, and gaining fast. Catholics now make up 50 percent of the worldwide Christian church, while Pentecostals make up 20 percent.

Dynamic, Charismatic Spirituality at the Center

From the beginning, Pentecostalism has been characterized by variety, and therefore, any classifications are at their best generalizations. Two obvious reasons for its variety are its multicultural, multinational beginnings and its growth within many cultural settings.[111] We should actually speak of Pentecostalisms rather than Pentecostalism (as a single phenomenon).[112]

The variety of Pentecostalism can be seen in its main "theologies," and consequently, in the differing emphases with regard to the understanding of the Holy Spirit—as they appear now.[113] (1) Wesleyan Pentecostals emphasize the Wesleyan doctrine of "second blessing" instant sanctification. They simply added the baptism in the Holy Spirit evi-

109. L. Grant McClung Jr., "Pentecostal/Charismatic Perspectives on a Missiology for the Twenty-First Century," *Pneuma* 16, no. 1 (1994): 11 states, "David Barrett's description of the Pentecostal/Charismatic tradition, now numbering more than 400 million and growing by 19 million a year and 54,000 a day, is that it comes in an 'amazing variety' of 38 major categories, 11,000 Pentecostal denominations and 3,000 independent Charismatic denominations spread across 8,000 ethnolinguistic cultures and 7,000 languages. A cross section of worldwide Pentecostalism reveals a composite international Pentecostal/Charismatic who is more urban than rural, more female than male, more Third World (66%) than Western world, more impoverished (87%) than affluent, more family-oriented than individualistic, and, on the average younger than eighteen."

110. Hollenweger, "From Azusa Street," 3.

111. For a recent discussion, see Allen H. Anderson and Walter J. Hollenweger, eds., *Pentecostals after a Century: Global Perspectives on a Movement in Transition* (Sheffield: Sheffield Academic Press, 1999).

112. Cecil M. Robeck, "Taking Stock of Pentecostalism," *Pneuma* 15, no. 1 (1993): 45.

113. I am following here the categorization of Vinson Synan, "Pentecostalism: Varieties and Contributions," *Pneuma* 8, no. 2 (1986): 34–36.

denced by speaking in tongues as a "third blessing." (2) Baptistic Pentecostals came into being with the organization of the Assemblies of God in 1914, which is currently the largest Pentecostal denomination. They stress gradual sanctification and more presbyterial and congregational forms of church government than do most other Pentecostals. Most Pentecostal bodies in the world formed after 1914 reflect this strand. (3) Oneness Pentecostals, who today comprise roughly one-fourth of all Pentecostals and are also known as "Jesus' name" Pentecostals, represent the most radical theological departure of any Pentecostal group. Essentially, these churches teach a unitarianism of the Son that denies the traditional doctrine of the Trinity and claims that Jesus is Father, Son, and Holy Spirit. They (re)baptize in Jesus' name and are also the only major grouping of Pentecostals who teach (or at least imply) that speaking in tongues is necessary for salvation. (4) Charismatic Pentecostals (later known simply as "Charismatics") are those who decided to stay in their churches after experiencing the new work of the Holy Spirit and who incorporate aspects of Pentecostal practice and theology into the theological frameworks of their own traditions. (5) Independent Pentecostal Charismatic theologies and spiritualities have diverse agendas. Two of the most recent and most famous are the "Toronto blessing," which began in 1994, and the "Pensacola revival," which began a few years later. (6) The endless variety of Pentecostal and Charismatic movements, especially in the Two-Thirds world, contribute to the heterogeneity of Pentecostalism; some of these groups clearly border on being non-Christian religions (especially in Africa).

Pentecostalism represents a grassroots spiritual movement rather than a novel theological construction. It has not so much produced new theology as a new kind of spirituality and aggressive evangelism methods. Therefore, it has provoked controversy at almost every stage of its development. Negative attitudes have not arisen merely because of Pentecostalism's tradition-breaking forms of worship and practice. They have arisen, significantly, because it has challenged the so-called cessationist principle, which holds that miracles or extraordinary *charismata* were terminated at or near the end of the apostolic age.[114] Scholars of church history and historical theology had asserted and explained the disappearance of the "religion of the Spirit and of power" in the earliest church. Against this view, "the salient characteristic of Pentecostalism is its belief in the present-day manifestation of spiritual gifts, such as miraculous healing, prophecy and, most distinctively, glossolalia. Pentecostals affirm that these spiritual gifts (charismata)

114. See further Jon Ruthven, *On the Cessation of the Charismata: The Protestant Polemic on Postbiblical Miracles* (Sheffield: Sheffield Academic Press, 1993).

are granted by the Holy Spirit and are normative in contemporary church life and ministry."[115] Many observers of the movement hold that the "revalorization of the Charismata"[116] rather than theological analysis is the most important contribution that Pentecostalism and later Charismatic movements have made to the history of Christianity.[117]

Pentecostalism has (re)introduced a dynamic, enthusiastic type of spirituality to the modern church.[118] The focus of Pentecostal spirituality is experiencing God mystically as supernatural. The category of experience is essential to understanding the spirituality of Pentecostals and thus their worship. In the words of Daniel Albrecht, a researcher of Pentecostal spirituality:

> In a very real sense the Sunday services of . . . [Pentecostal] churches are designed to provide a context for a mystical *encounter*, an experience with the divine. This encounter is mediated by the sense of the immediate divine presence. The primary rites of worship and altar/response are particularly structured to sensitize the congregants to the presence of the divine and to stimulate conscious experience of God. . . . The gestures, ritual actions, and symbols all function within this context to speak of the manifest presence.[119]

For Pentecostals, "worship" is another way of saying "presence of God."[120] Their worship service is an interesting mixture of spontaneity; the exercise of spiritual gifts such as speaking in tongues, prophesying, and prayer for healing; and attentiveness to the mystical encounter with God. The Holy Spirit is not the center of the worship. Rather, in the power of the Spirit, the focus is on Jesus Christ and God. Often called "emotionalism" or "enthusiasm" by the public and scholars alike, the expressive worship of Pentecostalism carries on the tradition of Montanists, Anabaptists, Quakers, Shakers, and other revival movements. This type of worship is often accompanied by singing in tongues, applause to the Lord, the raising of hands, and the shouting of loud "amens" and "hallelujahs."[121] More traditional and established denominations, though, have recently come to appreciate the Pentecostal dynamism and have shown a desire to express it through more liturgi-

115. Ibid., 14.

116. Synan, "Pentecostalism," 36.

117. Ibid., 37.

118. For a definitive description of Pentecostal spirituality, see Daniel E. Albrecht, *Rites in the Spirit: A Ritual Approach to Pentecostal/Charismatic Spirituality* (Sheffield: Sheffield Academic Press, 1999).

119. Daniel E. Albrecht, "Pentecostal Spirituality: Looking through the Lens of Ritual," *Pneuma* 14, no. 2 (1996): 21, italics added.

120. Ibid., 9

121. Synan, "Pentecostalism," 37.

cal forms, as was evident at the worship services led by Pentecostals at the World Council of Churches Assembly at Canberra (1991) and the World Missions Conference at San Antonio (1989).

Pentecostal/Charismatic approaches emphasize empowerment through the Spirit for witnessing and service. Personal and mass evangelism are given high priority, which is perhaps the main factor accounting for the phenomenal growth of the movement. Pentecostal spirituality and worship emphasize the supernatural. "The Pentecostals envision a world subject to invasions by the supernatural element. Pentecostals teach adherents to expect encounters with the supernatural. . . . Claims of signs, wonders, and miracles are not limited to the regions of the Sunday ritual. They are to be a part of daily life."[122]

Pointing to the fact that Pentecostalism is not normally based on doctrinal agreement but rather on a shared experience of the Holy Spirit, Hollenweger has suggested that

> taken seriously this offers a real possibility of discovering a methodology of theology in an *oral* culture where the medium of communication is— just as in biblical times—not the definition, but the description; not the statement, but the story; not the doctrine but the testimony. . . . Whoever denies that one can do proper theology in these categories will have to prove that the Bible is not a theological book. Our way of doing theology is a culturally biased form (yet necessarily so, in our culture!). There are other equally relevant forms of doing theology. Pentecostalism offers raw materials and elements for such an alternative methodology.[123]

Distinctive Features of Pentecostal Pneumatology

To come to a right understanding of the distinctive features of Pentecostal pneumatology, it is important to note that Pentecostals understand themselves first and foremost on the basis of their particular brand of spirituality.[124] That is the core of Pentecostal identity.[125] According to Margaret Poloma, Pentecostals have offered an "anthropological protest against modernity [by] providing a medium for encoun-

---

122. Albrecht, "Pentecostal Spirituality," 23.

123. W. J. Hollenweger, "Charisma and Oikumene: The Pentecostal Contribution to the Church Universal," *One in Christ* 7 (1971): 332–33.

124. Richard Israel, Daniel E. Albrecht, and Randal G. McNally, "Pentecostals and Hermeneutics: Texts, Rituals, and Community," *Pneuma* 15, no. 2 (1993): 146. See also Jean-Daniel Plüss, *Therapeutic and Prophetic Narratives in Worship: A Hermeneutic Study of Testimony and Vision* (Frankfurt: Peter Lang, 1993).

125. For details, see V.-M. Kärkkäinen, "On Free Churches' Identity in Ecumenical Context: Pentecostalism as a Case Study," *Mid-Stream: The Journal of the Ecumenical Movement* (forthcoming).

tering supernatural . . . [and] fus[ing] the natural and supernatural, the emotional and rational, the charismatic and institutional in a decidedly postmodern way." She has characterized this Pentecostal worldview by "its belief in and experience of the paranormal as an alternate *Weltanschauung* for our instrumental rational modern society."[126]

Donald Dayton, in his seminal work *Theological Roots of Pentecostalism*,[127] has urged Pentecostals to understand themselves through a paradigm involving several theological factors. The four he identifies were present in a slightly different form in the American Wesleyan-Holiness movement of the nineteenth century, but they were reconfigured in Pentecostal thinking and used in a powerful way in the form that Aimee Semple McPherson, the founder of the Foursquare Gospel, one of the oldest and largest Pentecostal bodies, popularized: Jesus was understood to be Savior, Baptizer in the Holy Spirit, Divine Healer, and Coming King. To these were added still one more aspect, rooted in the Holiness movements from which Pentecostalism came, and consequently, Pentecostals were known as "full gospel" Christians. This full gospel was comprised of the following five theological motifs:

1. justification by faith in Christ
2. sanctification by faith as a second definite work of grace
3. healing of the body as provided for all in the atonement
4. the premillennial return of Christ
5. the baptism in the Holy Spirit evidenced by speaking in tongues

This last motif came to be the most distinctive feature of classical Pentecostalism.[128] Perhaps the "prophethood" of all believers could be added as a sixth motif.[129]

Hollenweger has argued that the paradigm for defining Pentecostal identity must be understood more broadly. His classic description of the aspects that form Pentecostal identity includes the following:

- orality of liturgy
- narrativity of theology and witness

126. I found this citation in Timothy B. Cargal, "Beyond the Fundamentalist-Modernist Controversy: Pentecostals and Hermeneutics in a Postmodern Age," *Pneuma* 15, no. 2 (1993): 163.

127. Peabody, Mass.: Hendrickson, 1987.

128. Steven J. Land, *Pentecostal Spirituality: A Passion for the Kingdom* (Sheffield: Sheffield Academic Press, 1993), 18.

129. Ibid.

- maximum participation at the level of reflection, prayer, and decision making and therefore a form of community that is reconciliatory
- inclusion of dreams and visions into personal and public forms of worship; they function as a kind of icon for the individual and the community
- an understanding of the body/mind relationship that is informed by experiences of correspondence between body and mind; the most striking application of this insight is the ministry of healing by prayer[130]

Whether these descriptions of Pentecostalism are legitimate in the final analysis cannot be established in this presentation, and it is important to note that Pentecostalism emphasizes lived charismatic spirituality rather than discursive theology.

Distinctive Features of Charismatic Pneumatologies

Although Pentecostalism and the Charismatic movements share basic commonalities, they also possess definite differences, which come to the fore in regard to pneumatological orientations.[131] This is understandable in view of the fact that Charismatic theologies are shaped by their respective church traditions. For example, the Catholic Charismatic Movement is shaped as much (or more) by its commitment to the Catholic Church as it is by its commitment to a type of spiritual experience.[132]

While Spirit baptism is the core experience of most Charismatics, not all Charismatic theologians understand the baptism in the same

130. W. J. Hollenweger, "After Twenty Years' Research on Pentecostalism," *International Review of Missions* 75 (January 1986): 6. He has presented this kind of list in numerous other writings too, and it has been enthusiastically cited by most of the observers of the movement, both insiders and outsiders. More recently, Hollenweger ("From Azusa Street," 3–14) has summarized the "roots" of Pentecostalism in these terms: (1) the black oral root, (2) the Catholic root, (3) the evangelical root, (4) the critical root, and (5) the ecumenical root.

131. For basic documents on Charismatic pneumatologies, see Kilian McDonnell, ed., *Presence, Power, Praise: Documents on the Charismatic Renewal*, 3 vols. (Collegeville, Minn.: Liturgical Press, 1980).

132. See further Francis A. Sullivan, "Catholic Charismatic Renewal," in *The Dictionary of Pentecostal and Charismatic Movements*, 110–25; Kilian McDonnell, "Catholic Charismatic Renewal and Classical Pentecostalism: Growth and Critique of a Systematic Suspicion," *One in Christ* 23 (1987): 36–61; idem, *Charismatic Renewal and Churches* (New York: Seabury Press, 1976); idem, *Charismatic Renewal and Ecumenism* (New York: Paulist Press, 1978); and idem, ed., *The Holy Spirit and Power: The Catholic Charismatic Renewal* (Garden City, N.Y.: Doubleday, 1975).

way. Most Charismatic theologians view the baptism in an "organic" way by identifying it with water baptism, though it is not actualized through spiritual gifts until much later. For Charismatics, this view avoids the problems of the "initial evidence" doctrine, the idea of two baptisms, and the dividing of Christians into two classes: those baptized by the Spirit and those who are not.

Pentecostalism represents a revival movement with a restorationist tendency and consequently a low view of history and tradition. In contrast, Charismatic theologians usually pay much more attention to tradition and look at the Holy Spirit in light of the historical roots of their traditions. Catholic Charismatics especially often remind Christians that spiritual gifts have never been absent from the life of the church, finding examples, even of "singing in the Spirit," throughout their history.

Charismatic Christians usually focus more on community than do their Pentecostal counterparts. They have a greater sense of community life and the relationship between koinōnia and the work of the Spirit. This is especially true for Charismatics in more sacramental denominations. The Spirit is seen as working through tradition, which carries and interprets divine revelation. The new experience of the Spirit is interpreted in light of Scripture and tradition. Believing that the Spirit has been at work throughout the history of the church, Charismatics search for the continuity between their new experience and the faith handed down to them. For example, in the Catholic Renewal Movement, the Spirit is seen at work through the seven sacraments of the church, all of which depend on the grace of God and the faith of the recipient (or the faith of the parents in the case of infant baptism).

It has also been characteristic of Charismatics to strive to show how their experience adds to and can be a part of traditional theology. Nevertheless, Yves Congar is concerned that in many Charismatic theologies, there is an unhealthy opposition between "charism" and "institution,"[133] which is certainly true of Pentecostalism. In other words, the "free" ministry of the Spirit is appreciated while the necessity of structures and even leadership "control" or guidance of the Spirit's ministry is questioned.

Theologies of Spirit Baptism

The single most important aspect of Pentecostal pneumatology is the doctrine of Spirit baptism.[134] In recent years, this much disputed idea has become one of the more widely discussed pneumatological

133. Congar, *I Believe in the Holy Spirit*, 2:165–69.
134. The standard source for different theologies of Spirit baptism is Lederle, *Treasures Old and New*. See also Kilian McDonnell and Arnold Bittlinger, *The Baptism in the Holy Spirit as an Ecumenical Problem* (Notre Dame: Charismatic Renewal Service, 1972).

topics in dialogues between Pentecostals/Charismatics and other Christian theologians. It has even been suggested recently that baptism in the Holy Spirit has become as important today as justification by faith was in the time of Luther. The late "Mr. Pentecost," David du Plessis, has contended that the distinctive feature of Pentecostalism is neither evangelical zeal nor healing but the baptism in the Holy Spirit with the manifestation of the spiritual gifts.[135] For many, the doctrine of Spirit baptism is a "distinctive aspect" of not just Pentecostalism but also the Charismatic movement.[136]

Pentecostals view the event of Spirit baptism as distinct from and subsequent to conversion. In other words, Spirit baptism and conversion are two different, though usually related, events. Consequently, Pentecostals believe that the Holy Spirit acts differently in conversion/regeneration than in the work of Spirit baptism.

There are actually two versions of *ordo salutis* (order of salvation) among Pentecostals. Early Pentecostalism often stressed Spirit baptism as a third distinct experience, after justification/new birth/regeneration, which came first, and sanctification, which came second. As it was coined, "Baptism with the Holy Ghost is a gift of power upon the sanctified life."[137] Later classical Pentecostal teaching has increasingly minimized or even disregarded a second work of sanctification as a prerequisite to Spirit baptism. Currently, therefore, Pentecostals by and large speak of Spirit baptism as a second experience of God's grace, not so much for sanctification of life as for empowerment to witness. Sanctification, on the one hand, is understood as being included in conversion (as an initial stage), and, on the other hand, as a lifelong growth process.

In addition to empowerment, Pentecostals convey the meaning of Spirit baptism using various other terms: a new sense of the reality of faith, power to witness, fullness of life, reception of God's charismatic gifts, and so on. The most peculiar feature of Pentecostalism is the close identification of baptism in the Spirit with speaking in tongues. By far the largest section of Pentecostals believe that speaking in tongues is "the initial (physical) evidence" of baptism in the Spirit.[138]

135. Sandidge, *Roman Catholic-Pentecostal Dialogue*, 1:41. Du Plessis, already at the early stage of his emerging ecumenical career, noted that baptism in the Holy Spirit could fit into various ecclesiological polities.

136. Lederle, *Treasures Old and New*, xi: "The major distinctive doctrines of the charismatic movement certainly are Spirit baptism and the charisms of the Holy Spirit."

137. J. Rodman Williams, "Pentecostal Spirituality," *One in Christ* 10 (1974): 180–92. See also Tak-Ming Cheung, "Understandings of Spirit-Baptism," *Journal of Pentecostal Theology* 8 (1996): 115–28.

138. See further Gary B. McGee, ed., *Initial Evidence: Historical and Biblical Perspectives on the Pentecostal Doctrine of Spirit Baptism* (Peabody, Mass.: Hendrickson, 1991).

Other Pentecostal interpretations of Spirit baptism include both the *sacramental* view and the *non-sacramental/integrative* view. According to the sacramental view, Spirit baptism is a breakthrough to a conscious awareness of the Spirit already received and present through water baptism. Rather than being a new imparting, it is an actualization of the graces already received. Some Pentecostals use the term *release* to describe this event.[139] This view has been called the "original Catholic interpretation of Spirit baptism." It "comes close to being the official Catholic position and has also received support from Lutheran, Anglican, and Presbyterian circles."[140]

A non-sacramental view sees in Spirit baptism a "new imparting" unrelated to any immediate sacramental context. In other words, the reception of the Spirit does not come (automatically) in the moment of water baptism. A separate imparting is needed. The background for this view can be found in Thomas Aquinas's understanding of several impartings of the Spirit. According to the non-sacramental interpretation, in Spirit baptism people receive a real imparting of the Spirit.[141]

In addition to these interpretations, a third has been called the "dominant view" or "the unified pattern of Christian experience." According to this view, one can see a pattern of gradual development in a believer who is at the same time justified and sinful, without any two-level (justification and Spirit baptism) or three-level (justification, sanctification, and Spirit baptism) models. Karl Barth's understanding of Spirit baptism illustrates this idea: "We thus regard it as legitimate to understand by the baptism of the Holy Ghost . . . the divine preparation of man for the Christian life in its totality."[142]

Catholic theologians Kilian McDonnell and George Montague have done groundbreaking research on the early understandings of Spirit baptism. They have shown undisputed evidence that during the first centuries Christians regarded it as an integral part of Christian initiation and that it was usually accompanied by Pentecostal-type spiritual manifestations.

A text from Tertullian exemplifies the patristic understanding of Christian initiation, Spirit baptism, and gifts. The rite of initiation as

139. See further Kilian McDonnell and George T. Montague, *Christian Initiation and Baptism in the Holy Spirit: Evidence from the First Eight Centuries* (Collegeville, Minn.: Liturgical Press, 1991).

140. Lederle, *Treasures Old and New*, 105, 106.

141. Francis Sullivan, *Charisms and Charismatic Renewal* (Ann Arbor, Mich.: Servant Publications, 1982).

142. Karl Barth, *Church Dogmatics*, vol. 4/1 (Edinburgh: T & T Clark, 1969), 31. Barth seems to identify the baptism of the Holy Spirit with the reconciling act of God in Christ.

Tertullian knew it consisted of a water bath, anointing, the laying-on of hands, and the celebration of the Eucharist.[143] To use Tertullian's own words, the church "seals with water, clothes with the Holy Spirit, and feeds with the Eucharist."[144] Tertullian's *On Baptism* then goes on to state:

> Therefore, you blessed ones, for whom the grace of God is waiting, you who are about to come up from the most sacred bath of the new birth, you who for the first time spread out your hands in your mother's house: With your brethren ask your Father, ask your Lord, for a special gift of His patrimony, the abundance of charisms. Ask, He says, and you shall receive. In fact, you have sought, and you have found; you have knocked, and it has been opened to you.[145]

This passage shows convincingly that the basic elements of Christian initiation during this early time in the church were water baptism, "inviting and welcoming the Holy Spirit," with accompanying gifts such as prophecy and tongues as "patrimony." This experience took place for a believer after serving as a catechumenate for a considerable length of time, perhaps as much as three years. On the basis of their investigation, McDonnell and Montague summarize: "The research supports the classical Pentecostal teaching that baptism in the Holy Spirit is not peripheral but central. The gifts of the Spirit were expected and received during the rite of initiation because they belong to the Christian equipment, to building up of the community."[146]

The Spirit in the Ecumenical Movement's Theologies

The Ecumenical Potential of Pneumatology

To conclude our survey of how the Spirit has been understood and appropriated in various Christian traditions, old and new, we turn to

143. Kilian McDonnell, "Communion Ecclesiology and Baptism in the Spirit: Tertullian and the Early Church," *TS* 49 (1988): 678–79.

144. *Prescription against the Heretics* 36 (*SC* 46, 138–39).

145. *De baptisme* 20 (*SC* 35, 96). Tertullian's phrase "the first time spread out your hands" *(primas manus . . . aperitis)* refers to prayer, and the expression "in your mother's house" *(apud matrem)* refers to the church.

146. Kilian McDonnell, "Five Defining Issues: The International Classical Pentecostal/Roman Catholic Dialogue," *Pneuma* 17, no. 2 (1995): 180. In *Christian Initiation*, McDonnell and Montague investigate thirteen post-biblical texts. The witnesses include five doctors of the church (Hilary, Cyril, John Chrysostom, Basil, Gregory of Nazianzus), in addition to Tertullian, Origen, and Philoxenus, and embrace Latin, Greek, and Syrian cultures.

the theologies and conceptions of the Spirit in the ecumenical movement. It is safe to say that, besides the emergence of the Pentecostal/Charismatic movements, no development has so reshaped the essence of Christianity as has the ecumenical movement. Support for this statement can be found in the fact that since Vatican Council II in the 1960s, even the Roman Catholic Church has opened its door to ecumenism, even though—like Pentecostals—it is not a member of the World Council of Churches (WCC).

Of course, it has to be noted that ecumenism is a far more comprehensive concept than the WCC or other formal ecumenical organizations; by far the majority of Christians are not members of WCC churches. At the same time, however, it is true that the role of the WCC is unsurpassed in the efforts of Christian churches to give united testimony and find ways to overcome existing barriers.

Recently, several Catholic ecumenists spoke of the importance of pneumatology in the work for Christian unity. Avery Dulles thinks that the rules of ecumenical theology must be "biblically rooted, ecclesially responsible, open to criticism, and sensitive to the present leading of the Holy Spirit."[147] Philip Rosato declares confidently that pneumatology offers the divided Christian communities a new meeting place for dialogue.[148] Dietrich Ritschl has elaborated on a "therapeutic task of theology," in which the plurality and diversity promoted by the Holy Spirit is acknowledged as a condition for unity.[149]

It is noteworthy that the Roman Catholic Church has been the first and, until 1996, when the International Dialogue between the World Alliance of Reformed Churches and World Pentecostal Churches was initiated, the only church to begin official dialogues with Pentecostals and Charismatics, who represent the youngest strand of Christian experience of and reflection on the Spirit. Ecumenically, this dialogue carries enormous potential for several reasons. First, it is a dialogue between the two largest Christian churches, which together represent almost two-thirds of all Christians. Second, its focus is on the Spirit and spirituality, and therefore, it may

147. Avery Dulles, "Method in Ecumenical Theology," in *The Craft of Theology: From Symbol to System*, ed. Avery Dulles (New York: Crossroad, 1992), 195. In this sense, we could criticize the model of ecumenical theology posed by Hans Küng for its total lack of pneumatological reference, as is clearly seen in his definition of ecumenism, found in Hans Küng, *Theology for the Third Millennium: An Ecumenical View* (New York: Doubleday, 1988), 169, 206.

148. Philip Rosato, "Called by God, in the Holy Spirit: Pneumatological Insights into Ecumenism," *The Ecumenical Review* 30 (1978): 110–26.

149. Dietrich Ritschl, "The Search for Implicit Axioms behind Doctrinal Texts," *Greg* 74 (1993): 219.

open up new vistas for unity.[150] Third, it is a dialogue between an established church with a long history of tradition and a movement of independent churches worldwide; in terms of ecumenical methodology, it represents the challenges and potentials of the future of ecumenism.

The Catholic Paul D. Lee, who wrote his doctoral dissertation on some aspects of this dialogue, has argued that the dialogue has helped Catholic theologians test a truly pneumatological approach to Christian unity.

> This science [i.e., pneumatology] provides a fresh ecumenical meeting-ground, especially as regards a theologically more agreeable understanding of the Church. The Spirit continuously brings to the Church hope, vigor, and new insights. Today's renewed interest in pneumatology among Christians has positive implications for a more comprehensive and theo-centric ecclesiology. A growing convergence in the theology of the Holy Spirit promises new breakthroughs, for instance, in the traditional ecclesiological tensions between "the charismatic" and "the institutional," between the laity and the clergy, between the historical and the eschatological, and between understandings of the Church as "an event" and as "an organization."[151]

Pneumatology offers "an eschatological hope to be experienced and realized now," "a new meeting place for dialogue" in the midst of divided Christendom, Lee further contends.[152] It brings with it new hope and new challenges for ecumenical work.[153]

Similarly, an interesting pneumatological outlook is emerging in WCC-related theologies, the topic to which we now turn.[154]

The Emergence of a Pneumatological Perspective in WCC Theologies[155]

The Seventh General Assembly of the World Council of Churches in Canberra in 1991 focused on the Holy Spirit. Rather than analyzing the

150. For an analysis of pneumatology during the first three quinquennia of the dialogue, see V.-M. Kärkkäinen, *Spiritus ubi vult spirat: Pneumatology in the Roman Catholic-Pentecostal Dialogue (1972–1989)*, Schriften der Luther-Agricola-Gesellschaft 42 (Helsinki: Luther-Agricola Society, 1998).

151. Lee, "Pneumatological Ecclesiology," 2.

152. Ibid., 277.

153. Ibid., 287.

154. See further, V.-M. Kärkkäinen, "Pneumatology as a New Ecumenical 'Model,'" *Ecumenical Trends* 27, no. 9 (1998): 10–16; and idem, "The Ecumenical Potential of Pneumatology," *Greg* 80 (1999): 121–45.

155. My use of the term WCC theologies (in the plural rather than the singular) reflects the conviction that there is no definite WCC theology, since that would be a contradiction in terms for a constituency that provides a forum for cooperation but not a defined communion.

outcomes of that particular meeting—the results of which are well documented and easily accessible[156]—I will trace briefly the development of a pneumatological perspective in the WCC, which culminated in Canberra.[157]

In the reports of the major ecumenical conferences held prior to the formation of the WCC in 1948, references to the Holy Spirit remained fairly traditional, following the lines of general Protestant thinking. The trinitarian confession of faith was formally acknowledged, but the affirmation of the Spirit as a person in communion with the Father and the Son remained largely undeveloped. According to Konrad Raiser, this relative subordination of the Holy Spirit to the person of Jesus was fairly representative of Protestant theology and evangelical piety of those years.[158]

The Faith and Order conferences at Lausanne (1927) and Edinburgh (1937) referred to the Holy Spirit mainly in relation to the church, as the one who gives life to the church. The Spirit sanctifies and renews the church through Word and sacrament and draws it into unity.[159]

The reports of the First Assembly of the WCC at Amsterdam (1948) concentrated on Christ, who brings forth the church. They affirmed that the church persisted in continuity throughout history through the presence and power of the Holy Spirit.[160] Interestingly enough, the expression "recover[ing] the spirit of prophecy to discern the signs of the times," which became one of the catchwords of Vatican II, was employed here.[161]

The International Missionary Conference at Willingen and the Faith and Order Conference at Lund, both held in 1952, reached a new understanding of the missionary task as participation in the *missio Dei*. Through the Spirit, the church can proclaim God's saving work in Christ and wait for his final victory. The Lund conference affirmed many earlier pronouncements on the Spirit. The continuity of the church in history was assured "by the constant action of the risen Lord through the Holy Spirit," and it is through the "unifying power

156. Michael Kinnamon, ed., *Signs of the Spirit: Official Report*, Seventh Assembly (Geneva: WCC, 1991).

157. In this section, I am heavily indebted to Konrad Raiser, "The Holy Spirit in Modern Ecumenical Thought," *The Ecumenical Review* 41, no. 3 (1989): 376ff. Useful information and insights can also be found in Albert C. Outler, "Pneumatology as an Ecumenical Frontier," *The Ecumenical Review* 41, no. 3 (1989): 363–74.

158. Raiser, "The Holy Spirit," 376.

159. Edinburgh, section III, in *A Documentary History of the Faith and Order Movement 1927–1963*, ed. L. Vischer (St. Louis: Bethany, 1963), 45, #29.

160. Amsterdam, section I, in *A Documentary History*, 78, #11.

161. Amsterdam, section II, in *The Church's Witness to God's Design* (New York: Harper & Brothers, 1948), 222.

of His indwelling Spirit" that the organic unity of the body of Christ is sustained.[162]

At the Third Assembly of the WCC at New Delhi (1961) a new orientation became clearly visible. The basis of the WCC was enlarged to affirm an explicitly trinitarian, doxological formulation: "to the glory of the one God, Father, Son and Holy Spirit."[163] The preamble to the statement placed the understanding of unity in a trinitarian, pneumatological setting:

> The love of the Father and the Son in the unity of the Holy Spirit is the source and goal of the unity which the triune God wills for all men and creation. We believe that we share in this unity in the Church of Jesus Christ. . . . The reality of this unity was made manifest at Pentecost in the gift of the Holy Spirit, through whom we know in this present age the first fruits of that perfect union of the Son with his Father, which will be known in its fullness only when all things are consummated by Christ in his glory.[164]

The Montreal Faith and Order Conference (1963) built on the conference held at New Delhi and developed a pneumatological perspective, especially in relation to Scripture and tradition as well as to the delicate issue of ministry. The statement on ministry anticipated the rise of the Charismatic movements and the renaissance of *charismata* in the church: "The Holy Spirit dwells in the Church. . . . He also bestows differing gifts *(charismata)* on groups and individuals. . . . All members of the Church are thus gifted for the common good."[165] After the Montreal meeting came new studies on pneumatology, especially studies involving the pneumatological understanding between East and West, based on patristic studies, as well as further study on "Christ, the Holy Spirit, and the Ministry." Another influential study involved the relationship between the sacraments and the Spirit (Bristol, 1967). But it was the Uppsala Assembly (1968) that produced "the fullest summary of ecumenical thinking on the Holy Spirit up to that

162. Lund, section I, in *A Documentary History*, 90, #19.

163. W. A. Visser't Hooft, "The Basis: Its History and Significance," *The Ecumenical Review* 37, no. 2 (1985): 170–74.

164. New Delhi section on unity, in *A Documentary History*, 144, #1. Raiser ("The Holy Spirit," 378) pays special attention to the Orthodox contribution to this unity formula and refers to the important article by Nikos Nissiotis, "The Witness and the Service of Eastern Orthodoxy to the One Undivided Church," in *The Orthodox Church in the Ecumenical Movement*, ed. C. Patelos (Geneva: WCC, 1978), 231ff.

165. Montreal, section III, in *The Fourth World Conference on Faith and Order: The Report from Montreal 1963*, ed. P. C. Rodger and L. Vischer (New York: Association Press, 1964), 65, #92.

moment."[166] The Assembly studied the relationship between the traditions and the Spirit, the relationship between the church and the Spirit, and the significance of the Spirit in relation to Christian unity.

The Faith and Order meeting at Louvain (1971) gathered together studies initiated at Montreal and paved the way for the most important document of Faith and Order, *Baptism, Eucharist, and Ministry*, issued roughly ten years later.[167] Raiser synthesized the pneumatological perspective after Louvain in the following way:

1. The first statement involved the role of the Holy Spirit in the confession of the faith. The influential study on *filioque* suggested that there needs to be "a new sensitivity to the person and work of the Holy Spirit as the one who in his fullness both rests upon Jesus Christ and is the gift of Christ to the church, the Lord and Giver of life to humankind and all creation."[168] The project *Confessing One Faith* has been far-reaching in the study of the Spirit in confessions.[169] It explicates the classical affirmation about the Holy Spirit in the Nicene-Constantinopolitan Creed.

2. Second is the relationship between the Spirit and the church. Here, of course, *Baptism, Eucharist, and Ministry* stands in the forefront. The pneumatological perspective, though not the focus of the study, is present in relation to sacraments and ministry, based on the pneumatological understanding of the church.

3. As more churches from the Third World have joined the WCC, issues of the Spirit and religious pluralism, the third topic in Raiser's summary, have come into focus.[170] The recent works of Jürgen Moltmann and others have provided additional analysis of the developments that have come out of the theology of religions and the role of the Spirit.

4. The fourth aspect of development is the emergence of charismatic renewal among WCC churches as well as in the Roman Catholic Church. Beginning in the 1960s, many member churches

166. Raiser, "The Holy Spirit," 380; see *The Uppsala 68 Report*, ed. N. Goodall (Geneva: WCC, 1968).

167. *Faith and Order Paper 111* (Geneva: WCC, 1982).

168. Lukas Vischer, ed., *Spirit of God, Spirit of Christ: Ecumenical Reflections on the Filioque Controversy* (London: SPCK; Geneva: WCC, 1981), 18.

169. *Confessing One Faith: Towards an Ecumenical Explication of the Apostolic Faith*, Faith and Order Paper 140 (Geneva: WCC, 1987).

170. See Stanley J. Samartha, "The Holy Spirit and Peoples of Various Faiths," *Courage for Dialogue* (Geneva: WCC, 1981).

experienced manifestations of a charismatic renewal that focused on the baptism of the Holy Spirit, charismatic ministry, and various *charismata*. In 1999, in the aftermath of the last General Assembly (Harare, Zimbabwe, 1997), a Joint Working Group between the WCC and the Pentecostals was formed to foster cooperation and mutual knowledge, especially with regard to the doctrine and spirituality of the Holy Spirit.

One of the most noteworthy recent developments in the WCC that bears on the ecumenical pneumatological perspective is the influence of the Faith and Order Conference at Santiago de Compostela (1993).[171] Its emphasis on *koinōnia*-theology carries potential for pneumatological developments, since there is a growing consensus that the church is a "communion in the Spirit."

The various approaches to the Holy Spirit discussed in this chapter have arisen out of their respective theological and ecclesiastical contexts. Pneumatology, as any other theological locus, is integrally connected to the underlying guiding principles of a theological system. The same principle is evident in the next chapter, which delves into the role and significance of the Holy Spirit in the writings of some leading theologians of our time. Some of these thinkers have devoted much energy to pneumatological topics specifically, while others have considered the Spirit mainly as a necessary part of a theological program. What is evident is that the topics related to pneumatology are gaining ascendancy in most theologies, both in the West and in the two-thirds world.

171. For conference proceedings, see *On the Way to Fuller Koinonia: Messages to the Churches*, WCC, Fifth Conference on Faith and Order, Santiago de Compostela, Spain, 3–14 August 1993 (Geneva: WCC, 1993).

5

Leading Contemporary Theologians on the Spirit

A Pneumatological Smorgasbord

Having inquired into various approaches taken by major Christian traditions concerning the doctrine and spirituality of the Holy Spirit, it is time to focus on the role of the Spirit in the thought of some leading theologians of our day. Six representatives will illustrate the richness and variety of perspectives on pneumatology: John Zizioulas of the Eastern Orthodox tradition, Karl Rahner of the Roman Catholic Church, Wolfhart Pannenberg of the Lutheran tradition, Jürgen Moltmann and Michael Welker of the Reformed Church, and Clark Pinnock of the Baptist/evangelical tradition, who has in recent years identified himself with Charismatic theologies.

In a legitimate sense, all of these theologians represent their respective traditions. Inquiry into their distinctive understandings of the Holy Spirit reveals the connection between their theologies and their overall theological contexts. Rahner's theology cannot be divorced from his commitment to the Catholic faith, nor Zizioulas's from his Orthodox views. But it should be noted that, for example, Rahner's theology and Catholic theology are not synonymous; there are several contemporary Catholic theologies, of which Rahner's is just a representative example. The same applies to Pannenberg. Certainly, reading Pannenberg's writings gives one the sense that he is a theologian who draws from the rich sources of Lutheranism, but Pannenberg could hardly be labeled a "Lutheran-only" theologian. He not only criticizes some Lutheran views but also expands them to create an ecumenical, conciliar theology. Similar examples could be given in regard to Moltmann and Welker.

All of this is to say that focusing on individual theologians both clarifies some dominant pneumatological themes already covered in relation to major Christian traditions, but it also confuses the picture. Both perspectives are theologically helpful. If there is any single dimension to the endless variety of contemporary theologies, it is the unity-in-diversity nature of even "confessional" theologies. There are several Lutheran, or Catholic, or Pentecostal/Charismatic theologies.

Furthermore, what makes the study of individual theologians' ideas about the Spirit so exciting—and a learning experience, indeed—is the fact that in each theological approach, the doctrine of the Spirit is, of course, integrally related to the rest of the theology. Pannenberg's or Zizioulas's distinctive views of pneumatology could never be understood without reference to the specific structures and emphases of their theologies. Even though in the confines of this chapter I cannot offer a comprehensive introduction to the wider theological outlook of the selected theologians, I will, however, connect what they believe about the Spirit with some leading themes of their theologies.

John Zizioulas: Communion Pneumatology

"Ontology of Communion"

John Zizioulas, the Bishop of Pergamon, Greece, is the most significant Eastern Orthodox theologian of our day. Like Bishop Kallistos (originally, Timothy Ware of England), Zizioulas has built bridges between the East and the West.

Zizioulas's most distinctive idea that permeates all of his theology and his view of the church is that of *koinōnia*, communion. Zizioulas draws an analogy between the being of God and the being of humans. What is most characteristic of God is his being in relation. As the Trinity, the three Persons of the Godhead interrelate with each other. There is an intra-trinitarian love relationship. With this same love, the Triune God relates to human beings and the world and embraces them in divine-human *koinōnia*. Zizioulas's basic argument, therefore, runs as follows:

> From the fact that a human being is a member of the Church, he becomes an "image of God," he exists as God Himself exists, he takes on God's

"way of being." This way of being . . . is a way of *relationship* with the world, with other people and with God, an event of *communion*, and that is why it cannot be realized as the achievement of an *individual*, but only as an *ecclesial* fact.[1]

In fact, Zizioulas insists that communion is not just another way of describing being, whether individual or ecclesial, but that it belongs to the *ontology* of being. Thus, we should speak of an actual "ontology of communion." The Vatican II view of the church basically says the same when it states that God "has, however, willed to make men holy and save them, not as individuals without any bond or link between them, but rather to make them into a people who might acknowledge him and serve him in holiness."[2]

Zizioulas makes a distinction between "biological" and "ecclesial" being: The former refers to a human being apart from communion with God and others, while the latter denotes a person living in *koinōnia*. Further, Zizioulas's communion ecclesiology is based on an integral relationship between Christology and pneumatology, the topic we discuss before delving into his ecclesiology.

Christ and the Spirit

Zizioulas attempts to work for a proper synthesis between Christology and pneumatology as the basis for his ecclesiology.[3] He rightly notes that in the New Testament, there is a mutuality between the two rather than a priority given to either one. On the one hand, the Spirit is given by Christ (John 7:39); on the other hand, there is no Christ until the Spirit is at work either at his baptism (Mark) or at his birth (Matthew and Luke). Both of these views could coexist in the one and the same canon. In the early centuries, however, especially in the Christian West, confusion came on the liturgical level due to the separation of baptism and confirmation. As long as these two rites were united, it could be argued that pneumatology (confirmation) and baptism (Christology) form one entity.[4]

1. John D. Zizioulas, *Being as Communion: Studies in Personhood and the Church* (Crestwood, N.Y.: St. Vladimir's Seminary Press, 1985), 15, italics added.
2. *LG* 9.
3. See further J. Zizioulas, "Die Kirche als Gemeinschaft," in *Santiago de Compostela 1993*, Fünfte Weltkonferenz für Glauben und Kirchenverfassung; Beiheft zur Ökonomischen Rundschau 67, ed. G. Gassmann und D. Heller (Frankfurt: Otto Lembeck Verlag, 1994), 100; idem, "Die pneumatologische Dimension der Kirche," *Internationale Katholische Zeitschrift "Communio"* 2 (1973): 134ff.
4. Zizioulas, *Being as Communion*, 126–29.

In other words, according to Zizioulas's distinctive vocabulary, Christ is a historical person only in the Spirit (Matt. 1:18–20; Luke 1:35). Zizioulas is even ready to say that "Christ exists only pneumatologically." In line with the Eastern trinitarian sensitivity, he adds that to speak of Christ is to speak at the same time of the Father and the Holy Spirit. He also says, "Thus the mystery of the Church has its birth in the entire economy of the Trinity and in a pneumatologially constituted Christology."[5]

In line with his communion theology, Zizioulas contends that there are two kinds of Christologies. First, we may understand Christ as an individual, and second, as a "corporate personality"[6] in his relationship with his body, the church. In the former case, Christ is an "individual," in the latter, a "person." The role of the Spirit comes to the fore here: "The Holy Spirit is not one who *aids* us in bridging the distance between Christ and ourselves, but he is the person of the Trinity who actually realizes in history that which we call Christ. . . . In this case, our Christology is *essentially* conditioned by pneumatology, not just secondarily as in the first case; in fact it is *constituted* pneumatologically."[7]

One could also express this by saying that the corporate personality of Christ comes into being pneumatologically. Therefore, it is significant that since the time of Paul the Spirit has been associated with the notion of *koinōnia*. Pneumatology creates for Christology (and consequently, for ecclesiology) the dimension of communion.[8]

The Church as Communion in the Spirit[9]

Zizioulas points out the obvious fact that in the New Testament Easter (the work of Christ) and Pentecost (the outpouring of the Spirit) belong together.[10] From ancient times on, the pneumatological aspect of the church is highlighted by the fact that its confessions of faith connected the church with the Holy Spirit. But what exactly are the ecclesi-

5. Ibid., 112.
6. Ibid., 130.
7. Ibid., 110–11, italics in the original.
8. Zizioulas, "Die pneumatologische Dimension der Kirche," 95–104.
9. See further V.-M. Kärkkäinen, "Spirit, Christ, and Church: An Ecumenical Inquiry into a Pneumatological Ecclesiology," *One in Christ* 36, no. 4 (2000): especially 340–43. A fine study of Zizioulas's communion ecclesiology, in dialogue with the Catholic and Free Church ecclesiologies, is offered by Miroslav Volf, *After Our Likeness: The Church as the Image of the Trinity* (Grand Rapids: Eerdmans, 1998).
10. For a detailed analysis, see also James D. G. Dunn, *The Parting of the Ways between Christianity and Judaism and Their Significance for the Character of Christianity* (London: SCM Press; Philadelphia: Trinity Press International, 1991), 265ff.; and idem, "Unity and Diversity in the Church: A New Testament Perspective," *Greg* 71 (1990): 629–56.

ological ramifications of the role of the Spirit? What is the role of pneumatology in Zizioulas's view of the church?[11]

The New Testament calls the church the body of Christ (1 Cor. 12:12–13; Eph. 1:22–23; 4:15–16; etc.). Never is the church labeled the "body of the Spirit," and never are Christians said to be "members of the Spirit."[12] Therefore, the traditional christological grounding of the church seems well-founded. Zizioulas takes note of the fact that ecclesiologies traditionally have been built on either of the two classical rules, that of Ignatius of Antioch or of Irenaeus. Ignatius suggested the ecclesiality of the church could be secured by reference to Christ's presence: "Wherever Jesus Christ is, there is the universal church."[13] According to Irenaeus, what is decisive is the presence of the Spirit of God: "Wherever the Spirit of God is, there is the church, and all grace."[14]

Zizioulas joins with the tradition of Eastern theology that speaks of the church as founded on a twofold divine economy: the work of Christ and the work of the Holy Spirit.[15] On the basis of biblical language, Eastern theologians speak about the church as the body of Christ and the fullness of the Holy Spirit. We see the mutual relationship between the Son and Spirit in that just as the Son came down to earth and accomplished his work through the Spirit, so the Spirit came into the world, sent by the Son (John 15:26). The work of the Spirit is not subordinate to the work of the Son, nor is Pentecost a continuation of the incarnation but rather its sequel, its result.

But as Zizioulas builds on the long tradition of Eastern ecclesiology, he does so critically.[16] While sympathetic to Vladimir Lossky and other Eastern theologians, he sees as problematic both the idea of a distinct "economy of the Spirit" as well as a distinction between "objective" (Christology) and "subjective" (pneumatology).[17] Self-critically, he also insists that even Eastern ecclesiology falls short of a proper balance between Christology and pneumatology.[18]

---

11. Zizioulas, "Die pneumatologische Dimension der Kirche," 133.

12. Zizioulas, "Implications ecclésiologiques de deux types de pneumatologic," in *Communio Sanctorum: Mélanges offerts à Jean-Jacques von Allmen* (Geneva: Labor et fides, 1982), 141–54.

13. Ignatius, *Smyrn.* 8.2.

14. Irenaeus, *Adversus haereses* 3.24.1.

15. E.g., Vladimir Lossky, *The Mystical Theology of the Eastern Church* (Crestwood, N.Y.: St. Vladimir's Seminary Press, 1976), 156–57; and idem, "Concerning the Third Mark of the Church: Catholicity," in *In the Image and Likeness of God*, ed. John H. Erickson and Thomas E. Bird (Crestwood, N.Y.: St. Vladimir's Seminary Press, 1985), 177–78.

16. Zizioulas, *Being as Communion*, 124–25.

17. Two other Eastern theologians with whom Zizioulas interacts constantly are Nikos Nissiotis and Boris Bobrinskoy.

18. Zizioulas, *Being as Communion*, 124–26.

In a helpful way, Zizioulas speaks of the church as "instituted" by Christ and "constituted" by the Spirit.[19] He contends that it is not enough to speak of pneumatology in relation to the church but rather to make pneumatology (along with eschatology[20]) constitutive in regard to ecclesiology; in other words, pneumatology must qualify the very ontology of the church. The Spirit is not something that "animates" a church that already exists. "Pneumatology does not refer to the well-being but to the very being of the Church." Consequently, pneumatology is an ontological category in ecclesiology.[21]

What then are the main consequences of this pneumatological orientation for the life of the church? First of all, it guards against over-institutionalization. When there is a pneumatological deficit, one result is a hierarchical, centralized concept of the church. Second, it rehabilitates the local church as the primary entity, which is a teaching of the New Testament. In doing so, it brings church closer to the members and encourages the priesthood of all. If pneumatology is not ontologically constitutive of Christology, then there can be first one church and then many churches. However, if pneumatology is constitutive in regard to ecclesiology, the body of Christ is ontologically constituted by the Spirit. In other words, the Pentecost event is an ecclesiologically constitutive event. Further, when the church has a christological foundation only, it becomes hierarchical in the sense that what matters primarily is the universal body of Christ. When the Spirit is made co-constitutive of the church, each member of the church and each local church has the presence and charism of Christ and belongs to the whole church, but the church does not receive its ecclesiality from that.[22] Third, all pyramidal notions disappear in a pneumatological ecclesiology in which the "one" and the "many" coexist as two aspects of the same being.[23] Fourth, according to Zizioulas, pneumatology helps ecclesiology open up to the eschatological perspective. Incorporating the eschatological perspective avoids both "meta-historicism," in which the doctrine of the church is divorced from historical reality (sometimes attributed to Eastern tradition), and "historization" of ecclesial institutions, in which the doctrine of the church says nothing more than what the church has been as a historical reality (a danger

19. Ibid., 132, 136, 140.

20. For the role of eschatology in ecclesiology, see ibid., 131ff.

21. Ibid., 131–32 (citation on 132).

22. Ibid., 132–33. Zizioulas, however, sees as problematic the older Eastern emphasis on the local church, which, in his assessment, led to a sort of "congregationalism." This was the fault of the eucharistic ecclesiology of Afanasiev and others that gave priority to pneumatology rather than balancing pneumatology and Christology (133).

23. Ibid., 139.

within Western churches).[24] Fifth, the pneumatological orientation has consequences for ministry. The ministry of the church is the ministry of Christ. But when Christology is pneumatologically constituted, the Spirit constitutes the relationship between Christ and the ministry. This, in fact, agrees with what Paul argues in 1 Corinthians 12. The life and ministry of the body of Christ is conceived pneumatologically, in terms of the gifts of the Spirit. Be it the question of ordination or of the role of the laity, the proper context is the *koinōnia* of the Spirit among the members of the body of Christ. The charismatic life constitutes, rather than being derived from, the church's being.[25]

Interestingly enough, Zizioulas remarks that Orthodoxy's freedom from some of the experiences of the Western churches, such as the problems of clericalism or anti-institutionalism, may be taken as an indication that for the most part pneumatology has saved the life of Orthodoxy up to now.[26] Whatever one thinks of the accuracy of this statement in the real life of Orthodox churches, it contains a theological insight worth pondering.

Karl Rahner: Transcendental Pneumatology

Universal Transcendental Revelation in the Spirit

While it is an overstatement to claim that Karl Rahner[27] was the most significant Catholic pneumatologist of our time,[28] it certainly is true that he was the single most influential theologian of the post-conciliar Catholic Church. From within his unbelievably extensive theological production, a groundbreaking view of the Spirit emerged as an in-

24. Ibid., 139–40. For the significance of eschatology and pneumatology to ecclesiology, see the seminal work of Gerhard Ebeling, *Dogmatik des Christlichen Glaubens* (Tübingen: Mohr, 1979), 3:5–32.

25. Zizioulas, *Being as Communion*, 210–12, 217 n. 20.

26. Ibid., 140.

27. A very helpful recent summary of Rahner's pneumatology can be found in John R. Sachs, "'Do Not Stifle the Spirit': Karl Rahner, the Legacy of Vatican II, and Its Urgency for Theology Today," in *Catholic Theological Society Proceedings*, ed. E. Dreyer, 51 (1996): 15–38.

28. The Annual Meeting of Catholic Theological Society of America in 1996, with its focus on pneumatology, made a comprehensive assessment of Rahner's influence on pneumatology and ecclesiology. As often happens in eulogies, overstatements replace sound judgment; Sachs ("'Do Not Stifle the Spirit,'" 20), and Philip S. Keane ("The Role of the Holy Spirit in Contemporary Moral Theology," in *Catholic Theological Society Proceedings*, 109 n. 41) contended that Rahner has been the most influential pneumatologist of our time. Without denying Rahner's unbelievable productivity and unsurpassed influence, it simply isn't true that he would surpass, e.g., Congar and Muehlen, specifically in the field of pneumatology.

tegral part of his overall theological program. Rahner's role was that of a mediator between two dominant Catholic theologies, that of "modernism," which sought to adapt to the modern mind-set, and "integralism," which emphasized the integrity of the Catholic tradition and opposed accommodation to modern culture.

Rahner set himself the ambitious task of holding together two premises that appear contradictory: on the one hand, the universal saving action of the Spirit, and on the other hand, the necessity of supernatural revelation and faith. In order for these two premises to hold, revelation and faith must occur at a universal, transcendental level. His basic thesis was that God reveals himself to every human person in the very experience of that person's own finite, yet absolutely open-ended transcendence. God is the Holy Mystery who is the ground and horizon of human subjectivity.[29] A human being may exist as a person whose life gets ultimate meaning from that person's openness to God.

The background for this universal orientation was in Rahner's "transcendental method." "Transcendental experiences" show that humans are naturally oriented toward the Holy Mystery, called God. The human being is by nature "spirit," which means that the human being is open to receive revelation. God is not alien to human nature but an intrinsic part of it as the necessary condition for human subjectivity.[30] It is through "transcendental reflection" that one seeks to discover the necessary preconditions for human experience. Human beings are not only part of nature, but they are also oriented toward an infinite, mysterious horizon of being that Christians know as God. For Rahner:

> not only are humans always by nature open to God *(potentia oboedientalis),* they are also always supernaturally elevated by God in that transcendental openness so that such elevation becomes an actual experience of God in every human life. God actually communicates himself to every human person in a gracious offer of free grace, so that God's presence becomes an existential, a constitutive element, in every person's humanity.[31]

The human person, therefore, is "the event of a free, unmerited and forgiving, and absolute self-communication of God."[32] God's self-com-

29. Karl Rahner, "Experience of Self," in *Theological Investigations* 13 (New York: Seabury Press, 1975), 122–32; and Sachs, "'Do Not Stifle the Spirit,'" 20–21.
30. Here Rahner agrees with Wolfhart Pannenberg.
31. Stanley J. Grenz, and Roger E. Olson, *Twentieth-Century Theology: God and the World in a Transitional Age* (Downers Grove, Ill.: InterVarsity Press, 1992), 245.
32. Karl Rahner, *Foundations of Christian Faith* (New York: Seabury Press, 1978), 116.

munication means that God makes his very own self the innermost constitutive element of the human person; this is the mystery of the Spirit for Rahner: "God . . . has already communicated himself in his Holy Spirit always and everywhere and to every person as the innermost center of his existence."[33]

The spirited experience of self and God is never an individualistic experience but rather something that takes place in relation to others: "The act of personal love for another human being is therefore the all-embracing basic act . . . which gives meaning, direction and measure to everything else."[34] In other words, at its most basic level, our encounter with God takes place precisely in our encounters with others. Genuine human transcendence in love is possible only because of the gracious self-communication of God in the Spirit.[35]

What about the need for special revelation in Rahner's theology? His answer was that "categorical revelation," specific revelation in history through events, words, and symbols, is needed to fulfill what the transcendental, implicit, unthematic revelation reveals about God. These two are distinct yet interdependent. The categorical revelation discloses the inner reality of God that cannot be discovered through transcendental revelation alone: the personal character of God and his free relationship with spiritual creatures. Therefore, universal, transcendental experience of God in the Spirit does not make void the necessity of historical, special revelation.

> This Spirit is always, everywhere, and from the outset the entelechy, the determining principle, of the history of revelation and salvation; and its communication and acceptance, by its very nature, never takes place in a merely abstract, transcendental form. It always comes about through the mediation of history.[36]

The Dynamic Element in the Church [37]

Rahner's interest in pneumatology was long-standing. On the eve of Vatican II, he wrote a passionate appeal for openness to the Spirit, titled "Do Not Stifle the Spirit,"[38] in which he spoke about the great potentialities and challenges facing the church. He issued a serious warn-

---

33. Ibid., 139; Sachs, "'Do Not Stifle the Spirit,'" 21.

34. Karl Rahner, "Reflections on the Unity of the Love of Neighbour and the Love of God," in *Theological Investigations* 6 (Baltimore: Helicon, 1969), 241.

35. Ibid., 237–39.

36. Karl Rahner, "Jesus Christ in the Non-Christian Religions," in *Theological Investigations* 17 (New York: Crossroad, 1981), 46; Sachs, "'Do Not Stifle the Spirit,'" 22.

37. See further Kärkkäinen, "Spirit, Christ, and Church," 346–50.

38. In *Theological Investigations* 7 (New York: Herder, 1971), 72–87.

ing: The Spirit who blows everywhere "can never find adequate expression simply in the forms of what we call the church's official life, her principles, sacramental system and teaching."[39] He was very concerned about the charismatic element of the church:

> It is a situation by a spirit which has been rather too hasty and too uncompromising in taking the dogmatic definition of the primacy of the pope in the Church as the bond of unity and the guarantee of truth, this attitude objectifying itself in a not inconsiderable degree of centralization of government in an ecclesiastical bureaucracy at Rome.[40]

A couple of years later, while the council was still going on, he published another appeal for the charismatic element in the church titled *The Dynamic Element in the Church*.[41] Rahner issued a powerful call for the charismatic structure of the church by pointing out that the Holy Spirit is promised and given first and foremost to ecclesiastical ministry not to suppress the free flow of the Spirit but to make room for it.[42] The church should be to the end the "Church of the abiding Spirit."[43]

Rahner suggested that one must learn to perceive *charismata* when they first appear. Rather than canonizing charismatic persons after their death:

> it is almost of greater importance to perceive such gifts of the Spirit on their first appearance, so that they may be furthered and not choked by the incomprehension and intellectual laziness, if not ill-will and hatred, of those around them, ecclesiastics included. . . . But the charismatic is essentially new and always surprising. To be sure it also stands in inner though hidden continuity with what came earlier in the Church. . . . Yet it is new and incalculable, and it is not immediately evident at first sight that everything is as it was in the enduring totality of the Church. . . . And so the charismatic feature, when it is new, and one might almost say it is only charismatic if it is so, has something shocking about it.[44]

According to Rahner, the Spirit is constitutive of the church in a way more basic than its institutional structure.[45] When there is one-sided

---

39. Rahner, "'Do Not Stifle the Spirit,'" 75.
40. Ibid., 76.
41. New York: Herder & Herder, 1964.
42. Karl Rahner, *The Dynamic Element*, 42ff.
43. Ibid., 47–48.
44. Ibid., 82–83.
45. Karl Rahner, "Observations of the Factor of the Charismatic in the Church," in *Theological Investigations* 12 (New York: Seabury Press, 1974), 97.

emphasis on Christology, church structures tend to become dominating (this has also been the result of the older Catholic view of the church as continued incarnation). The charismatic element "does not merely stand in a dialectical relationship to the institutional factor as its opposite pole, existing on the same plane. Rather it is the first and the most ultimate among the formal characteristics inherent in the very nature of the Church as such."[46] Rahner also said that the church is primarily the "historical concretization of the charismatic as brought about by the Spirit of Christ."[47] And it is clear that in Rahner's view the term *charismatic* does not refer to any specific group in the church but to the life and ministry of all believers.

If the church is founded by the sovereign action of the Spirit, then the church has to be understood as an "open system."[48] In other words, the church cannot be understood or defined from a point within the church itself but rather from outside, from the Spirit of God.[49]

The practical results of Rahner's view of the charismatic structure of the church are obvious. First, this view creates an openness to the promptings of the Spirit. Second, it gives primacy to the Spirit over the structures and offices of the church, even if the structures in themselves express the Spirit (Rahner never championed individualism). Third, legitimate plurality results from the sovereign action of the Spirit.[50] Fourth, Rahner's pneumatological ecclesiology is open to ecumenism. There is an ultimate unity that already exists among all Christians, a unity brought about by the Spirit of God. In the Spirit, "all of us 'know' something more simple, more true and more real than we can know or express at the level of our theological concepts."[51]

The Universality of the Spirit

Rahner's approach to the urgent question of theology of religions (that is, what role, if any, do other religions play in salvation?) is distinctively pneumatological in that it is the Spirit who enables human reception of divine grace and the self's experience of existential tran-

46. Ibid.

47. Ibid., 86.

48. Ibid., 88.

49. See Sachs, "'Do Not Stifle the Spirit,'" 30.

50. See Karl Rahner, "Heresies in the Church Today?" in *Theological Investigations* 12 (New York: Seabury Press, 1974), 117–41.

51. Karl Rahner, "Some Problems in Contemporary Ecumenism," in *Theological Investigations* 14 (London: Darton, Longman & Todd, 1976), 245–53, here 251; see also his "Church, Churches, and Religions," *Theological Investigations* 10 (New York: Herder, 1973), 42ff.

scendence.[52] Transcendental experience of the Spirit is oriented toward explicit awareness. For Rahner, this is expressed in the religious traditions of the world and reaches its apex in the final self-revelation of God in Christ. Other religions also have "individual moments" of this kind, which make those people "anonymous Christians." However, because of human depravity, every such event of revelation remains partial and intermixed with error. The value of religions is in the mediation of these experiences of the Spirit, even when it is less than perfect.[53]

In that sense, all religious traditions potentially express truth about God's self-communication in the Spirit and therefore are part of the history of revelation. This does not mean, of course, that all religions express equally valid expressions of divine self-revelation: There is error in any religion. But through Christ's death and resurrection, God's gracious self-communication in the Spirit has become manifest in history: The "world is drawn to its spiritual fulfillment by the Spirit of God, who directs the whole history of the world in all its length and breadth towards its proper goal."[54]

Rahner built on Yves Congar's "mystical body of Christ" in his argument that there is thus a state of being of explicit faith prior to the hearing of the gospel when a person can respond positively to the grace of God. A person in this state qualifies himself or herself as "anonymous Christian" insofar as this acceptance of grace is "present in an implicit form whereby [the] person undertakes and lives the duty of each day in the quiet sincerity of patience, in devotion to his material duties and the demands made upon him by the person under his care."[55] According to Rahner, Christ is present and efficacious in the non-Christian believer (and therefore in the non-Christian religions) through his Spirit. And furthermore, anonymous Christians are "justified by God's grace and possess the Holy Spirit."[56]

52. Gary Badcock, "Karl Rahner, the Trinity, and Pluralism," in *The Trinity in a Pluralistic Age: Theological Essays on Culture and Religion*, ed. Kevin J. Vanhoozer (Grand Rapids: Eerdmans, 1997), 149.

53. Amos Yong, *Discerning the Spirit(s): A Pentecostal-Charismatic Contribution to Christian Theology of Religions* (Sheffield: Sheffield Academic Press, 2000), 42–44, 72–76; Sachs, "'Do Not Stifle the Spirit,'" 22–23.

54. Karl Rahner, "The One Christ and the Universality of Salvation," in *Theological Investigations* 16 (New York: Crossroad, 1983), 203.

55. Karl Rahner, "Anonymous Christians," in *Theological Investigations* 6 (Baltimore: Helicon, 1969), 394.

56. Karl Rahner, "Jesus Christ in the Non-Christian Religions," 43.

I am indebted to Joseph Wong, who sees the following passage as an adequate summary of Rahner's pneumatological theology of religions:[57]

> Wherever persons surrender themselves to God or the ultimate reality, under whatever name, and dedicate themselves to the cause of justice, peace, fraternity, and solidarity with other people, they have implicitly accepted Christ and, to some degree, entered into this Christic existence. Just as it was through the Spirit that Christ established this new sphere of existence, in the same way, anyone who enters into this Christic existence of love and freedom is acting under the guidance of the Spirit of Christ.[58]

In line with the Catholic standpoint, rather than seeing the "anonymous Christians" thesis as undermining the validity of the church or the mission, Rahner argued that the individual should be brought to the fullness of faith by the church obediently carrying out its evangelistic mandate.[59]

Wolfhart Pannenberg: Universal Pneumatology

The Danger of Subjectivization of the Spirit

Since Karl Barth's publication of his massive *Church Dogmatics*, no other theologian except for Wolfhart Pannenberg has attempted to formulate a full-scale, comprehensive theological system. Pannenberg's entire life's work has come to maturity in his three-volume *Systematic Theology*.

For Pannenberg, theology—and consequently, pneumatology—is a public discipline rather than an exercise in piety. He adamantly opposes the widespread privatization of faith and theology. Theology has to speak to common concerns, since there is no special "religious truth." Therefore, the relationship between science and theology is essential. They are not two separate fields but have the same object of study, namely, creation. What theology claims has to be in consonance with what other fields of inquiry claim: There can be only one truth. As Pannenberg untiringly insists, if something is true, it has to be true for everyone, not just for one person.

---

57. Joseph H. Wong, "Anonymous Christians: Karl Rahner's Pneuma-Christocentrism and an East-West Dialogue," *TS* 55 (1994): 630.

58. Karl Rahner, "Observations on the Problem of the 'Anonymous Christian,'" in *Theological Investigations* 10 (New York: Seabury Press, 1976), 291.

59. Karl Rahner, "Anonymous Christianity and the Missionary Task of the Church," in *Theological Investigations* 12 (New York: Seabury Press, 1974), 161–80.

In fact, for him the truth question is the main question of theology. To its detriment, modern theology has by and large left behind the truth question, but Pannenberg has not been willing to surrender the quest for one truth. Consequently, Pannenberg's theology focuses on reason and argumentation; theological statements—in the form of "hypotheses"—have to be subjected to the rigor of critical questioning. Faith is not a blind act or a leap of faith; rather, it is grounded in public, historical knowledge.

In Pannenberg's theology, God is the object and determining reality of all theology: God is the power that determines everything. If the idea of God must be able to illumine not only human life but also experience of the world, then pneumatology must also. Similar to Rahner, Pannenberg regards human beings as naturally religious: "open to God." The human being is a question mark pointing toward God.

Although Pannenberg is undeniably one of the most noteworthy pneumatologists for the third millennium, interestingly enough, he has not produced a separate pneumatology.[60] Rather, he incorporated his doctrine of the Spirit into his ambitious theological program. In fact, pneumatology is interwoven throughout every major loci of his systematics, especially God, creation, human beings, Christology, the church, and eschatology. His theology also contains a rich discussion on the Spirit with regard to salvation, as typical Protestant pneumatologies do, but he tries to avoid the dangers of privatization of the Spirit to only subjective areas. He is critical of the secondary place given to pneumatology in theology since the Middle Ages and of the restriction on the action of the Spirit in regard to soteriology in Reformation theology: "The Spirit of which the New Testament speaks is no 'haven of ignorance' *(asylum ignorantiae)* for pious experience, which exempts one from all obligation to account for its contents. The Christian message will not regain its missionary power . . . unless this falsification of the Holy Spirit is set aside which has developed in the history of piety."[61]

60. He has written only a few articles distinctively on pneumatology: Wolfhart Pannenberg, "The Doctrine of the Spirit and the Task of a Theology of Nature," in *Beginning with the End: God, Science, and Wolfhart Pannenberg*, ed. C. R. Albright and J. Haugen (Chicago: Open Court, 1997), 65–79 (first published in *Theology* 75, no. 1 [1972]: 8–20); and idem, "The Working of the Spirit in the Creation and in the People of God," in *Spirit, Faith, and Church*, ed. W. Pannenberg, A. Dulles, and C. E. Braaten (Philadelphia: Westminster, 1970), 13–31.

61. Wolfhart Pannenberg, "The Doctrine of the Spirit and the Task of a Theology of Nature," *Theology* 75, no. 1 (1972): 10.

The Spirit as "Force Field"

In the Bible, the Spirit is depicted as the life-giving principle to which all creatures owe life, movement, and activity. This is true of animals, plants, and humans: "When you send your Spirit, they are created, and you renew the face of the earth" (Ps. 104:30). In keeping with this is the second creation account, which says that God "formed the man from the dust of the ground and breathed into his nostrils the breath of life, and the man became a living being" (Gen. 2:7). Conversely, all life perishes when God withdraws his Spirit (Job 34:13–15; Ps. 104:29). The souls of all living things and the breath of all people are in the hands of the Spirit (Job 12:10).[62]

Pannenberg asks how this biblical view of life can be reconciled with modern biology in which life is a function of the living cell of the living creature as a self-sustaining and reproducing system? Pannenberg addresses this crucial question by utilizing the "field concept," borrowed from modern physics (Michael Faraday). The most distinctive idea of Pannenberg's pneumatology is his depiction of the Spirit in terms of a force field.[63]

Pannenberg believes this is in consonance with the biblical usage of *ruach/pneuma*, and he sees "surprising possibilities" for agreement between the newer scientific theories and theological concepts. This is so given the changes in contemporary physics from a "physical" to a more "spiritual" view; even bodies themselves are forms of forces that are no longer qualities of bodies but independent realities. Pannenberg also notes that the field concept has a metaphysical origin in pre-Socratic philosophy. Science has adapted a concept that is not "scientific" in origin. This modern scientific concept is not foreign to religious interpretations.[64]

Pannenberg uses the term *Spirit* in two ways: of God as spirit and of the Third Person of the Trinity, the Holy Spirit. The first usage denotes God as spirit. In other words, Pannenberg defines God as infinite spir-

---

62. Wolfhart Pannenberg, *Systematic Theology* (Grand Rapids: Eerdmans, 1994), 2:76–77.

63. With Pannenberg, several modern systematicians and pneumatologists have come to speak about the Spirit as "field of force/field force," using a standard concept of modern physics: Michael Welker, *God the Spirit,* trans. John F. Hoffmeyer (Minneapolis: Fortress Press, 1994); Bernd Jochen Hilberath, *Pneumatologie* (Düsseldorf: Patmos, 1994); even Karl Rahner, already in the 1970s, referred to the concept of "energy field" in his "Experience of Self," in *Theological Investigations* 13 (New York: Seabury Press, 1975).

64. Pannenberg, *Systematic Theology,* 2:79–83. Illustrative of Pannenberg's creative theologizing is his application of the Spirit as understood with the field concept to several philosophical and theological topics, such as "Space and Time as Agents of the Spirit's Working" (2:84–102) and the doctrine of angels (2:102–9).

itual essence. Traditionally, two approaches have been taken regarding the essence of God. On the one hand, the patristic interest in clarifying the otherness of God and rejecting the idea of God as physical because of the Stoic doctrine of physical *pneuma* led to the understanding of God as supreme reason. This concern, however, is no longer an issue, since *spirit* is conceived of as a nonphysical entity. On the other hand, in high scholasticism, the idea of God as reason was complemented with the idea of God as will. Pannenberg is critical of these two concepts of God (God as reason and as will) and sides with the biblical description of God as spirit.[65]

Furthermore, Spirit also denotes the Third Person of the Trinity, the Holy Spirit: "Although both the Father and the Son are differentiated from the essence of the Godhead that is Spirit, they are bound together through the Spirit, the third person of the Trinity. Likewise, in that the personal Spirit glorifies the others, that is, differentiates himself from them, he 'knows' himself as connected to the Father and the Son."[66]

Both of these aspects of the Spirit are needed. If the Spirit were solely the impersonal divine field, the divine essence (=spirit) would be impersonal; in the Bible, the Spirit is not only the common life of the Father and the Son but also appears as a personal center of activity.

God as spirit encompasses both immanence and transcendence. The Spirit transcends the world but at the same time is the immanent source, the life-principle.

The Spirit in the Trinity

One of the most distinctive features of Pannenberg's treatment of the doctrine of the Triune God is that the doctrine of the Trinity precedes that of the unity of God.[67] Almost always the opposite is the case. This reversal is significant in view of the fact that trinity is not something added to the unity of God; God in fact exists as trinity. Pannenberg makes use of G. W. F. Hegel, who derived the Trinity from the concept of God as Spirit, but he differs from Hegel in one important respect. Pannenberg does not want to derive the Trinity from God's unity, be it as Spirit or otherwise, since it leads to modalism[68] or subordinationism.[69] Rather, the doctrine of the Trinity must be grounded on revela-

---

65. Wolfhart Pannenberg, *Systematic Theology* (Grand Rapids: Eerdmans, 1991), especially 1:370–78.

66. Stanley J. Grenz, *Reason for Hope: The Systematic Theology of Wolfhart Pannenberg* (New York: Oxford University Press, 1990), 61.

67. Pannenberg, *Systematic Theology*, 2:280–99.

68. The view that the trinitarian persons are not real persons but rather appearances or modes of acting.

69. The view that either the Son or the Spirit is subordinate to the Father.

tion, namely, on the way the Father, Son, and Spirit came to appearance in the event of revelation. Therefore, the point of departure for trinitarian doctrine is Jesus' message of the fatherly care of God and the kingdom of God, his rulership over all creation.[70]

At the heart of Pannenberg's doctrine is his concept of "self-differentiation" (in line with Hegel), namely, that the essence of a person lies in the act of giving oneself to one's counterpart and thereby gaining one's identity from the other. This is a correction of the traditional notion of trinitarian "self-differentiation," which refers to the bringing forth of the second and third trinitarian persons through the Father and so implies the priority of the Father. According to Pannenberg, the one who differentiates oneself from another is dependent on the other for one's identity. In that sense, the Father's fatherhood is dependent on the activity of the Son and the Spirit and vice versa. In this understanding, Pannenberg follows the rule of Athanasius[71] (according to which the Father would not be the Father without the Son and vice versa); even here it is manifest that the Trinity is essential to God's ontological being. Jesus differentiated himself from God and voluntarily submitted himself to serve God and his kingdom, giving place to the Father's claim to deity (Phil. 2:6–8). Conversely, the Father handed over the lordship to the Son until the Son hands it back at the eschaton (1 Cor. 15:24–25; Phil. 2:9–11). The Father's kingdom is dependent on the Son and his obedience.[72]

This paradigm also explains the differentiation of the Spirit from both the Father and the Son. Pannenberg appeals to the Johannine statements concerning the glorifying of the Son by the Spirit. He notes that the trinitarian concept of the Spirit likewise developed from the coming of Jesus; the early church viewed the Spirit of God as the mediator of Jesus' community with the Father and of believers' participation in Christ. This act constitutes the Spirit as a distinct person alongside the Father and the Son; as Jesus glorified the Father, not himself, and thereby is one with him, so the Spirit glorifies the Son and with him the Father.[73]

It has now become evident that Pannenberg rejects the *filioque* view (that the Spirit proceeds from both the Father and the Son). He sees it as wrong because it presupposes that Father-Son is a primary relationship of origin to which the spiration of the Spirit is added. This makes the Spirit secondary and represents subordination of the Spirit.[74]

70. Pannenberg, *Systematic Theology*, 2:259–80.
71. Ibid., 279.
72. Ibid., 308–19 especially.
73. Ibid., 314–16 especially; see also 304–5.
74. Ibid., 317–19.

The Spirit in Creation

Pannenberg calls for a "new understanding of the Spirit in relation to the biblical statement of his role in creation."[75] He has a decidedly pneumatological approach to the doctrine of creation and humanity. The field theory of the Spirit lays the background for Pannenberg's idea of creation.

Pannenberg strongly supports the evolutionary view of creation and regards the earlier, widespread opposition of the Christian church, both Catholic and Protestant, as a serious mistake in that it has hindered dialogue between faith and science.[76]

He presents a trinitarian doctrine of creation in which the Spirit plays a crucial role. The Son is the model of an "otherness" different from the Father. The Son's self-differentiation from the Father is the basis for the existence of the world as independent from the Father. In that sense, the Son is the mediator of creation. The Spirit is the principle of the immanence of God in creation and the principle of the participation of creation in the divine life. There is an interesting paradox here: The goal of creation is the independence grounded in the Son, but participation in God—in the divine life—is likewise necessary; the latter is the role of the Spirit.[77]

The biblical idea of the Spirit as the life-principle comes to the fore in Pannenberg's pneumatology against the background idea according to which "life is essentially ecstatic." This means that each organism lives in an environment that nurtures it, and each organism is oriented by its own drives beyond its immediate environment, on which it is dependent, to its future and to the future of its species. The Spirit is the environmental network or "field" in which and from which creatures live. By virtue of the fact that they are alive, creatures participate in God through the Spirit. The Spirit is the "force" that lifts creatures above their environment and orients them toward the future. So the Spirit as force field is the most comprehensive and powerful field in which creatures move.[78]

Pneumatological Ecclesiology

The most characteristic feature of Pannenberg's theology and pneumatology is his holistic, comprehensive approach.[79] Creation, salvation, church, and eschaton belong together. It is the same Holy Spirit

75. Grenz, *Reason for Hope*, 82.
76. Pannenberg, *Systematic Theology*, especially 2:118–23.
77. Ibid., 20–34.
78. Ibid., 198–99, 451–52.
79. See further V.-M. Kärkkäinen, "Spirit, Christ, and Church," 343–46.

of God who works united in all of these spheres: "The doctrine of the Spirit as an eschatological gift . . . aims at the eschatological consummation of salvation."[80] The same Holy Spirit of God who is active in salvation is active in creation and in the consummation of God's eternal plan:

> The same Holy Spirit of God who is given to believers in a wholly specific way, namely, so as to dwell in them (Rom. 5:9; 1 Cor. 3:16), is none other than the Creator of all life in the whole range of natural occurrence and also in the new creation of the resurrection of the dead. . . . The work of the Spirit of God in his church and in believers serves the consummating of this work in the world of creation.[81]

Pannenberg begins his third volume, the theme of which is ecclesiology and pneumatology, with the chapter titled "The Outpouring of the Spirit, the Kingdom of God, and the Church." Pannenberg's ecclesiological vision sees an integral, dialogical relationship between the Spirit and the Son. "The christological constitution and the pneumatological constitution do not exclude one another but belong together because the Spirit and the Son mutually indwell one another as Trinitarian persons."[82] Everywhere the work of the Spirit is closely related to that of the Son, from creation to salvation to the consummation of creation in the eschaton.

The reciprocity, rather than asymmetry (usually in the form of Christology taking precedence), is accentuated by the fact that in the New Testament,[83] Jesus Christ himself is seen as a recipient of the Spirit and his work in conception (Luke 1:35), baptism (Mark 1:10), and resurrection (Rom. 1:4; 8:11).[84] According to John, the Spirit is given to Jesus Christ "without limit" (John 3:34), whereas for believers the Spirit is a gift related to their becoming sons and daughters by fellowship with Jesus Christ (Rom. 5:15; 6:3ff.).[85] Since the risen Lord is

80. Pannenberg, *Systematic Theology* (Grand Rapids: Eerdmans, 1998), 3:xiii; see also especially Pannenberg, "The Working of the Spirit."

81. Pannenberg, *Systematic Theology*, 3:2.

82. Ibid., 16–17 especially; this emphasis is evident throughout his discussion of the foundations of the church in the earlier part of volume 3.

83. Pannenberg (*Systematic Theology*, 3:6–7) rightly notes that the concepts of the Holy Spirit in the New Testament are by no means uniform. While Paul (but also 1 Peter 3:18) traces the resurrection of Jesus to the Spirit, Luke and John say nothing on the theme. Other differences could be added; suffice it to say here, however, that according to Pannenberg, the different concepts of the Holy Spirit simply express different aspects that have their basis in the Old Testament and obviously belong together in this context.

84. Pannenberg, *Systematic Theology*, 1:316; Pannenberg, *Systematic Theology*, 2:84; Pannenberg, *Systematic Theology*, 3:4–5.

85. Pannenberg, *Systematic Theology*, 3:9.

wholly permeated by the divine Spirit of life, he can impart the Spirit to others insofar as they have fellowship with the Lord.[86]

The gift of the Spirit is not just for individual believers but aims at the building up of the fellowship of believers, "at the founding and the constant giving of new life to the church."[87] The Spirit thus unites believers with Christ and into fellowship with others. The story of Pentecost (Acts 2) expresses the fact that the Spirit does not simply assure each believer individually of his or her fellowship with Jesus Christ but at the same time founds the fellowship of believers.[88]

Pannenberg rightly notes that in Paul's writings, Jesus Christ is the foundation of the church (1 Cor. 3:11), whereas in Acts, the church seems to be founded by the "power" of the Holy Spirit (Acts 2). In constructing a systematic appraisal of the New Testament teaching, it is important not to see alternatives in these various ideas nor suppress the differences by harmonizing. Each theological concept of the church must integrate into itself the material aspects articulated in these various orientations that are found in the same canon. To this effect, the Johannine statements are helpful because they share with Luke's writings an interest in the Spirit as an independent entity, and yet at the same time, they deal with the theme of the link between his work and Jesus Christ. The Spirit's work is to glorify Jesus (John 16:13–14), but as that takes place, Jesus himself through the Spirit's work is one with the Father (John 14:20).[89]

In short, the church is thus the creation of both the Spirit and the Son. Therefore, Pannenberg argues, a one-sided christological grounding for the church has to be judged as a distortion of its full reality. It leads, as the history of the Western church shows, to an overemphasis on official church structures derived directly from Jesus Christ.[90] Christology, on the one hand, and the integral relationship between pneumatology and creation and pneumatology and eschatology, on the other hand, together help avoid a defective constriction of pneumatology from a christological angle that finds the Spirit's work only in the fellowship of believers. In this limitation of the Spirit's work, Pannenberg further sees an exaggeration of one side of the Spirit's work, which manifests itself in a harmful enthusiasm, such as that of the Montanists, evident throughout church history.[91]

86. Ibid., 1:269.
87. Ibid., 3:12.
88. Ibid., 13.
89. Ibid., 15–16.
90. Ibid., 17–19.
91. Ibid., 19–20.

Pannenberg joins in the classical twofold description of the church as the body[92] of Christ, which highlights the christological orientation, and as the fellowship of believers, which highlights the pneumatological orientation.[93] It is the Spirit who by his work builds up the body of Christ as he testifies to Jesus Christ in the hearts of believers.[94] The Holy Spirit is the agent who makes possible for individual believers the immediacy of Jesus Christ in the church that is his body.[95] The same Spirit is not merely the basis of their immediacy but also the basis of the fellowship of believers in the unity of the body of Christ.

From all this Pannenberg draws an all-important ecclesiological principle, namely, that the work of the Spirit releases and reconciles the tension between the fellowship and the individual in the concept of the church, and hence, the underlying anthropological tension between society and individual freedom. The work of the Spirit lifts individuals ecstatically above their own particularity, not only to participation in the sonship of Christ but at the same time also to the experience of the fellowship in the body of Christ that unites individual Christians to all other Christians. Furthermore, the Spirit's work is ecstatic not merely in individual Christians but also in the life of the church.[96] The Spirit's role in the church is accentuated in the Lord's Supper, in which the Spirit mediates Christ's presence among his people gathered at the table.[97]

Jürgen Moltmann: Holistic Pneumatology

The Spirit of Life

Jürgen Moltmann has distinguished himself as one of the most productive and creative contemporary theologians. His first three contributions to theology were *Theology of Hope* (1964), *The Crucified God* (1972), and the pneumatological ecclesiology titled *The Church in the Power of the Spirit* (1975). His later contributions include the following books: *The Trinity and the Kingdom of God* (1981), *God in Creation* (1985), *The Way of Jesus Christ* (1990), and his main pneumatological work, *The Spirit of Life* (1992). Even though pneumatology plays an im-

---

92. For Pannenberg (*Systematic Theology*, 3:102) the body of Christ is no mere metaphor, nor it is just one of the biblical ways of depicting the nature of the church. Instead, it reveals the realism of the inseparable union of believers with Christ.

93. Pannenberg, *Systematic Theology*, 3:99–110.

94. Ibid., 151.

95. Ibid., 122ff.

96. Ibid., 130, 133–34.

97. Ibid., 304–24.

portant role in all of Moltmann's writings, for example, in his account of creation, he has written two volumes specifically on the various aspects of the Spirit.

The English subtitle for Moltmann's main pneumatological work, *The Spirit of Life*, is *A Universal Affirmation*. This translation does not quite capture all the nuances of the original German, *Eine ganzheitliche Pneumatologie*, which suggests a pneumatology that is "holistic," "all-encompassing," or "comprehensive." The title of the book gives a clue regarding Moltmann's aim. First of all, he highlights the critical role of the Spirit of God in giving birth and sustaining life; second, he aims to create a pneumatology that does not exclude any area of life.

What makes Moltmann's pneumatology so appealing and exciting is that in his discussion he takes note of a wide ecumenical array of materials, from the patristic pneumatology of the Orthodox Church to the Pentecostal experience of young churches. He places between these two opposite poles the questions of the contemporary (European) era, for example, questions related to subjectivity and experience.[98] His approach is also ecumenical in that he notices the latest developments in the ecumenical movement, the work in which he has actively participated for many years, as has Pannenberg. The ecumenical movement has come up against questions of pneumatology in many ways, for example, through the encounters of churches with differing experiences and theologies of the Holy Spirit. In fact, the ecumenical movement was seen by the pioneers as begun by the Spirit.[99]

Moltmann's basic thesis is that wherever there is passion for life, there the Spirit of God is operating: life over against death, liberation over against oppression, justice over against injustice, and so on. Therefore, the only legitimate attitude is to affirm life:

> So the essential thing is to affirm life—the life of other creatures—the life of other people—our own lives. If we do not, there will be no rebirth and no restoration of the life that is threatened. But anyone who really says "yes" to life says "no" to war. Anyone who really loves life says "no" to poverty. So the people who truly affirm and love life take up the struggle against violence and injustice. They refuse to get used to it.[100]

98. Jürgen Moltmann, *The Spirit of Life: A Universal Affirmation*, trans. Margaret Kohl (Minneapolis: Fortress Press, 1992), 2–3.
99. Ibid., 3–5.
100. Ibid., xii.

Immanent Transcendence: God in All Things

Moltmann sees a mutual relationship between the Spirit and the Word. Since there are no human words about God without human experiences of God's Spirit, the words of proclamation spoken by the Bible and the church must also be related to the experiences of people today. This is possible if Word and Spirit are seen as existing in a mutual relationship. On the one hand, the Spirit is the subject determining the Word, not just the operation of the Word. Therefore, the efficacy of the Spirit reaches beyond the Word. On the other hand, the experiences of the Spirit do not find expression in words alone. The Spirit also has "unspeakable" words.[101]

While the opposition between the Word and Spirit goes further back in history, the false alternative between divine revelation and human experience of the Holy Spirit is largely due to the dialectical theology of Karl Barth, who overreacted to what he regarded as a "theology from below" by Friedrich Schleiermacher and the liberals. Moltmann insists that divine revelation and human experience belong together; they are not opposite of one another.[102]

Consequently, rather than positing revelation about God and our experience of God the Spirit as antitheses, Moltmann states that revelation "is to be found in God's immanence in human experience, and in the transcendence of human beings in God." Because God's Spirit is present in human beings, the human spirit is self-transcendently aligned toward God.[103] This possibility of perceiving God in all things and all things in God—in Moltmann's terminology, "immanent transcendence"—is grounded theologically in an understanding of the Spirit of God as the power of creation and the wellspring of life (Job 33:4; Ps. 104:29ff.). Every experience of a creation of the Spirit is hence also an experience of the Spirit itself. And every true experience of the self becomes also an experience of the divine spirit of life in the human being. "Every lived moment can be lived in the inconceivable closeness of God in the Spirit."[104]

The Cosmic Spirit

Moltmann describes vividly the limited pneumatological approach of the past:

101. Ibid., 3.
102. Ibid., 5–8.
103. Ibid., 7.
104. Ibid., 35.

In both Protestant and Catholic theology and devotion, there is a tendency to view the Holy Spirit solely as the Spirit of redemption. Its place
is in the church, and it gives men and women the assurance of the eternal
blessedness of their souls. This redemptive Spirit is cut off both from
bodily life and from the life of nature. It makes people turn away from
"this world" and hope for a better world beyond. They then seek and experience in the Spirit of Christ a power that is different from the divine
energy of life, which according to the Old Testament ideas interpene-
trates all the living. The theological textbooks therefore talk about the
Holy Spirit in connection with God, faith, the Christian life, the church
and prayer, but seldom in connection with the body and nature.[105]

The results have been tragic. This limited view of the Spirit has impoverished and emptied the churches while the "Spirit emigrates to spontaneous groups and personal experiences."[106]

Moltmann believes that one reason for this neglect of the role of the
Spirit in the world and creation has been the *filioque:* Theology has spoken of the Spirit of Christ and of redemption rather than of the Spirit
of the Father, the Creator. Consequently, Christ's Spirit and Yahweh's
ruach have had nothing to do with each other. Thus, the continuity between the work of the Spirit in creation and in the new creation has
been severed.[107] In classical terminology, there has been discontinuity
between the *Spiritus sanctificans* and the *Spiritus vivificans*.

As a result, Moltmann greets with enthusiasm new approaches to the
study of the Spirit, such as ecological theology, cosmic Christology, the
rediscovery of the body in theology, and so on. These approaches begin
with the Hebrew understanding of the Spirit as the Spirit of creation.
"So experience of the life-giving Spirit in the faith of the heart and in
the sociality of love leads of itself beyond the limits of the church to the
rediscovery of the same Spirit in nature, in plants, in animals, and in
the ecosystems of the earth."[108] "God's *ruach* is the life force immanent
in all the living, in body, sexuality, ecology, and politics."[109]

Moltmann radically expands the traditional notion of the "communion of the Holy Spirit" to encompass the whole "community of creation," from the most elementary particles to atoms to molecules to
cells to living organisms to animals to human beings to communities
of humanity. In this "fellowship as process," all human communities
are embedded in the ecosystems of the natural communities and live

105. Ibid., 8.
106. Ibid., 2.
107. Ibid., 8–9.
108. Ibid., 9–10.
109. Ibid., 225–26.

based on the exchange of energy with them.[110] Any kind of community of creation is the fellowship of the Holy Spirit. To capture this, a holistic doctrine of the Spirit is needed.[111]

Moltmann insists that the Spirit is working even in the arena of politics. He makes use of the Johannine *paraklētos* (counsel for the defense), who works for righteousness and liberation. Justification and liberation do not apply only to individual liberation from sin as has traditionally been the interpretation of Christian soteriologies.[112]

As another way of expanding traditional pneumatological categories, Moltmann speaks of *charismata*, the gifts of the Spirit, in broader terms. Traditionally, the *charismata* have been divided into two groups: "supernatural" (1 Cor. 12:6–10) and "natural" (Rom. 12:6–8). But both groups have operated within the confines of the church and individual piety. Moltmann insists that the Holy Spirit gives spiritual gifts for service in the world, for example, prophetic speech in liberation and ecology movements.

> If charismata are not given to us so that we can flee from this world into a world of religious dreams, but if they are intended to witness to the liberating lordship of Christ in this world's conflicts, then the charismatic movement must not become a non-political religion, let alone a de-politicized one.[113]

The Sanctification of Life

Traditionally, sanctification has been associated with the ministry of the Spirit as is evident in the ancient creeds. Commensurate with how the doctrine of justification has been understood in traditional theologies, the doctrine of sanctification has referred to the development of spiritual life in an individual believer. Moltmann's point of departure is the observation that since all life is meant to continue, to grow, sanctification has to do with the furtherance and facilitation of growing life.

Sanctification, seen in this more comprehensive perspective, encompasses several aspects. It means rediscovering the sanctity of life and the divine mystery of creation and defending them from life's manipulation, the secularization of nature, and the destruction of the world through human violence. The earth belongs to God and therefore is something to be protected. Out of this attitude grows a rever-

---

110. Ibid.

111. Moltmann actually explicitly labels his pneumatology "holistic" in *Spirit of Life*, xiii.

112. For his distinctive way of approaching the traditional doctrine of justification, see further ibid., chap. 6.

113. Ibid., 186.

ence for life. This attitude links a religious attitude toward life with a moral respect for it. Sanctification in this sense also means the renunciation of violence toward life. Any kind of violence that threatens life and growth opposes the purposes of the Spirit of life. Sanctification of life also includes the search for the "harmonies and accords of life."[114]

The Church in the Power of the Spirit

Along with Hans Küng's *The Church*, Moltmann's major work on ecclesiology, the name of which gives a clue about its orientation, *The Church in the Power of the Spirit*,[115] is a significant step in the development of the contemporary doctrine of the church, especially as a pneumatological ecclesiology. Prior to this book, Moltmann had already begun to develop his principal ecclesiological ideas in other works. For example, in his *Theology of Hope*,[116] he spoke about the eschatological promise given in the resurrection of Christ in the power of the Spirit that creates a missionary church and a church of "dialectical hope" (the Christ who was crucified and separated from God was also raised from the dead and united with God). This eschatological promise equips it to serve the world, and that includes political involvement.

Moltmann discusses his view of the church through four categories: the church of Jesus Christ, the missionary church, the ecumenical church, and the political church.[117] The overall context and background is not only permeated with pneumatology but is also thoroughly trinitarian.[118] He locates the church in the trinitarian history of God and, more specifically, in the history of the Spirit.[119]

A host of determinative factors have shaped Moltmann's view of the church, and the result is a highly intercultural, even contextual, pneumatological doctrine of the church: ecumenical contacts and work (especially with the WCC and the Eastern Orthodox Church); extensive travel in the Third World; interest in and contact with the Pentecostal/

114. Ibid., 171–74 (citation on 173).

115. Subtitled *A Contribution to Messianic Ecclesiology* (New York: Harper & Row, 1977).

116. With the subtitle *On the Ground and the Implications of a Christian Eschatology* (London: SCM Press, 1967).

117. Moltmann, *The Church in the Power of the Spirit*, 1–18.

118. The Trinitarian outlook of Moltmann's ecclesiology comes to focus also in the structure of his *Church in the Power of the Spirit*, part 3: "The Church of Jesus Christ"; part 4: "The Church of the Kingdom of God"; and parts 5 and 6: "The Church in the Presence [and Power, respectively] of the Holy Spirit."

119. See especially *The Church in the Power of the Spirit*, 28–36.

Charismatic movements;[120] interaction with the "voluntary religion" of Protestant free churches as over against the German state church, with liberation theologies of Latin America and elsewhere, with Catholic base communities in Latin America, and with the persecuted church and his own prison years.

On the one hand, ecclesiology can be developed only from Christology. Statements about Christ also point beyond the church to the kingdom, the future reign of Christ, the Messiah who brings his kingdom into being by the power of the Spirit, the same power that raised him from the dead. In what Moltmann occasionally calls "charismatic ecclesiology," the Holy Spirit mediates the eschatological future to us as the church lives between the history of Jesus and the anticipation of the coming of the kingdom; the Spirit serves the coming of the kingdom of the Son. In that sense, the church participates in the mission of the Spirit.[121]

The church was born on the day of Pentecost, and *glōssolalia* was the sign of its birth.[122] But since the work of the Spirit is not confined to the church—the Spirit works everywhere in creation—the church cannot absolutize itself but is always provisional in nature.

Moltmann's "relational ecclesiology" contends that the church never exists for itself but is always in relation to God and the world; therefore, it is a serving, missionary church. In fact, everything, including God, exists only in relationships. God is an "open Trinity": In creation, he opens himself to the world and is also vulnerable to happenings in history. This is the thrust of Moltmann's "social trinity."[123]

For this missionary, suffering church, the cross and resurrection set the tone. The church participates in the passion of Christ and the "sighings of the Spirit" until God's kingdom of joy and peace arrives. *Glōssolalia,* speaking in tongues, is "such a strong inner grasp of the Spirit that its expression leaves the realm of understandable speech and expresses itself in extraordinary manner, just as intense pain is expressed in unrestrained crying or great joy in jumping and dancing."[124]

120. See, e.g., vol 4 of the *Journal of Pentecostal Theology* (1994), which was devoted to his keynote address, "The Spirit Gives Life: Spirituality and Vitality," and the discussion between Moltmann and his respondents, who represented every continent, in *All Together in One Place: Theological Papers from the Brighton Conference on World Evangelization,* ed. Harold D. Hunter and Peter D. Hocken (Sheffield: Sheffield Academic Press, 1993).

121. Moltmann, *The Church in the Power of the Spirit,* 33ff., 197ff.

122. Moltmann, "The Spirit Gives Life," 26

123. See further Moltmann, *Spirit of Life,* 289–308, from a pneumatological perspective.

124. Moltmann, "The Spirit Gives Life," 27.

For Moltmann, the church is a "charismatic fellowship" of equal persons. There is no division between the office-bearers and the people.[125] The church for Paul (1 Cor. 12–14)—and for Moltmann—is where the Spirit's self-manifestation takes place in overflowing powers, *charismata*. Consequently, the people of God see themselves in their existence as "the creation of the Spirit": "The Spirit calls them into life; the Spirit gives the community the authority for its mission; the Spirit makes its living powers and the ministries that spring from them effective; the Spirit unites, orders and preserves it."[126] Consequently, the ministry of the church is charismatic in essence. According to Moltmann, "ecclesiology becomes hierarchology if we do not start from the fact that every believer, whether he be an office-bearer or not, is a member of the messianic people of God." The ministry is turned into an insipid "spiritless, kind of civil service, and the charisma becomes a cult of the religious genius, if we do not make the one charismatically living community our point of departure."[127]

Likewise, Moltmann places the celebration of the sacraments in a pneumatological context:

> When it listens to the language of the messianic era and celebrates the signs of dawn and hope in baptism and the Lord's Supper, the church sees itself in the presence of the Holy Spirit as the messianic people destined for the coming kingdom. In the messianic feast it becomes conscious of its freedom and its charge. In the power of the Holy Spirit the church experiences itself as the messianic fellowship of service for the kingdom of God in the world.[128]

It is fully understandable that on the basis of his view of the church as an open, charismatic fellowship, a form of inclusive "open friendship,"[129] he is critical of the state church model and in favor of a voluntary "free church" model. The church is a fellowship of committed believers, submitting their lives under Christ's lordship in the power of the Spirit.

Michael Welker: Realistic Pneumatology

Pluralistic Pneumatology

Of all the pneumatologies produced during the past decade or so, Michael Welker's *God the Spirit*[130] is the most distinct in its form and

125. Moltmann, *The Church in the Power of the Spirit*, 298.
126. Ibid., 294.
127. Ibid., 289–90.
128. Ibid., 289.
129. Moltmann, *Spirit of Life*, 255–59.
130. Trans. John F. Hoffmeyer (Minneapolis: Fortress Press, 1994).

content. Rather than being a systematic or philosophical treatise, it is a thorough treatment of biblical texts from both the Old and New Testaments, as far as they relate to the Spirit of God. As Welker himself notes, the book could also be called "a biblical theology of the Holy Spirit,"[131] although not in a traditional way.

Welker's main critique addresses metaphysical, speculative, or abstract pneumatologies: "The book serves as a guide past the mistaken paths of totalistic metaphysics, merely speculative trinitarianism, abstract mysticism, and irrationalism undertaken by conventional understandings of the Holy Spirit." A case in point would be a theology captive to "old European metaphysics." In positive terms, "the book seeks first to articulate the broad spectrum of experiences of God's Spirit, searches and quests for the Spirit, and skepticism toward the Spirit that defines the contemporary world."[132]

Welker's main question is, Where is the Spirit of God? or Where can we discern the Spirit in life? His thesis states:

> In contrast to all so-called natural pneumatologies, it has . . . become clear that the Spirit does not "somehow or other" enlist the services of "everything." Instead, the Spirit who acts in the fullness of time "rests" decisively on the selfless, suffering, and despised Messiah. . . . But in contrast to all pneumatologies of the "beyond," it has become clear that God's Spirit acts in, on, and through fleshly, perishable, earthly life, and precisely in this way wills to attest to God's glory and to reveal the forces of eternal life.[133]

Thus, in this search, he wants to correct two kinds of errors. On the one hand, he is critical of natural pneumatologies that associate the Spirit with "life" in general and do not see any distinction between the Spirit and spirit(s). On the other hand, he is also uneasy with what he calls "pneumatologies of the beyond" that associate the Spirit with strange and obscure actions and experiences removed from real life. Welker argues that the few biblical passages that depict the Spirit as an incomprehensible, numinous power should be read in light of the majority of references that speak about the Spirit in concrete, understandable terms, not vice versa.[134]

He labels his own approach both "realistic" and "pluralistic." In his reading of the biblical canon, Welker comes to the conclusion that "we encounter the attested experiences of God's Spirit firmly embedded in

131. Welker, *God the Spirit*, xii.
132. Ibid., ix.
133. Ibid., 338–39.
134. Ibid., 50–51 especially.

various life experiences, particularly in experiences of life that is threat-
ened and endangered, but also life that has been delivered and liberated." A realistic theology of the Spirit is related to various structural
patterns of experience that cultivate sensitivity to the differences
among those various patterns.[135]

His approach is also at the same time pluralistic: It is sensitive to
various kinds of experiences and responses to the Spirit as manifested in the Bible and in life. A postmodern[136] pluralistic theology
takes seriously the various biblical traditions with their differing
"settings in life." This pluralism is also visible in the observation that
there is a development in the canon, from "Early, Unclear Experiences of the Spirit's Power"[137] in the first books to more clearly articulated conceptions.

Commensurate with his pluralistic approach, Welker criticizes traditional approaches in which the Spirit's function is to create union
and unity. Instead, he argues that the Spirit also champions diversity
and plurality: "The action of God's Spirit is pluralistic for the sake of
God's righteousness, for the sake of God's mercy, and for the sake of the
full testimony to God's plenitude and glory."[138] Pentecost is a grand example of this kind of diversity in that "through the pouring out of the
Spirit, God effects a world-encompassing, multilingual, polyindividual
testimony to Godself."[139] There is, however, a definite difference between "individually disintegrative pluralism" and "the life-enhancing,
invigorating pluralism of the Spirit." The (post)modern mind-set is sus-
ceptible to disintegrative pluralism, which opposes the life-enhancing
power of the Spirit.[140]

The Spirit and the "Modern Consciousness of the Distance of God"

For Welker, the catalyst for his realistic pneumatology is the experience in today's world that he calls "the modern consciousness of the
distance of God."[141] Welker contrasts this sense of being alienated from
God, which is felt by most modern (Western) people, with the Pente-
costal/Charismatic Christians' vivid, almost childlike enthusiasm of
God's presence here and now. Whereas for Pentecostals and Charismatics, God seems to be near, for other people, talk about the Spirit of

135. Ibid., x; see also 46–47.
136. Welker would also be willing to label his approach "postmodern." Ibid., xii.
137. The title for chap. 2 in Welker, *God the Spirit;* see especially 50–51.
138. Welker, *God the Spirit,* 25.
139. Ibid., 235.
140. Ibid., 25–27.
141. The title in Welker, *God the Spirit,* 1.

God makes no sense. People who possess the secular common sense of the West have great difficulty perceiving even a distant glimpse of anything approaching God's Spirit. If talk relates to anything spiritual, they instead see ghosts.[142]

The Spirit of God becomes central here in that only through the Spirit is knowledge of God and God's creative power possible. Even here one must not be naive; Welker does not believe that the Holy Spirit is the "most intimate friend of common sense," as Karl Barth once said. On the contrary:

> Today in many cultures common sense simply has difficulty reciprocating the friendship of the Holy Spirit, whether because common sense cannot even perceive that friendship or because common sense receives little help in its occasional attempts to make friends with the Holy Spirit. In this way the suspicion is solidified that the Holy Spirit is a phantom, a ghost. But common sense knows, especially since the Enlightenment, that there are no such things as ghosts.[143]

What has contributed to this abstract, numinous concept of the Spirit as "ghost" in Western culture is the traditional theology that emphasizes the abstract, transcendent, otherwordly, and mysterious nature of the Holy Spirit. In contrast, the many biblical testimonies to the action of God's Spirit talk about the Spirit entering into diverse realities of human life.[144]

It is the task of the Spirit of God to make God's power knowable. God's Spirit makes it possible to know the creative power of God, which brings the diversity of all that is creaturely into rich, fruitful, life-sustaining relations. Experiences of God's Spirit are not only private experiences (as the modern mind-set prefers to think), nor are they limited to some isolated groups (as the Charismatic mind-set often implies). Therefore, the main challenge of theological pneumatology is to confront the tensions and conflicts between the biblical attestation that in the Spirit God acts in concrete ways that can be experienced and the assertion of secular common sense that God is distant and powerless.[145]

The Spirit the Liberator

According to the messianic promises of the Bible, God establishes justice, mercy, and knowledge of God through the Messiah, on whom the Spirit of God rests. God pours out the Spirit on all flesh to make all

142. Ibid., especially 1–13.
143. Ibid., 2–5.
144. Ibid., 6.
145. Ibid.

people free to overcome the social and cultural boundaries that have been built to divide people. Welker sees in the emergence of liberation and feminist theologies clear signs of the mighty works of the Spirit. The Spirit works in various ways among diverse peoples and groups to set the captives free. This delivering work makes the various kinds of liberation theologies the most significant forms of theology for today.[146]

For Welker, one of the main forms of the ministry of the Spirit is his work for liberation, be it related to minorities, women, the poor, or any other group that thirsts for freedom. In his exposition of biblical pneumatology, Welker focuses especially on the stories about liberation. The Book of Judges especially receives detailed commentary in his book. In these situations, the Spirit works specifically in restoring solidarity and the community's capacity for action. Welker sees the stories in Judges not so much as miracle stories as narratives about the Spirit of God working toward the restoration of solidarity among people:

> God's Spirit does not "come upon" heroes and those who radiate the glory of victory. The Spirit produces a new unanimity in the people of God, frees the people from the consequences of the powerlessness brought about by their own "sin," and raises up the life that has been beaten down by oppression. . . .
>
> In all the early attestations to the experience of God's Spirit, what is initially and immediately at issue is the restoration of an internal order, at least of new commitment, solidarity, and loyalty. The direct result of the descent of God's Spirit is the gathering, the joining together of people who find themselves in distress. The support of their fellow persons is acquired; a new community, a new commitment is produced after the descent of the Spirit.[147]

At the same time, Welker presents the biblical story honestly and does not whitewash the personalities that the Spirit uses.[148] In fact, the action of the Spirit is by no means necessarily a good thing for the bearer of the Spirit.[149]

Welker goes on to say that in the Old Testament, the testimonies to the action of God's Spirit did not mediate clear knowledge, let alone exhaustive knowledge, of the Spirit. Consequently, the task of "discerning the spirits" was mandatory. Yet despite the ambiguity of the work of the Spirit, there were clear indications, even in the early experiences, that God's Spirit is "the Spirit of righteousness and mercy."[150]

146. Ibid., 16–17.
147. Ibid., 52, 57.
148. Ibid., chap. 2.
149. Ibid., 63.
150. Ibid., 55.

The Promised Spirit of Justice and Peace on the Messiah

Welker explains in detail Isaianic and other messianic passages that speak about the Spirit in the life of the Messiah. The focus is on the ministry of extending justice and morality, as well as God's knowledge, even beyond the borders of Israel. [151]

Welker likewise emphasizes the integral relationship between Christ and the Spirit in the New Testament: Christ was installed in mission by the Spirit, not by any self-serving public. Even though the Anointed One establishes justice and peace, the Messiah is no political figure. His voice cannot be heard on the streets; he is the suffering Messiah. [152]

Jesus' life was characterized by the concrete presence of the Spirit. In the power of the Spirit, he helped powerless individuals by driving out demons and liberating those trapped with no escape. The authority of the Spirit-filled Messiah was then passed on to his followers to heal the sick and free the prisoners. The presence and power of the Spirit was the determinative indication of his messiahship: "But if I drive out demons by the Spirit of God, then the kingdom of God has come upon you" (Matt 12:28). [153]

Welker provides an extensive list of the works wrought by the Spirit of Christ, such as bringing help to those caught in various forms of powerlessness, captivity, and entrapment; gathering people experiencing selflessness and without public means of power to the sphere of God's reign in which people are empowered to be who they are called by God to be; acting as the Spirit of deliverance from human distress and sin; and restoring both solidarity and the capacity for communal action. [154]

The Public Person of the Spirit

Welker's book on pneumatology is not systematic in nature but rather an extensive dialogue with the manifold and varied biblical testimony. Therefore, he does not engage questions regarding the Spirit in the Trinity or even the personhood of the Spirit. The closest Welker comes to defining the Spirit is when he uses the term "the public person of the Spirit." The Spirit is person, but more specifically, a public person: "Where a person is thought and conceived only as an individual-human center of action, the personhood of the Holy Spirit remains ob-

---

151. Ibid., chap. 3.
152. Ibid., 124ff.
153. Ibid., 195–96.
154. Ibid., 220–21.

scure."[155] One could also say that the Spirit is Christ's domain of resonance, a kind of force field.[156]

Welker contrasts two "spirits": the spirit of Western culture and philosophy and the Spirit of God. The spirit of the Western world has been
shaped and defined by a spirit that "exhibits another constitution,
other interests, other goals, and other power structures than the Spirit
of God. This spirit has also spread over the rest of the world."[157] What
is dangerous is that it has often been identified with the Spirit of God.
The Western spirit originates in the philosophies of Aristotle and Hegel. Welker describes it as self-referential and self-productive as over
against the selflessness of the Spirit of God.[158]

With the help of Aristotelian metaphysics, Western philosophy described the person (and personhood of the Spirit) as "self-referential,
outside the world and yet related to it, comprehending everything and
thus perfect, controlling everything and at the same time at one with
self."[159] Characteristic of this kind of spirit is individualism, self-cer-
tainty, self-possession, self-production, and especially domination of
people and nature. The results have been the domination of creation
and the environment and the subjugation of people.[160]

The Spirit of God, however, does not bear witness to the Spirit but
makes present the self-withdrawing and self-giving Crucified One.
Characteristic of the Spirit of God is a self-giving nature and self-with-
drawal, even selflessness. The Spirit is a turning to others.[161]

By turning to Christ and others, the Spirit creates solidarity and
communion. The true and real church, the ecumenical and transconti-
nental church that extends beyond particular epochs, concretely
present here and now, was and is built up by the Holy Spirit: "Inas-
much as human beings are taken into this communion, their isolation
as weak, consumeristically corrupted individualities, intoxicated by the
mass media and without public resonance, is dissolved both for them
and through them."[162]

155. Ibid., 312.
156. Ibid., 314. Here Welker utilizes the concept of "domain of resonance" (from Ni-
klas Luhmann): Human beings acquire the features of personhood only by being formed
in diverse webs of relationships (we are persons as much as we are children, relatives,
friends, etc.); these webs of resonance are only partially dependent on our activity.
157. Ibid., 279.
158. Ibid., 283.
159. Aristotle, *Metaphysics XII* 7.
160. Ibid., 284ff.
161. Ibid., 280–83.
162. Ibid., 308.

But the Spirit of God is not content to work only in visible churches, Welker insists. The One Spirit also becomes recognizable in the many religious and secular environments.[163]

Clark Pinnock: Systematic Pneumatology

Clark Pinnock is one of the leading theologians of the evangelical movement, which in recent years has established itself especially in the English-speaking world as an influential theological force. Distinguishing itself from more reactionary, conservative fundamentalism, evangelicalism purports to preserve the classical doctrines of the Christian tradition but at the same time to face openly the challenges of the post-Enlightenment and postmodern world. In the last decade, Pinnock has contributed significantly both to pneumatology in general and also to charismatic issues. As a Free Church theologian, he has highlighted the baptistic heritage.

His primary pneumatological work, *Flame of Love: A Theology of the Holy Spirit*,[164] is unique in that rather than producing a pneumatology on its own terms, it discusses the main systematic topics, such as the Trinity, creation, revelation, Christology, and the church, from an explicitly pneumatological perspective. Pinnock wants to challenge theology that in general has given the Spirit a secondary role.[165] The appeal of this work is its experiential, almost enthusiastic style. Clearly, this is a sort of "testimony book" that is also a systematic theology.[166] Unlike most theologians, Pinnock wants to engage both the mind and the heart.

A Pneumatological Theology of Religions

One of the most urgent challenges of contemporary theology and missiology is the question of a theology of religions: Is there salvation, or at least salvific elements, outside the church/Christ?

In evangelical theology, the most significant appeal for a truly pneumatological theology of religions has come from Pinnock, who for years has written extensively on a responsible inclusivist position. Such

163. Ibid.

164. Downers Grove, Ill.: InterVarsity Press, 1996.

165. Pinnock, *Flame of Love*, 10–11. His comment is incisive: "Our language is often revealing—the Spirit is a third person in a third place" (10).

166. Ibid., 12. Actually, Pinnock says that "though this is not a testimony book, I hope the reader will sense how in love with God I am and how much practical usefulness there is in improved theology." "Improved theology" in this sense means a theology properly imbued by pneumatological perspectives.

a position holds that although Christ is the normative and absolute Savior, salvation cannot necessarily be limited to the proclamation of the gospel.[167] Pinnock started his move toward inclusivism primarily on a christological[168] basis but later shifted to a definite pneumatological view.[169]

Pinnock rightly grasps the basic errors to be avoided: One error is to say dogmatically that all will be saved, and the other is to say that only a few will be saved. The two poles of the Christian message, the universal will of God to save all and the finality of salvation only in Christ, are to be handled in a way that neither discourages evangelism nor makes salvation unavailable to most. In Pinnock's view, counting against restrictivism is not only God's nature as Father and the universality of the atonement of Christ, but also the ever-present Spirit, "who can foster transforming friendships with God anywhere and everywhere."[170]

The gateway for Pinnock to an appreciation of a more unlimited ministry of the Spirit is the "cosmic range to the operations of the Spirit."[171] The emphasis on the Spirit's work in salvation should not be read as a denial of the creative work on which it is based, as too often has been the case.[172] Often in theology (especially evangelical theology),

167. Clark H. Pinnock, "The Finality of Jesus Christ in a World of Religions," in *Christian Faith and Practice in the Modern World: Theology from an Evangelical Point of View*, ed. M. A. Noll and D. F. Wells (Grand Rapids: Eerdmans, 1988), 152–68; idem, "Toward an Evangelical Theology of Religions," *Journal of the Evangelical Theological Society* 33 (1990): 359–68; idem, "Evangelism and Other Living Faiths: An Evangelical Charismatic Perspective," in *All Together in One Place*, 208–18; idem, "An Inclusivist View," in *More Than One Way? Four Views of Salvation in a Pluralistic World*, ed. D. L. Ockholm and T. R. Phillips (Grand Rapids: Zondervan, 1995), 93–148; idem, *Flame of Love*, 185–215 especially; see also 49–78 for his treatment of the role of the Spirit in creation and its implications for our topic.

168. See further Clark Pinnock, *A Wideness in God's Mercy: The Finality of Jesus Christ in a World of Religions* (Grand Rapids: Zondervan, 1992).

169. His *Flame of Love* is actually a comprehensive systematic theology written from the perspective of the Spirit. Chapter 6, titled "Spirit and Universalism," focuses on theology of religions, but several other chapters, especially chapter 4, "Spirit and Christology," lay the foundation, as does his masterful treatment of revelation in the final chapter 7.

170. Pinnock, *Flame of Love*, 186–87.

171. Ibid., 49. In ecumenical spirit, Pinnock quotes here in approval of Pope John Paul II, who speaks of "the breath of life which causes all creation, all history, to flow together to its ultimate end, in the infinite ocean of God" (Pope John Paul II, *On the Holy Spirit in the Life of the Church and the World*, Encyclical of the Supreme Pontiff [Sherbrooke, Quebec: Editions Paulines, 1986], 95).

172. Ibid., 51. A case in point is the evangelical theologian W. H. Griffith Thomas (*The Holy Spirit of God* [Grand Rapids: Eerdmans, 1964], 187, 196, 201), who prefers to bypass the cosmic activities of the Spirit, as he sees them threatening the uniqueness of the gospel.

there is no correlation between the role of the Spirit in creation and in salvation. Consequently, salvation is understood in quite limited terms. What God has provided to all people on the basis of creation is ignored. Pinnock argues that by acknowledging the work of the Spirit in creation, we are actually allowed a more universal perspective of the Spirit's ministry in which the preparatory work for hearing the gospel is not set as an antithesis to the fulfillment of the gospel in Christ.[173] "What one encounters in Jesus is the fulfillment of previous invitations of the Spirit."[174]

Pinnock argues that access to grace is less of a problem for a pneumatologically based theology of religions than it is for an exclusively christologically anchored one. Whereas the incarnation of the Son was confined to a specific place in time and history, its universal effects, through the ministry of the Spirit, can be transmitted to the farthest ends of the earth.[175]

A truly revolutionary insight for an evangelical theologian is that religions, rather than being either futile human attempts to reach God (conservatives) or outright obstacles to a saving knowledge of God (the young Barth), can be Spirit-used means of pointing to and making contact with God.[176] Further, everyday human experiences can likewise be used by the Spirit, since human beings "as spirit" are created to be open to God.[177]

In the final analysis, the ministries of the Son and the Spirit can be seen as "both-and." "Christ, the only mediator, sustains partic-

173. Pinnock, *Flame of Love*, 63.

174. Ibid., 63.

175. Ibid., 188.

176. Ibid., 203. He asks, "If the Spirit gives life to creation and offers grace to every creature, one would expect him to be present and make himself felt (at least occasionally) in the religious dimension of cultural life. Why would the Spirit be working everywhere else but not here? God is reaching out to all nations and does not leave himself without witness (Acts 14:17). Would this witness not crop up sometimes in the religious realm?" (200–201).

177. Ibid., 73. Here one can see the influence of Karl Rahner on Pinnock's thinking, although he doesn't explicate it in this context. Also, Wolfhart Pannenberg's theological anthropology operates with this idea. Another sign of Pinnock's open ecumenical attitude is that he quotes with approval from the Catholic feminist theologian Elizabeth A. Johnson (*She Who Is: The Mystery of God in Feminist Theological Discourse* [New York: Crossroad, 1992], 125): "The breath and depth of experience that may mediate holy mystery is genuinely inclusive. It embraces not only, and in many instances not even primarily, events associated with explicitly religious meaning such as church, word, sacraments, and prayer, although these are obviously intended as mediations of the divine. Since the mystery of God undergirds the whole world, the wide range of what is considered secular or just plain ordinary human life can be grist for the mill of experience of Spirit-Sophia, drawing near and passing by."

ularity, while Spirit, the presence of God everywhere, safeguards universality."[178]

The Spirit and Revelation

Pinnock engages the questions of truth and revelation from a pneumatological perspective; in other words, he asks how the Spirit reveals God's identity and brings revelation to fruition.[179] A pneumatological outlook focuses on "the imperative of timeliness," that is, on the relevance of God's revelation to the present. Doctrines are timebound witnesses rather than timeless abstractions.[180] At the same time, God's Spirit is never confined to parochial interests but is always intended for the nations. The Spirit is "guiding, luring, wooing, influencing, drawing all humanity, not just the church."[181]

Pinnock's concern in his discussion of revelation is not so much divine inspiration—which has been the focus of much of traditional theology—but rather the growth of Christians and all peoples as hearers of the Word. The issue is the appropriation of God's Word. The Spirit cares for truth in the locus of Christ's body and fosters movement toward truth, despite our mistakes and errors, Pinnock claims. But the Spirit plays a crucial role not only in hearing but also in the development of doctrine. Pinnock rightly notes that the evangelical emphasis on the propositional nature of truth has directed attention almost entirely toward biblical exegesis, to the neglect of other dynamics involved in interpretation.[182] He distinguishes himself as an evangelical theologian in proposing a theory of the development of doctrine in which the Spirit brings to the believers' minds new dimensions of God's truth and also works in the tradition of the church. The Spirit has been guiding Christian understanding toward a sounder grasp of truth. These developments do not necessarily indicate past corruption, but they represent an ever clearer comprehension of a revelation that is unsurpassable.[183]

Interestingly enough, Pinnock approaches the nature of revelation in a way similar to the Roman Catholic Church's *Dei Verbum:*

178. Pinnock, *Flame of Love*, 192. For an appreciation of Pinnock's overall scheme but also a critique of his theological methodology here, see Amos Yong, "Whither Theological Inclusivism? The Development and Critique of an Evangelical Theology of Religions," *Evangelical Quarterly* 71 (1999): 327–48.

179. The basic argumentation is found in Pinnock, "Word and Spirit," *The Scripture Principle* (San Francisco: Harper & Row, 1984).

180. Pinnock, *Flame of Love*, 215–16.

181. Ibid., 216.

182. Ibid., 218–20.

183. Ibid., 231–35.

Revelation is neither contentless experience (liberalism) nor timeless propositions (conservativism). It is the dynamic self-disclosure of God, who makes his goodness known in the history of salvation, in the process of disclosure culminating in Jesus Christ. Revelation is not primarily existential impact or infallible truths but divine self-revelation that both impacts and instructs. The mode of revelation is self-disclosure and interpersonal communication. As such it is pregnant with significance and possible development.[184]

To accomplish this work, the Spirit employs both inspiration, bringing God's plans to fruition, and illumination, help in ongoing appropriation and interpretation. Or we could speak of an inspiration of text and reader. "Past inspiration secures Scripture, and present inspiration empowers readers."[185]

The Spirit and Salvation

Pinnock's approach to soteriology is unique in comparison with most Protestant theologians, for it draws heavily from the Eastern pneumatological doctrine of salvation. Not insignificantly, the chapter on salvation in *Flame of Love* is titled "Spirit and Union." He reminds us that when we look at salvation from the standpoint of the Spirit, we view it in relational and affective terms. Rather than focusing on standard Protestant guilt and sin categories, Pinnock searches for a concept of salvation that has its goal in transformation, personal relationship, union. He describes beautifully the image of salvation as the embrace of God, following Bernard of Clairvaux: "If the Father kisses the Son and the Son receives the kiss, it is appropriate to think of the Holy Spirit as the kiss."[186]

Although there are various facets to salvation, the goal is glorification and union with God, the Spirit. "We are destined to find our true selves in God, in whom we live and move and have our being. Christ dwells in our hearts by faith, and the Spirit sweeps us up into the love of God."[187] The ancient concept that has captured this union dimension is the Eastern doctrine of *theōsis*. Insightfully, Pinnock notes that if we appreciated the prospect of union with God more, we would not think to complain as much about the arduousness of the journey. At the end of our journey we will be enfolded in trinitarian love through the Spirit.[188]

184. Ibid., 226.
185. Ibid., 227–31 (citation on 230).
186. Ibid., 150.
187. Ibid.
188. Ibid., 151–52.

When the Bible—and Pinnock—comes the closest to describing the overall goal of the Christian life, namely union, it employs sexual imagery. In Paul's writings, the love of husband and wife points to the mystery of Christ's love for us (Eph. 5:29–31). This intimate imagery links salvation to the fulfillment of our deepest desires as gendered creatures. This joyful celebration of the holy mysteries of Christian faith rings out in the Orthodox liturgy: "Let us rejoice and exult and give him glory, for the marriage of the Lamb has come, and his bride has made herself ready."[189]

Employing the imagery of love and sexuality, Pinnock says that if salvation is union, conversion is awakening to love. The Spirit is calling the wayward to return back to the Father's embrace. On the one hand, the invitation from the Father comes by grace, and he is the initiator. On the other hand, the Spirit may draw, but people must consent. The Spirit helps us, but we are also coworkers with God. We work out our salvation, while God is at work in us (Phil. 2:12–13). Conversion requires an interplay of grace and assent.[190]

In a pneumatological soteriology, conversion can also be described as an event of the life-giving Spirit (2 Cor. 3:6). It is living water within, springing up to eternal life (John 4:10, 14; 7:37–39). The risen Lord breathed on the apostles and said, "Receive the Holy Spirit" (John 20:22), which was reminiscent of God breathing life into Adam's nostrils and of the breath blowing over the valley of dead bones.[191]

The Significance of Glōssolalia

Even though Pinnock contends that it is not necessary for every believer to speak in tongues since there is no law of tongues in the New Testament, he sees glōssolalia as related to renewal. Glōssolalia is one evidence of the Spirit's presence. Therefore, it is better to say that speaking in tongues is normal rather than normative. The apostles spoke in tongues when they were filled with the Spirit, but this may not be the pattern for everybody always.[192]

Speaking in tongues for Pinnock is a noble and edifying gift (1 Cor. 14:12). The Christian who speaks in tongues edifies himself or herself. In this context, then, tongues are not an intelligible language but a way of responding to the inexpressibility of God, "a way of crying to God from the depths and expressing the too-deep-for-words sighings of the

189. Ibid., 152–53 (citation on 153).
190. Ibid., 159.
191. Ibid., 163.
192. Ibid., 172.

heart." Tongues is prayer without concepts, prayer at a deep, noncognitive level.[193]

Pinnock argues that the Spirit is given in baptism and is realized in experience throughout life. Believers whose experience runs dry and who are unaware of charisms should seek renewal. Each Christian receives the Spirit in the shape of a particular charisma: "Each has a particular gift from God" (1 Cor 7:7 NRSV).[194]

Theologizing about the Spirit does not take place only in the confines of the Western theological academy. Rich, creative approaches to pneumatology are emerging in the various contextual and local theologies of the two-thirds world as well as among theological movements in the West such as feminist and process thought. To these varied and complementary approaches we now turn.

193. Ibid., 173.
194. Ibid.

6

Contextual Pneumatologies

The Spirit in Context

According to the biblical promise, the Spirit will be poured out on "all flesh," in other words, on all kinds of people, both young and old, from all cultures and environments (Joel 2:28–29; Acts 2:17–18). The ministry of the Spirit is always particular, specific. The one Spirit of God is not a numinous power hovering above the cosmos but a person living in and permeating people in various life situations and contexts. Even though the purpose of the work of the Spirit always remains the same—to glorify the Son and to bring into fulfillment the new creation of the Father—the Spirit relates to each person and people group in a very specific way.

In our contemporary world, theology has the burden of showing its cultural sensitivity. Theology can no longer be the privilege of one people group. Instead, it must be context specific as it addresses God and God's world in specific situations and in response to varying needs and challenges.

In recent decades, contextual understandings of the Spirit have emerged to correct and complement the mainly Western approach that has dominated. This chapter highlights the richness of pneumatology. Process pneumatology builds on the foundation of process philosophy and theology and attempts to understand the Spirit in dynamic, evolving, mystical terms. Liberation theology, which evolved in the womb of the poor of Latin America but soon spread to other continents as well, approaches the Spirit from the questions of freedom and survival. Ecological or green pneumatologies purport to address the impending crises of the future of creation—pollution, the depletion of natural resources, and ecological disaster—by utilizing pneumatological insights and resources. Feminist pneumatologies attempt to interpret the Spirit experience from the perspecive of women and find feminine counterparts for addressing the deity and the divine Spirit. An example of the rich variety of "area studies" is the African concept of the Spirit. As is well known, the most rapid growth of Christian churches is taking place outside the West, and African Instituted Churches (AIC) and other nontraditional churches are heavily pneumatologically and charismatically loaded in their spirituality and theology.

Process Pneumatology

The World in Process

While process philosophy did not enter Christian theology until the last half of the twentieth century, its principal ideas are not new. The ancient philosopher Heraclitus (540–475 B.C.) expressed the mind-set of process thought in his often-quoted dictum: "You cannot step twice into the same river; for fresh waters are ever flowing in upon you." Several philosophers of the modern era developed this thought. Hegel, for example, talked about the Absolute in terms of the Whole that contains and is contained in each part, thereby ascribing finiteness and freedom to ultimate reality. Einstein's principle of relativity, which finally discredited static Newtonian physics, the philosopher Henri Bergson's idea of the organic view of reality, and William James's view of human consciousness as a stream are more recent developments that laid a foundation for process philosophy. The mathematician Alfred Whitehead wrote Process and Reality,[1] which presents the main ideas of process thought.

In process thought, one of the leading ideas is the contingency of all things. We live in an interdependent world in which each event must be seen as part of an endless flow of preceding causes and succeeding consequences. Nothing exists in isolation. Everything is related to some degree, directly or indirectly, to every other thing or entity. Nothing exists except by participation. Process thought applies the idea of Einstein's principle of relativity to reality as a whole. Each entity,

1. New York: Free Press, 1957.

whether object or organism, is a nexus of relations within a given context; thus, no entity, experience, or achievement can be absolute.

The sense of the transience of all things is a related idea. Nothing in the universe is static—either at the inorganic or the organic level. We live in a world of becoming where things, events, societies, and especially persons come to be and pass away. In opposition to the older static view, in process philosophy reality itself exhibits novelty, spontaneity, and self-creation. This view challenges the traditional emphasis on cause and effect. Thus, in recent decades, terms such as "becoming," "process," "change," "participation," and "dynamic" have been widely used.

Process theology makes an honest attempt to find compatibility between contemporary science and God's creative presence in the world. Since "creation continues," there is openness to God's "new" actions.

Like all actual entities, God is dipolar and consists of a "primordial" and a "consequent" dimension. The primordial dimension (or nontemporal or mental) refers to God's grasp of all possibilities. This is the dimension of God as the principal of the process of the world with the infinite range of possibilities. The consequent (or physical or concrete) pole in God is "God's feeling of the world," "a fullness of physical feeling": He becomes the fellow-sufferer who understands.[2] God responds to the choices and processes of creation; God exists in genuine dynamic interaction with the world.

The Spirit as Divine Immanence

Process theology has roots in classical theism but serves also as its critic. The main complaint against the classical theistic view is its denial of the principle of reciprocity (between God and the world). For process thinkers, Christian theology qualifies the reciprocity to an extent that makes it almost meaningless. Philosophical prejudices such as "aseity, immutability, and impassibility" truncate the concept of mutual reciprocity. Thus, process theology centers around questions related to the relationships of static versus dynamic, being versus becoming, eternal versus temporal, and unchanging versus ever-changing.[3]

The major study introducing a pneumatology built on process thought is Blair Reynolds's *Toward a Process Pneumatology*. The purpose of that book "is to take the first step toward formulation of a doctrine of the Holy Spirit, God as immanent in ourselves and our uni-

2. See further John B. Cobb and David Ray Griffin, *Process Theology* (Philadelphia: Westminster, 1976).
3. Blair Reynolds, *Toward a Process Pneumatology* (London: Associated University Presses, 1990), chap. 4 especially.

verse, within the categories of process theology."[4] The point of departure for Reynolds is to interpret pneumatologically White-head's idea of divine immanence. In process theology, God's imma-nence in creation is the central theme, which can be explained in terms of the doctrine of the Holy Spirit. Whitehead never made an ex-plicit reference to the term *Holy Spirit*, but his idea can be explicated pneumatologically.

Whitehead tried at all cost to avoid dualism (or as he calls it, bifur-cationalism): "The universe, assumed to be ever-changing, is the only reality."[5] Pneumatologically this principle is important since it elimi-nates the traditional ontological dualism between God and the world. Even though there is a distinction between God and the world, there is also an intimate, two-way relationship. This idea also has profound *theo*-logical consequences. It is Whitehead's contention that unless placed within a unified metaphysical schematization, the concept of God acquires a meaning so indefinite and indeterminate as to be unin-telligible. God and the world require each other for the intelligibility of each.[6]

Furthermore, God is present in human experience. God is accessi-ble, close at hand: "God dwells within the universe, among us, not in some remote atemporal realm above and beyond the world."[7] If this principle holds, then it means that to experience the world, we also at some level experience God. In other words, the Spirit functions as a real contact between God and us. God is encountered within our expe-riences. Using the terminology of process thought, we could also say that every actual entity prehends every other actual entity (God being one entity among others).[8]

Christian Mysticism and Process Pneumatology

One of the most challenging and exciting features of Reynolds's book is that he offers Christian mysticism as a potential bridge between more traditional Christian theology and process theology. He surveys various mystical authors, such as Dionysius the Areopagite, Meister Eckhart, Teresa of Avila, and John of the Cross, and seeks to show that even though the mystical tradition contains dualistic elements, such as

4. Ibid., 9.
5. Ibid., 13.
6. Donald W. Sherburne, "Whitehead without God," in *Process Philosophy and Christian Thought*, ed. D. Brown, R. James, and G. Reeves (New York: Bobbs-Merrill, 1971), 313; Reynolds, *Toward a Process Pneumatology*, 14.
7. Reynolds, *Toward a Process Pneumatology*, 35.
8. See further ibid., 40–41.

dualism between spirit and matter, holy and secular, it also perceives dynamic, relativistic attributes of deity, making it more accessible to process thought. He shows that several mystics struggled to find a balance between the Christian dogma of God and their own mystical experiences. For example, Dionysius the Areopagite sought a more dynamic view of God than orthodoxy had. Many mystics also struggled with the question of obvious change in the Godhead as well as with the soul-body dialectic.[9] All of these are themes that process theology sees as critical challenges to classical theism.

Reynolds is quite right that historically mysticism has yielded the most detailed accounts of the experience of having the Spirit. In Reynolds's interpretation, there is an affinity between mystical ecstasy and the aesthetic experience of Whitehead.[10] Mystical ecstasy centers on a mutual reciprocity between God and the world, and in turn, God's presence is objectified or manifested in and through fullness of feeling.[11] The ecstatic desires that God "might pervade her [the soul] wholly in the deepest affections and to the very ground of the heart."[12]

Consequently, Reynolds sees several common elements between process pneumatology and Christian mysticism. In both traditions, God's touch is exercised gently. Process theology makes central the sensitive, tender elements of God. Similarly, the mystics tended to allegorize God as an artist, not unlike the mystics. The feelings of sweetness, gentleness, and tenderness characterize the life of the mystics. Finally, both the mystics and many process thinkers allegorize God in the feminine form.[13]

"Affective redemption" is Reynolds's shorthand for the mystical ecstatic experience. He notes that often mysticism is depicted in pervasive, dualistic, "cold" terms, but he seeks to show that mysticism draws on the affective side of life, with passion for union. Still another noteworthy feature is that in the mystical tradition ecstasy is a process, not a static repose. Reynolds summarizes:

> The mystical literature provides a concrete illustration of an aesthetic-affective pneumatology that is of meaning and value. . . . The fundamental mystical intuition of God as diffuse in the cosmos provides the basis for a spirituality in which purity is not found in a separation from the temporal-material world but is formed in a deeper penetration of the universe.[14]

9. Ibid., chap. 2.
10. See further Alfred Whitehead, *Adventures of Ideas* (New York: Free Press, 1967).
11. Reynolds, *Toward a Process Pneumatology*, 78.
12. David Butler, *Western Mysticism* (London: Everyman's Library, 1919), 50.
13. Reynolds, *Toward a Process Pneumatology*, 80–83.
14. Ibid., 103.

The Dynamic Spirit

One of the main struggles of pneumatology has been to relate the Holy Spirit to the temporal-material order. According to Reynolds, from earliest times it was assumed that God as pure Spirit was the antithesis of the mutability, multiplicity, and temporality of the spaciotemporal world. This made it difficult if not impossible to speak of God as literally present or penetrating throughout the universe.

In facing this challenge, Reynolds offers an intriguing dialogue with Irenaeus. Irenaeus denied that the Holy Spirit was the Giver of life or the principal explanatory element of nature: "The breath of life which renders man alive is one thing, the quickening spirit that renders him Spiritual is another."[15] However, certain aspects of Irenaeus's thought reveal a concept of divine immanence, what Reynolds calls "process soteriology," with the cosmic Christ. Irenaeus's refutation of Gnosticism suggests for Reynolds that Irenaeus attempted to transcend any sort of spirit-matter dualism. Rather, he strove to synthesize or to unify nature and spirit, body and soul, creation and redemption. Irenaeus's recapitulation theory suggests a dynamic rather than a static view of the world and creation. Furthermore, his view of salvation as maturation and fulfillment leans toward a "process notion of an empathic bond between God and the world and also of the Holy Spirit as creative transforming love."[16]

Reynolds also notes that over against the tradition of the Cappadocians and Athanasius, the singular and distinct characteristic of the Holy Spirit is procession, a moving forth. This suggests a dynamic side of God.[17] Reynolds's dialogue with Augustine, similarly, is enlightening as he seeks to find commonalities between classical tradition and process emphases. For Augustine, immutability and other theistic attributes, on the one hand, were important. But on the other hand, Augustine also seemed to suggest that we are all sharers and participants in the very being of God. Even though serious ambiguities exist in Augustine's concept of the Spirit, the Spirit is depicted as God dynamically related to the world.[18] Reynolds's summary concerning less well-known features of Augustinian pneumatology is revealing:

> In a sense, then, creation is continuous, a dynamic process by which God's immanence keeps us in being by successive acts of will. There is,

15. Ibid., 110.
16. Ibid., 111.
17. Ibid., 116–19.
18. Ibid., 119–31.

in Augustine, a strong recognition of the Spirit as the presence of a loving, vital will rather than of an abstract will. There is strong appeal here
to the contingency and interdependency of all reality: The universe continues if it continues to please God. So there is novelty in nature. Were all
things predetermined, nothing would be contingent. Indeed, the emphasis that Augustine places here upon the Spirit as perfecter suggests that
it is best thought of as the creative Spirit and that its activity is continu-
ous. Thus, the Spirit is a dynamic reality: It is the radiation of life-giving,
creative energy. . . . The Spirit is continually at work in history as Creator
and Redeemer, so that the Spirit is concerned with all of life, not only
with those aspects specifically seen as spiritual or ecclesiastical. It is to
be noted that a comparable theme is to be found in a magnificent passage
in Calvin's *Institutes* [2.15].[19]

One of the most creative aspects of Reynolds's thought is that he sees
the Spirit's place in the Trinity as a bridge to process thought: "The
Trinity suggests that there are elements of relativity, complexity, or
multiformity and change within an otherwise simple, immutable, self-
contained deity."[20] In addition, the incarnation of one person of the
Trinity shows that God can take material form and can overcome the
dualism so prevalent in theism. In fact, Reynolds argues that the doctrine of incarnation and atonement might serve to qualify the mono-
polar concept of Spirit as immutable: These doctrines imply an infinite
being suffering for our sins. Jesus is a temporal being; Jesus suffered.

Pneumatology in the Making

The development of a full-scale doctrine of the Spirit of God on the
basis of process philosophy and theology has taken its first steps. Several features in the thought make the endeavor both promising and
challenging. The following comments offer summaries as well as sug-
gestions for further reflection:

- Process pneumatology takes the immanence of God seriously:
  God in Spirit is present in all creation and all people.
- The Spirit is depicted as passible and sensitive—even vulnera-
  ble—to the contingencies of nature and history.
- The notion of God/Spirit as love presupposes relationality, the
  ability to suffer, and change. Some process theologians fittingly
  call the Spirit "creative-responsive love."
- There is a distinctive "trinitarian" view; the Holy Spirit as conse-

19. Ibid., 125.
20. Ibid., 132.

quent nature of God signifies God's intimate responsiveness to creation.

- Life in the Spirit is not flight from the world but the fullest possible actualization of our capacities for creaturely existence; there is a mutual relationship between the world, including us, and God.
- The relationship between the Spirit of God and the human spirit is mutual: All persons have the power to shape their own destinies, but the fulfillment of this creative potential is grounded in the presence of God's creative-responsive or persuasive love.
- The Holy Spirit in process theology is not a miraculous supernatural energy overwhelming and filling up persons (depersonalization); in contrast, the Spirit denotes the fullest expression of the potentials for creaturely existence.

Liberation Pneumatology

In Search of Freedom

According to Jürgen Moltmann, the liberation theology of Latin America is the first convincing outline to combine belief in God with the will to be free, as the biblical traditions enjoin. Because of this orientation, liberation theology has challenged not only political establishments but also traditional Christian theology and pneumatology.[21] Michael Welker sees in the emergence of liberation theologies a sure sign of the Spirit's new work in the world.[22]

Even though Moltmann sees the potential danger of making theology captive to a particular context when beginning a pneumatology with historical, religious experience, as liberation theology does, he also sees this as a helpful corrective to "metaphysical, transcendental or personalist theologies," which often include traditional theologies. By focusing on real history, liberation theology does not separate two kinds of histories, secular and salvation histories, nor does it separate creation and redemption, nature and grace.[23]

Joseph Comblin, a Belgian Catholic theologian, pastor, and social critic who has been living and working in Latin America since 1958, has taken the experience of the Spirit in Latin America as the starting

21. Jürgen Moltmann, *The Spirit of Life: A Universal Affirmation,* trans. Margaret Kohl (Minneapolis: Fortress Press, 1992), 109.
22. Michael Welker, *God the Spirit,* trans. John F. Hoffmeyer (Minneapolis: Fortress Press, 1994), 16–17.
23. Moltmann, *Spirit of Life,* 110–12.

point for his pneumatology, titled *The Holy Spirit and Liberation*.[24] His basic thesis is that "the experience of God found in the new Christian communities of Latin America can properly be called experience of the Holy Spirit." But it is the fault of Western theology, with its neglect of the Spirit, Comblin claims, that "most of the Christians who make up these communities do not know that this [experience of the Spirit] is their experience; because of their religious upbringing, this Holy Spirit is still the Great Unknown for them."[25] In fact, Comblin insists that Christianity itself rests on experience of the Holy Spirit; the New Testament is quite definite on this point. As a way of introducing his study, Comblin surveys the New Testament.

Poverty, the other main concern of liberation theologies, has always been a challenge to the church. One way in which the church has responded in the past has been with voluntary poverty. In the Middle Ages, movements of spiritual poverty, invoking the inspiration of the Spirit and attributing their calling to the Spirit, went hand in hand with popular political movements. Franciscan orders provide an example of this kind of spiritual renewal. Comblin is concerned about the dominance of the spirituality of the "elite" as over against the spirituality of the "poor."[26]

The Reappearance of the Experience of the Spirit

In the liberation communities such as the Catholic base communities in Latin America, Comblin sees today a reappearance of the experience of the Spirit, manifested in Bible reading, praying, and vitality. Other aspects of this experience of the Spirit include the following.

First, it is an experience of action. Usually the poor are acted upon by others; now they take action. People who are usually passive, such as Amerindians, black slaves, slum dwellers, the unemployed, and the peasants, are energized by the Spirit to take action for the betterment of their lives. There may not even be a consciousness of being empowered by the Spirit, a self-awareness of engaging in activity. Rather, the community may just feel that something new is coming about in their midst. Comblin calls it "the experience of rebirth" and attributes it to the Spirit.[27]

Second, it is an experience of freedom. For five hundred years, the peoples of Latin America have had little experience of freedom. They feel that the natural world and material needs hold dominion over

24. Maryknoll, N.Y.: Orbis, 1989
25. Comblin, *Holy Spirit and Liberation*, xi.
26. Ibid., 51–55 especially.
27. Ibid., 21.

them. With regard to other people, this feeling of subjection is even stronger. Moreover, Comblin notes, ecclesiastical laws of the Catholic Church are felt by the poor as laws of domination.

The Spirit, however, liberates people, even from the fear of death. What is most significant here is that this freedom does not come from outside: "No one can make anyone else free."[28] Moltmann talks about the liberating work of the Spirit in three dimensions, associating them with the three classical virtues: (1) liberating faith: freedom as subjectivity; (2) liberating love: freedom as sociality; and (3) liberating hope: freedom as future.[29] According to Comblin, even though the liberation has direct social and economic implications, it is not in the first place a political or economic event but the birth of a new personality.[30]

Third, it is an experience of speech. The poor are speaking out, and this is a new reality in Latin America. They have always talked at home, in the fields and markets, but only of unimportant things. Empowered and encouraged by the Spirit, everyone has something worth saying, even to authorities. If the people speaking out were educated, it would be a natural occurrence, but the people now speaking out do not have intellectual training.

Fourth, it is an experience of community. "For practically all Latin Americans, community is a discovery."[31] The society has tried to stifle any manifestation of community spirit among the poor. The Amerindians were forced to disperse, to emigrate; peasants were not allowed to come together in villages but had to live where the landlord lived; slums were not communities. This is why community is a miracle. It is not natural for a new sense of community, a new consciousness to spring from the midst of a population that has been, by history and geography, alienated from any sort of association; it is a miracle from God.[32]

Finally, it is an experience of life, which comes out of an experience of death. There is a new aspiration for life. Death comes from the isolation of individuals; life springs from communities. The liberated and empowered communities cultivate an attitude of "not having more, but being more."

Comblin rightly acknowledges that each of these aspects could be explained in purely human terms. There are, however, legitimate reasons for attributing them to the Spirit of God:

28. Ibid., 24.
29. Moltmann, *Spirit of Life*, 114–20.
30. Comblin, *Holy Spirit and Liberation*, 25.
31. Ibid., 27.
32. Ibid., 28.

This experience has one single object: God and creation united. It is experience of God in creation and of creation in God. It is experience of God acting on us and on the world at the same time, relating us to the world and the world to us, not in some vague, cosmic contact, but in a specific and limited course of action.[33]

The Holy Spirit in the World

Liberation and freedom come from the Spirit of Christ, but we should not limit the Spirit's action or confine the Spirit to the church. The Holy Spirit was sent to the people of God, but this people exists for the sake of the world. The Holy Spirit was sent to the whole world to bring about a new creation, and the Spirit's action in the church is subordinate to this goal.[34]

The one and the same Spirit who effected the resurrection also gives birth to the new humanity fashioned after the image of God and even works mightily in the midst of the nations. Pentecost represents a call from the Creator. By accepting this call, the nations do not lose their identity, since in the kingdom each speaks in its own language and the diversity of cultures is maintained in the unity in Christ. "The Spirit does not oblige the nations all to wear the same clothing."[35]

This understanding is in line with Vatican II when it spoke of "the Spirit of the Lord, who fills the earth."[36] The document titled "The Church in the Modern World" expanded the traditional ecclesiocentric understanding of the Spirit:

Christ is now at work in the heart of men through the energy of his Spirit. He arouses not only a desire for the age to come, but, by that very fact, he animates, purifies and strengthens those noble longings too by which the human family strives to make its life more human and to render the whole earth submissive to this goal.[37]

Clearly, the council recognized the presence of the Spirit not only in movements for social and political change but also in the economic advances brought by science, technology, and labor, since "man is constantly worked upon by God's Spirit."[38]

33. Ibid., 31.
34. Ibid., 43.
35. Ibid., 47.
36. *Gaudium et Spes* 11.
37. Ibid., 38.
38. Ibid., 41; Comblin, *Holy Spirit and Liberation,* 48–49.

The Spirit and Evangelization

The 1990s were a decade of evangelization for the Catholic Church worldwide. "New evangelization" in terms of evangelization campaigns and training of evangelists was enthusiastically welcomed by both the hierarchy and the laity. Much of the new enthusiasm for evangelism emerged in Latin America, involving even the common people.

Strangely enough, however, "the Holy Spirit has been little invoked in missionary debate. This is a reflection of the absence of the Holy Spirit from Western theology."[39] While Comblin is critical of earlier approaches to evangelization, especially among indigenous people, he challenges the church and its theology to be awakened by the Spirit to a new enthusiasm for bringing the Christian gospel to those who have not yet heard it. The mutual involvement of Son and Holy Spirit has to be the rule in mission as much as in any other aspect of Christianity. The Christian message is not a proclamation of Christ alone but of the Holy Spirit as well.

In addition, it is clear that the Spirit is active long before the Christian message reaches non-Christian peoples. The Spirit is working mysteriously amidst the nations:

> Now the Spirit has been acting in pagan peoples and in all religions since humanity began. The Spirit leads peoples and religions in directions we cannot know in advance. All we can do is observe the signs of the Spirit at work and go along with it. There is no way we can anticipate it. If the Spirit leads nations to Christ, we do not know what steps or ways it has actually taken; about this we are as ignorant as pagans. We in fact know less than them, since the signs of the Spirit were given to them first and not to us. We have to learn from them how the Spirit has acted in their evolution.[40]

Along with preparing the nations for reception of the gospel and acceptance of God's righteous will, the Spirit is also preparing the church in the midst of the nations. The church is learning to present Christ in the same way as he presented himself: the way of humility and the cross. Christ sprang from poverty, from the midst of poor people. He presented himself as one without power. It is the Spirit who directs people in this way of humility and poverty. "In this way, Christ and the Spirit are united in mission too, and it is only their unity in mission that makes mission possible at this juncture of human history."[41]

39. Comblin, *Holy Spirit and Liberation*, 161.
40. Ibid., 161.
41. Ibid., 162.

Ecological Pneumatology

Toward a "Green" Doctrine of the Spirit

In recent years, new vocabulary has emerged in Christian theology: ecological/creation spirituality, deep ecology, ecofeminism, animal rights' movement, earth healing, Gaia-hypothesis,[42] ecological pneumatology, green pneumatology, and so on. There has been a definite shift from an anthropocentric to ecocentric framework.

In a provocative essay, Lynn White charged Christianity with an exploitative outlook that has engendered the ecological crisis in the West.[43] The impending eco-crisis, according to this view, results from the Judeo-Christian tradition, based on Genesis 1:26 and related texts. According to this interpretation, nature has served humans, and Christianity has sanctioned an exploitative ethic allowing science and technology to serve as instruments of exploitation.

While sensitive to the damages done to creation, Moltmann, in his seminal work God in Creation: A New Theology of Creation and the Spirit of God,[44] argues that the biblical charge to subdue is a dietary command: Human beings and animals alike are to live from the fruits of the earth; a seizure of power over nature is not intended. Moltmann also highlights the sociopolitical dimension of the ecological crisis and calls for an examination of structures of societal power. Science is not neutral; it is linked with politics. Therefore, Moltmann calls for a new stage in the relationship between theology and science: If human beings are to survive, these two areas of study must see themselves as companions in the ecological crisis. The theologian's task is to clarify the question, "How is nature to be understood as God's creation?" Moltmann answers by saying that nature is neither divine nor demonic. It should not be divinized as in New Age thought nor denied as in some extreme forms of religious thought.

Moltmann's "immanent transcendence" helps us focus on the integral relationship between the Spirit and nature. The Father is the creating origin of creation; the cosmic Christ is the ground for the existence of creation; and the Spirit of life is the life-giving origin. Through the Spirit, God participates in the destiny of creation; through the Spirit, God suffers with the suffering of creatures. Thus, the immanence of the Spirit undercuts the dualism of God and nature that has

42. The Gaia-hypothesis posits a necessary mutual relationship between human, animal, and natural life and the state of creation.

43. Lynn White, "The Historical Roots of Our Ecological Crisis," Science 155 (1967): 1203–7.

44. San Francisco: Harper & Row, 1985.

characterized the Western tradition. There is also an eschatological emphasis: It is not enough to affirm the goodness of creation in the past (Genesis 1). We must also affirm the anxious waiting of creation under futility as the Spirit "groans" for the liberation of creation and its children (Rom. 8:19–21).[45]

Sallie McFague, among others, has recently argued for the importance of pneumatology for the preservation of the earth. In her earlier work, *Models of God: Theology for an Ecological, Nuclear Age*,[46] McFague was much more critical of the value of pneumatology for the doctrine of nature. She criticized traditional descriptions of the Spirit as ethereal and vacant and concluded that Spirit language is an inadequate resource for the task of earth healing because such language is "amorphous, vague, colorless." In her more recent work, though, *The Body of God: An Ecological Theology*,[47] McFague appreciates the role of pneumatology in earth healing because it reveals the immanent presence of God in creation through the Spirit.

"Rediscovering the Spirit in an Age of Radical Ecology"[48]

Theologically, the most significant "green pneumatology" can be found in Mark Wallace's *Fragments of the Spirit: Nature, Violence, and the Renewal of Creation*.[49] Wallace argues that there has been a profound change in the spiritual sensibilities of our culture: Many people sense that we live in the "age of the Spirit." As a result, a new appreciation of nature-based religion practitioners, from native peoples to modern neopagans, has emerged. Those with spiritual sensibilities claim that a reverence for the Spirit in all life-forms is the most promising response to the threat of global ecological collapse:

45. Moltmann, *Spirit of Life*, 31–38 especially. See also Moltmann, *The Source of Life: The Holy Spirit and the Theology of Life* (Minneapolis: Fortress Press, 1997).

46. Philadelphia: Fortress, 1987, 169–72 especially.

47. Minneapolis: Fortress Press, 141–50.

48. This title is borrowed from Mark I. Wallace, "The Green Face of God: Rediscovering the Spirit in an Age of Radical Ecology," in *Advent of the Spirit: Orientations in Pneumatology*, Conference Papers from a Symposium at Marquette University, 17–19 April 1998 (unpublished).

49. New York: Continuum, 1996. For other contributions to this emerging topic, see Peter C. Hodgson, *Winds of the Spirit: A Constructive Christian Theology* (Louisville: Westminster John Knox, 1994); Chung Hyun-Kyung, "Welcome the Spirit, Hear Her Cries: The Holy Spirit, Creation, and the Culture of Life," *Christianity and Crisis* 51 (15 July 1991): 220–23; and Elizabeth A. Johnson, *She Who Is: The Mystery of God in Feminist Theological Discourse* (New York: Crossroad, 1992).

There appears to be an emerging sentiment that the topic of Pneumatology is the right focus for an ecumenical theology that speaks to the spiritual hopes and desires of our age. . . .

Could it be that the most compelling response to the threat of ecocide lies in a recovery of the Holy Spirit as a natural, living being who indwells and sustains all life-forms? Could it be that an earth-centered re-envisioning of the Spirit as the green face of God in the world is the best grounds for hope and renewal at a point in human history when our rapacious appetites seemed destined to destroy the earth?[50]

Significantly, Wallace delves deeply into the theological tradition to find resources for contemporary purposes. He makes the obvious note that in the Nicene Creed, the Spirit was named "the Lord, the Giver of Life." The life-centered model of the Spirit expands the intra-trinitarian role of the Spirit to encompass a biocentric role as the power of healing and renewal within all creation. This model retrieves certain biblical images of the Spirit in the Bible for the purpose of addressing the environmental crisis.

For Wallace, the Spirit is best understood not as a metaphysical entity but as a healing life-force: He wants to talk about "ecological pneumatology" as over against "metaphysical pneumatology." On the basis of various biblical and literary images—water, light, dove, mother, fire, breath, and wind—the Spirit is understood, not as divine intellect or the principle of consciousness but as a healing and subversive life-form. In other words, Wallace prefers a "rhetorical" understanding (employs concrete images in the Bible) over a "philosophical" one (abstract, based on ideas, such as that of Hegel).[51]

Wallace questions the reason for the "deemphasis on the Spirit's ecological identity" in view of the fact that so many biblical images connect the Spirit with nature. For example, the Spirit is seen as:

- breath that animates all life (Gen. 1:2; Ps. 104:29–30)
- healing wind (Judg. 6:34; John 3:6; Acts 2:1–4)
- living water (John 4:14; 7:37–38)
- the purgative fire (Matt. 3:11–12; Acts 2:1–4)
- the divine dove (Gen. 8:11; Matt. 3:16; John 1:32ff.)[52]

In Western theology and philosophy, the concept of spirit has "for the most part been fraught with difficulties, conveying something

50. Wallace, "The Green Face of God," 2, 4.
51. Ibid., 5ff.
52. Ibid., 13–14.

vapid and dualistic, implying a separation of and a hierarchy between the mental and the physical, the soul and the body, the human and the natural, the male and the female, and the holy and the profane." Ecological pneumatology captures the Spirit as "a living embodied being" who works for healing of the environment and of communities, and as "a wild and insurgent natural" force of healing.[53] In this view, the Spirit's work is not domesticated by locating his activity simply alongside nature. Rather, nature itself is construed as the primary mode of being for the Spirit's work in the world.

The Spirit, Communion, and Nature

In a way similar to Moltmann's idea of the "fellowship of the Spirit,"[54] Wallace retrieves the idea of the Spirit as *communion*. Taking his point of departure from Augustine[55] and others but expanding the range of the concept, Wallace insists that the Spirit is not only the power of relation between the trinitarian persons but also between God and all of creation. Here he finds support from the Eastern fathers, especially Basil of Caesarea, for whom the Holy Spirit is the agent of inseparable union within the Trinity. The Spirit labors alongside the Creator and the Redeemer as the Perfector who strengthens and completes the divine work of salvation in the world.[56] Wallace also refers to later medieval iconographers who depicted the Spirit as the *vinculum caritatis*, "bond of love," as a "dove" whose wings enfold the Father and Son and whose large talons and tail provide points of intersection of all three figures.

In fact, the Spirit is also the *vinculum caritatis* within nature in order to promote the well-being of creation. God's presence in the living Christ through the Spirit's maintenance of the ecosphere is the basis for a biocentric trinitarian theology.

Theologically, it is important to note that this biocentric focus does not undermine nor negate the Spirit's other roles but complements the work of the Spirit.[57] This balanced view became evident in a WCC consultation at Geneva in 1980. The consultation suggested that there are three major orientations to the Spirit's role in the world: (1) the ecclesiological approach: The Spirit works for the unity and united witness of all churches; (2) the cosmological approach: The Spirit renews creation and bestows fullness of life; this encompasses physical healing

---

53. Hodgson, *Winds of the Spirit*, 276.
54. See further Moltmann, *Spirit of Life*, 225–28 especially.
55. Augustine, *De Trinitate*, bk. 15.
56. Basil of Caesarea, *De Spiritu Sancto*, bk. 16.
57. Wallace, "The Green Face of God," 14.

and healing of social relationships; and (3) the sacramental approach: The Spirit is mediated through personal conversion, baptism, confirmation, and ordination as sacramental theologies renew their focus on the Spirit.

An "embodied doctrine of God" consists of three parts. First, the Creator Spirit breathes the world into existence and thereby enfleshes itself in the creation and maintenance of the natural order. Second, the divine life is embodied in Jesus—an earth creature like Adam from the dust. Third, this leads to the perichoretic union of Jesus in the Spirit. All this for Wallace indicates the "procession of Godself into the biotic realm that sustains life."

> From this perspective, nature is the enfleshment of God's Trinitarian love. As Trinity, God embodies forth divine compassion for all life-forms in the rhythms of the natural order. The divine Trinity's boundless passion for the integrity of all living things is revealed in God's preservation of the life-web that is our common biological inheritance. God as Trinity is set forth in the Father/Mother God's creation of the biosphere, the Son's reconciliation of all beings to himself, and the Spirit's gift of life to every member of the created order who relies on her beneficence for daily sustenance. As creator, God is manifested in the ebb and flow of the seasons whose plantings and harvests are a constant reminder of earth's original blessings. As redeemer, God is revealed in the complex interactions of organisms and the earth in mutual sustenance—an economy of interdependence best symbolized by Jesus' reconciling work of the cross. And as sustainer, God shows Godself through breathing the breath of life into all members of the life-web, a living testimony to the Divine's compassion for all things.[58]

This understanding corrects the one-sidedness of Western pneumatology: Even though the Spirit has always been confessed as the Spirit of God and of creation, the former has taken almost exclusive precedence.

The Wounded Spirit

If the Spirit and the earth internally condition and permeate one another, then they are inseparable yet distinguishable. According to this view, the "earth is the body of the Spirit." "Metaphorically speaking, God as spirit corporealizes Godself through the interanimation of the biosphere."[59] In breathing life into humankind and otherkind, a funda-

58. Ibid., 11.
59. Ibid., 15. Here Wallace borrows a metaphor from McFague, *The Body of God;* for a sustained dialogue between these two writers, see Wallace, *Fragments of the Spirit,* 139–44.

mental transformation within Godself occurs. Wallace maintains that "God is fully incarnated in the green fuse that drives all forms of life to their natural fruition in a carnival of praise to the Creator Spirit."[60]

Just as God once became human in the body of Jesus, so God continually enfleshes Godself in the embodied reality of life on earth. Both the Spirit and the earth are life-givers. The Spirit ensouls the earth with the quickening breath of divine life, and the earth enfleshes the Spirit as it offers spiritual and physical sustenance to all living things. Wallace rightly notes that this is a major challenge to the traditional Aristotelian and early Christian doctrine of God as unchangeable and self-subsistent, fundamentally unaffected by the creation.

An important corollary is that if the Spirit and the earth condition each other, then "it appears that God as Spirit is vulnerable to serious loss and trauma just insofar as the earth is abused and despoiled."[61] The Spirit is still free in his decision, but having decided to be enfleshed in earth, the Spirit places himself at risk: "God, then, is so internally related to the universe that the specter of ecocide raises the risk of deicide."[62] Here Wallace pays tribute to Moltmann's paradoxical idea in *The Crucified God,* according to which on the cross God died the death of the godless and yet did not die![63]

Feminist Pneumatology

The Maternal Spirit

We live in an age of "hermeneutics of suspicion"; what was comforting before is questioned today. This applies to the image of God as Father. Mary Daly insists that the personification of God as Father is the foremost symbol of patriarchy. She also claims that the image of the Father-God validates the mechanisms for the oppression of women, out of which grows male dominance.[64] According to Rosemary Ruether, most images of God in religions are modeled after the ruling class of society.[65]

The challenge of feminist theology has to be faced honestly. There is no denying the fact that language of God as Father can lead—and has too often led—to the social oppression of women. Even though it might

60. Wallace, "The Green Face of God," 16–17.
61. Ibid., 17.
62. Ibid.
63. Jürgen Moltmann, *The Crucified God* (New York: Harper & Row, 1974), 244; Wallace, "The Green Face of God," 17–18.
64. Mary Daly, *Beyond God the Father* (Boston: Beacon, 1973).
65. Rosemary Ruether, *Sexism and God-Talk* (Boston: Beacon, 1983).

be an overstatement to say that the symbol of divine fatherhood has been the cause of the misuse of power for violence, rape, and war, it is true that language not only reflects reality but also constructs it.[66]

Interestingly enough, the questions posed by feminist theologians apply to all the persons of the Trinity. Are we to address God as Father or Mother or something else? How does Jesus' maleness relate to the other half of humankind? And is the Spirit masculine or feminine?

Even though Christian theology has been slow to confront the traditional masculine language, the problem is not new. Gregory of Nazianzus ridiculed his opponents who thought that God was male because God is called Father, or that deity is feminine because of the gender of the word, or that the Spirit is neuter because it does not have a personal name. Gregory insisted that God's fatherhood has nothing to do with marriage, pregnancy, midwifery, or sexuality.[67] It has also been noted that we do not often think of God as male, even though we call God *him*. It is just a conventional way of using language. Joseph Comblin rightly notes that in contrast to many other religions, the Christian God is not sexist: None of the divine Persons has gender. But still in their action in humanity and the world, each Person is manifested under borrowed names using gendered language.[68]

Recently, some writers have stressed the feminine or maternal characteristics of the Holy Spirit to counterbalance masculine pronouns for Father and Son. But it has been also argued that calling the Holy Spirit feminine does not mean the Spirit is feminine any more than Father indicates masculinity. On the contrary, each Person is he/she or transcends gender and sexism.

Be that as it may, addressing the Spirit in feminine or maternal terms has never been completely foreign to Christian or Jewish theology. In Hebrew and Syriac, the word for *spirit* is feminine, which helped to overcome the exclusively masculine language for deity. Several early writers compared the Spirit to Eve to complement the comparison of Christ to Adam. As Eve, the Spirit gives life and plays a maternal role. Some would say that the woman in Revelation 12 is the Holy Spirit. The Spirit would thereby be associated with the church.[69] Furthermore, Syrian pneumatology during the third and fourth centuries talked about the Holy Spirit as mother.[70]

66. See further Ted Peters, *God—The World's Future: Systematic Theology for a Postmodern Era* (Minneapolis: Fortress Press, 1992), 109–20.

67. Ibid., 109.

68. Comblin, *Holy Spirit and Liberation*, 50.

69. Ibid., 49.

70. Bernd Jochen Hilberath, "Pneumatologie," in *Handbuch der Dogmatik*, ed. von Theodor Schneider et al. (Düsseldorf: Patmos, 1992), 1:512–13.

Applying feminine images to the Spirit is biblically legitimate since in the Bible the role of the Spirit involves activities usually associated with maternity and femininity in general: inspiring, helping, supporting, enveloping, bringing to birth.[71] Even though under Augustine's influence in the West all feminine references were eliminated from theology, due to his unfortunate view that women were not fully made in the image of God,[72] his writings also display God's immanence in a warm, loving spirituality. By expressing the feminine quality of cherishing love, the Holy Spirit points to a distinctively feminine aspect of God—the preservative, receptive aspect of God. Thus, Augustine likens the Holy Spirit to a mother hen.[73]

Luis Bermejo has drawn attention to the fact that of all the trinitarian persons, the Holy Spirit is more often related to intimacy. Even though we are meant to have an intimate relationship with each divine person, psychologically, we cannot direct equal attention to all three persons at any given moment. We are meant to have a special closeness with the Holy Spirit, an intimacy so profound that our longing for completion by union with another is fulfilled in the person of the Spirit. In other words, we are not only invited to "believe" in the Holy Spirit but also to "feel and experience" the Spirit.[74]

"She Who Is"

Sally McFague has tried to escape the problem of sexist talk about God with the help of metaphorical talk. She sees literalism as "rampant in our time" and suggests the piling up of metaphors to relativize the father symbol and make room for complementary symbols such as God as mother, lover, or friend.[75]

Elizabeth Johnson's approach shares similarities with that of McFague. Johnson argues in her book *She Who Is: The Mystery of God in Feminist Theological Discourse,*[76] that we need to envision and speak of the mystery of God using female images and metaphors in order to free women from a subordination imposed by the patriarchal imaging of God. Her own preference is "She Who Is." She envisions the female counterpart of the mystery of God as "Sophia" or "Wisdom." Johnson is convinced that when people speak of "God" they most often refer to

---

71. Comblin, *Holy Spirit and Liberation,* 39; Hilberath, "Pneumatologie," 536–38.

72. Comblin, *Holy Spirit and Liberation,* 39.

73. Reynolds, *Toward a Process Pneumatology,* 125.

74. Luis Bermejo, *The Spirit of Life: The Holy Spirit in the Life of the Christian* (Chicago: Loyola University Press, 1989), 114–15; see also Fatula, *The Holy Spirit,* 100–101.

75. For details, see McFague, *Models of God.* For a critique, see Peters, *God—The World's Future,* 119–20.

76. New York: Crossroad, 1992.

the Spirit. They talk about Sophia's active presence in the world, empowering and drawing us to solidarity with others, especially those who are suffering.[77]

What makes Johnson's approach to pneumatology unique is that she is not in favor of referring to the Spirit in feminine terms for the supposed reason that the Spirit also includes "feminine traits." This practice subordinates women to men by reducing their identity by limiting them to roles that involve mothering or service. In contrast, Johnson contends, we need to model our relationships on Sophia, in whose "inner relatedness" there is no subordination. Sophia herself is "unknowable mother of all."[78] For Johnson, there is a mutual relationship between woman and Sophia. On the one hand, woman is the image of Sophia, but on the other hand, Sophia herself is the image of woman. Naming God as feminine Sophia "points to the mystery of triune Holy Wisdom as *imago feminae*."[79]

Jürgen Moltmann's use of personal metaphors, such as "Lord," "mother," and "judge," for the Holy Spirit bears resemblance to Johnson's concern about not limiting feminine aspects of the Spirit to one-sided "womanly" traits, as is often done. Taking his departure from the third article of the Nicene-Contantinopolitan Creed, which calls the Spirit "the Lord who gives life" or "the Lord and giver of life," depending on the translation, Moltmann claims that two complementary metaphors are applied here to the Spirit: the experience of liberation and of new life. The title *Lord* in the Bible, certainly in 2 Corinthians 3:17, has nothing to do with enslavement. Its context is liberation, uninhibited access to the Lord. If *Lord* denotes freedom and liberation, the name is misunderstood and brought into disrepute if it is interpreted in terms of masculine notions of rule. To avoid this, the title should be complemented by the name of the one who gives and quickens life. Whereas for Paul, it is Christ who has become the "life-giving spirit" (1 Cor. 15:45), for John, it is the Paraclete, who comforts as a mother comforts and from whom believers are "born anew" (John 3:3–6). Humans are born, nurtured, and accompanied by the life of the mother. She is *fons vitae* and *fons vivificans*. But living and freedom can endure only in justice and righteousness. In justice, human freedom ministers to life and life struggles for the freedom of everyone and everything. The Spirit is also the judge (John 16:7–11) and the Spirit of truth.

77. Johnson, *She Who Is*, 127–41.

78. Ibid., 51–53, 143–44, 215; I am indebted to Fatula, *The Holy Spirit*, 94, for this reference.

79. Johnson, *She Who Is*, 215.

The three experiences, then—the experience of "being set free," or "coming alive," and of being made "just"—belong together and complement one another, making up the fullness of life in the experience of God; and in the same way the three names given to the source of these experiences also belong together and complement one another: the Spirit as lord, as mother and as judge. Every countercheck will at once discover how one-sided the viewpoint becomes if any one of these facets is left out, or if one term is reduced to something different.[80]

The Spirit and the Social Experience of Women and Men

Moltmann places the question of sexism in relation to the Spirit of God in a wider perspective, namely, that of community. Theologically, it is not enough just to criticize traditional theologies for neglecting feminine terminology and attempt to replace the masculine with another limited, exclusive usage. Moltmann insists that according to biblical ideas, what makes us *imago Dei* is not the soul apart from the body. The image of God consists of men and women in their wholeness, in their full, sexually specific community with one another. God is not known in the inner chamber of the heart or at a solitary place but in the true community of women and men. As a result, the experience of God and God's Spirit is "the social experience of the self and the personal experience of sociality."[81]

Therefore, Moltmann asks questions such as: What fellowship do women and men arrive at in fellowship with Christ and in their experience of the Spirit, who desires to give life to all flesh? How do women and men experience one another in the community of Christ's people and in the fellowship of the life-engendering Mother Spirit? These are not questions of church politics but first of all questions of faith:

According to the promise in Joel 2:28–30, "It shall come to pass in the last days, says the Lord, that I will pour out my spirit on all flesh; and your sons and your daughters shall prophesy" (cf. Acts 2:17ff.). The eschatological hope for the experience of the Spirit is shared by women and men equally. Men and women will "prophesy" and proclaim the gospel. According to the prophecy in Joel 2, through the shared experience of the Spirit the privileges of men compared with women, of the old compared with the young, and of masters compared with "men servants and maidservants" will be abolished. In the kingdom of the Spirit, everyone will experience his and her own endowment and all will experience the new fellowship together.[82]

80. Moltmann, *Spirit of Life*, 270–74 (citation on 272).
81. Ibid., 94.
82. Ibid., 239–41.

Toward an Ecofeminist Pneumatology

Elizabeth Johnson's *Women, Earth, and Creator Spirit*[83] is a groundbreaking pneumatological study in that it combines the concerns of two complementary approaches: feminist and ecological theologies. The thesis of the book is that "the exploitation of the earth, which has reached crisis proportion in our day, is intimately linked to the marginalization of women, and that both of these predicaments are intrinsically related to forgetting the Creator Spirit who pervades the world in the dance of life."[84] Johnson attempts to approach the challenge of women and creation from a distinctive pneumatological perspective.

In the first part of the book, Johnson carefully surveys the current eco-crisis and claims that the only legitimate way to address the problem is through ecofeminism. An analysis of the ecological crisis does not get to the heart of the matter unless it sees the connection between exploitation of the earth and sexist exploitation.[85]

Johnson is weary of the prevailing "hierarchical" dualism in Christian theology that leads to abuse of nature, the other sex, and one's own body. It has also affected the Christian understanding of God; often God has been depicted in hierarchical terms, which leads to hierarchical conceptions of the church as well.[86] Sexism pervades Christian spirituality and theology, Johnson argues. Femininity, nature, the body, sexuality, and women are separated. It is the task of ecofeminist theology to seek a new wholeness, a new community of equals.[87] Ecofeminist theology emphasizes unity among nature, women and men, and bodies, and so looks favorably toward "kinship models."[88]

As the Giver of life, the Spirit is the creative origin of all life. The Creator Spirit is immanent and has a rejuvenating energy to renew the face of the earth.[89] An ecofeminist "theology of the Creator Spirit overcomes the dualism of spirit and matter with all of its ramifications, and leads to the realization of the sacredness of the earth."[90] It leads toward a life-centered, biocentric model as opposed to a one-sided anthropocentric or androcentric model.

83. New York/Mahwah, N. J.: Paulist Press, 1993.
84. Johnson, *Women, Earth, and Creator Spirit*, 2.
85. Ibid., 10.
86. Cf. Moltmann, *Spirit of Life*, 239–40.
87. Johnson, *Women, Earth, and Creator Spirit*, 25.
88. Ibid., 39.
89. Ibid., 42.
90. Ibid., 60.

African Pneumatologies

A Real Life Pneumatology

As I pointed out in the introduction to this chapter, theology always takes root and is shaped by its particular context. Therefore, each cultural and religious setting tends to promote distinctive ideas about God and the Spirit. Such is the case concerning various African approaches to the Spirit.

M. L. Daneel from the Dutch Reformed Church in South Africa has offered a contemporary picture of the unique understanding of the Holy Spirit among the Christians in the African Instituted Churches (AIC).[91] This dynamic pneumatology has arisen out of a painful struggle with the more traditional theologies of the Western missionary churches. Numerically, AIC churches and other independent churches have outstripped their mother churches. For example, the Zion Christian Church of Bishop Lekhanyane, with millions of adherents, has spread throughout South Africa. In Zimbabwe, Independent churches claim 50 percent or more of the Christians in rural areas.

African pneumatologies depict the Holy Spirit in four major roles. First, the Spirit is the Savior of humankind. The apostle Johane Maranke vaPostori of the AIC of Zimbabwe saw in a vision two books from God that he could understand through the inspiration of the Holy Spirit and not through education received at the European mission station. The content of these books was eternal life. In his vision, Johane saw himself as a Moses figure, leading his followers from many countries through hostile terrain and fires to a safe place.

Characteristic of AIC theologies is an awareness of the lostness and sinfulness of humanity and the urgent need for conversion and baptism. The new laws and customs of the church are justified by attributing them directly to the inspiration and command of the Holy Spirit. The black race of Africa—the neglected, the poor, and the oppressed—are now the exalted and the elect, called by the Spirit to spread the message of salvation.

Second, the Spirit is Healer and Protector. Beginning in the 1940s, churches in Africa focused on healing ministries. Healing and protection against evil forces manifested the power of the Spirit. Speaking in

91. My exposition in this section is based on M. L. Daneel, "African Independent Church Pneumatology and the Salvation of All Creation," in *All Together in One Place: Theological Papers from the Brighton Conference on World Evangelization,* ed. Harold D. Hunter and Peter D. Hocken (Sheffield: Sheffield Academic Press, 1993), 96–126. For other contributions, see also Allan H. Anderson, *Moya: The Holy Spirit from an African Perspective* (Pretoria: University of South Africa, 1994).

tongues became the prelude to all prophetic diagnostic sessions during which the Holy Spirit would reveal to the prophet the cause of a patient's illness. All symbols used during healing rituals, such as holy water, paper, staffs, and holy cords, symbolized the power of the Holy Spirit over all destructive forces. "Jordan" (water) baptisms increasingly became purificatory, healing, and exorcist sessions.

Third, AIC Christians speak of the Spirit of justice and liberation. The late bishop Samuel Mutendi of Zion Christian Church in Zimbabwe entered the political arena by opposing colonial administration of education, land, and religious issues. The spiritual mobilization of the community to take action was effected through sermons, prayer, and a role model, often accompanied by prophecies. At times the prophets acted in the forefront. However, it was the Holy Spirit, as the "guardian of the land," who directed the liberation fighters. The most disputed practice involved prophets helping in "community-cleansing" operations to sort out those who had betrayed their fellow men and women in the face of government oppression. Also, the conception of a "warring spirit" has elicited mixed reactions.

The fourth role of the Holy Spirit in AIC theology and spirituality involves earthkeeping. In the post-Independence period in Zimbabwe, starting in 1980, AIC churches increasingly turned their attention to various projects, for example, the development of several church nurseries for exotic fruit and indigenous trees at or near prophetic church headquarters. The Holy Spirit's role was seen both in the liberation of the people from bondage and now from poverty and economic despair. The Holy Spirit's function as healer and life-giver encompassed everything relating to human well-being, including the healing and protection of crops. The practice of prophets diagnosing the illnesses of mother earth is one way AIC Christians live out the charismatic life. In recent years, some attempts have been made to develop a written theology of the environment from the perspective of African churches.

Clearly, these roles reveal an emphasis on the this-worldly dimension of the Spirit's work, despite a strong evangelistic orientation. Yet the cosmic dimension of the Spirit's work is not set over against the Spirit's role in personal salvation.

The Contextualized Spirit

Derek B. Mutungu has argued that on the basis of their alternative worldview, the Africans see spiritual and physical beings as real entities that interact with each other in time and space. These African Christians reject both the securalist worldview as well as missionaries' "Western" conceptions of reality and spirit. "Orthodoxy" has left Christians helpless in real life, and therefore, an alternative pneumatology is needed that can relate to needs other than those of a spiritual nature alone.[92]

There is no way to survey African pneumatologies without reference to the largest segment of the African churches and spirituality, namely, the Pentecostal/Charismatic movements. Even those churches that do not formally identify themselves with Pentecostal/Charismatic movements often reflect the kind of spirituality that has been associated with those movements.[93]

Allan H. Anderson of South Africa, who has for years studied the extremely complex phenomenon of African Pentecostalism, has argued that Pentecostalism has been capable of incorporating into its spirituality various kinds of local customs, beliefs, and rituals. African Pentecostalism is in constant interaction with the African spirit world much in the same way that Latin American Pentecostalism conceptually encounters folk Catholicism and Brazilian spiritism, and Korean Pentecostals have made use of shamanistic traditions in their culture.

Anderson contends that in Africa, the Pentecostal and Pentecostal-like movements manifested in thousands of indigenous churches have radically changed the face of Christianity simply because they have proclaimed a holistic gospel of salvation that includes deliverance from all types of oppression, such as sickness, sorcery, evil spirits, and poverty. This gospel has met the needs of Africans more fundamentally than the rather "spiritualized" and intellectualized gospel that was the legacy primarily of European and North American missionaries:

> All the widely differing Pentecostal movements have important common features: they proclaim and celebrate a salvation (or "healing") that encompasses all of life's experiences and afflictions, and they offer an empowerment which provides a sense of dignity and a coping mechanism for life, and all this drives their messengers forward into a unique mission.[94]

92. Derek B. Mutungu, "A Response to M. L. Daneel," in *All Together in One Place*, 127–31.

93. Allan H. Anderson, "Gospel and Culture in Pentecostal Mission in the Third World," unpublished paper presented at the 11th Meeting of European-Pentecostal Charismatic Association at Missionsakademi of the University of Hamburg, Germany, 13–17 July 1999. Anderson's main argument can be found in Allen H. Anderson and Walter J. Hollenweger, eds., *Pentecostals after a Century: Global Perspectives on a Movement in Transition* (Sheffield: Sheffield Academic Press, 1999). See also A. H. Anderson, *Bazalwane: African Pentecostals in South Africa* (Pretoria: University of South Africa, 1992).

94. Anderson, "Gospel and Culture," 11.

The Spirit's Power and Defetishism

Erhard Kamphausen, in a most creative and to some extent provocative study, explored the practice of "defetishisation" (a sort of purification) among Ghanaian Presbyterians. In his study, Kamphausen attempted to locate the practice of "purifying" market commodities among Ghanaian Presbyterians, most of whom are strongly charismatically oriented, in the context of African symbolism.[95]

As is well known, many preachers in Africa exhort Christians not to buy and consume market commodities without proper spiritual discernment and protection because these goods are believed to contain dangerous spiritual powers harmful to the users. The markets are understood as a scene in which products of unknown origins produced under the conditions of globalization are sold and bought, thus finding their way into the privacy of homes. Kamphausen believes that the prayerful act of purification is structurally similar to the concept of defetishisation practiced by the Christian missionaries when they encountered African tribal religions. Defetishisation was used to expose and denounce certain aspects of paganism controlled by evil spirits.

During the first half of the twentieth century, Ghanaian Christians equated Christianity with Western civilizations. The ability to buy and consume goods imported by missionaries and colonial traders was respected. Unfortunately, Ghana's economy experienced a most catastrophic downfall at the end of the 1980s as the number of Pentecostals increased dramatically. Pentecostals and Charismatics do not accept the established mainline churches' theology because they believe it is unable to provide prosperity and health. They interpret the real world as a spiritual battlefield where God and Satan are engaged in war. Accordingly, they believe that beneath the visible market is another market of spirits.

According to Kamphausen, the hermeneutical key to decoding this symbolic system seems to be the strange origin of Western commodities. Because of their strange origin, they are believed to cause damage. Pentecostal/Charismatic theology employs here the concept of commodities having a "cultural biography."[96] Instead of owning and controlling the commodities, the owner risks being possessed by goods of

95. Erhard Kamphausen, "Pentecostalism and De-Fetishism: A Ghanaian Case Study," unpublished paper presented at the 11th Meeting of European-Pentecostal Charismatic Association at Missionsakademi of the University of Hamburg, Germany, 13–17 July 1999.

96. Igor Kopytoff, "The Cultural Biography of Things: Commoditization as Process," *The Social Life of Things: Commodities in Cultural Perspective* (Cambridge: Cambridge University Press, 1986), 64ff.

foreign origin. Kamphausen compares this concept of "animated commodities" to the Marxist concept of *Warenfetischismus* (commodities
as fetish). Marx used the term *fetishism* to denounce the capitalist interpretation of commodities as autonomous subjects over against the
workers who produced them under alienated conditions of production.
For Marx, the commodities turned into fetishes at the very moment
that their true character as products of alienated labor was denied.

Contrary to the Marxist view, the Ghanaian Christians believe in the
transformation of commodities into "real" fetishes because of their
strange origin. Ghanaian preachers claim to reveal and uncover the
hidden "cultural biographies" of market goods by prayer and exorcism.
Kamphausen summarizes his study:

> It is of utmost importance to add, that the Pentecostal discourse does not
> only reveal the dangers inherent in commodities but also offers counter-
> measures and spiritual alternatives. By transforming human beings into
> vessels of the Holy Spirit born again believers are empowered to combat
> Satan and his diabolical following thus enabling them to change poten-
> tial fetishes into harmless items.[97]

In other words, the appeal of Pentecostal/Charismatic faith to Africans
struggling with the influence of spirits is understandable because of its
ability to speak directly to everyday issues and to provide needed spiritual resources.

This all-too-brief sample of various approaches to the study of the
Holy Spirit reveals that there is a need to connect theology to specific
contexts. Even though Christian theology is based on the revelation of
God, it is always lived out in specific times and places. One need not be
a prophet to say that the future of pneumatology lies to a large extent
in the emergence and proliferation of these new, fresh, contextual approaches, which also help traditional Western pneumatologies come to
terms with their strengths and weaknesses.

---

97. Kamphausen, "Pentecostalism and De-Fetishism," 19.

Epilogue

The Spirit is breath, not a full outline, and therefore he wishes only to breathe through us, not to present himself to us as an object; he does not wish to be seen but to be the seeing eye of grace in us, and he is little concerned about whether we pray *to* him, provided that we pray *with* him, "Abba, Father," provided that we consent to his unutterable groaning in the depths of our soul. He is the light that cannot be seen except upon the object that is lit up; and he is the love between Father and Son that has appeared in Jesus. He does not wish to be glorified but "to glorify me," by "taking what is mine and revealing it to you" (John 16:14), in the same way that the Son neither wishes nor is able to glorify himself but glorifies only the Father (John 5:41; 7:18).[1]

With these words the great Catholic pneumatologist, Hans Urs von Balthasar, reminds us of the distinctive feature of the "object" of pneumatology; in fact, in pneumatology, the Spirit, rather than being an object to be studied, is a Subject who grants us the needed, albeit necessarily limited, lenses to look at him. Indeed, rather than wishing to be seen, the Spirit is the "seeing eye of grace," in that sense the Third Unknown in the blessed Trinity whose distinctive task is to turn our eyes away from himself to the Son and through the Son to the Father.

Paraphrasing the paradoxical rule of Ludwig Wittgenstein, we have to acknowledge that even though there is little that we could say of the lofty "object" of our study, the Spirit, that which cannot be said is even more profound and meaningful. If ever the limitations of human lan-

---

1. Hans Urs von Balthasar, *Explorations in Theology*, vol. 3, *Creator Spirit* (1967; reprint, San Francisco: Ignatius Press, 1993), 111.

guage and theologizing can be easily acknowledged, it is in pneumatological study. This acknowledgment, of course, never stops us from saying something about that which is unutterable. It is similar to some
postmodern philosophers who first affirm that nothing meaningful can
be said and then set themselves the task of writing thick books about
that which nothing can be said!

There is something honorable and enlightening in the reservation of
the theologians of the first centuries to say too much about the Spirit.
It is not that their Spirit experiences were not vivid or that their theology could be constructed without references to the Spirit; this hesi-
tancy, most probably, was due to their respectful attitude toward the
Spirit. Even St. Augustine refrained from saying anything that had not
already been said by others, earlier doctors and fathers of the undivided church. Therefore, it is highly important that in our beholding
the things divine we should have "pneumatic eyes" and not exclusively
"(philo-)logical" eyes.[2]

Walking the path of the Spirit, even though it is a highly personal
journey, is essentially a communal event. We experience the Spirit in
relation to God and to fellow people. We receive the Spirit through the
church, which represents continuity with others who came before us.
As the bond of love, the Spirit unites us with the rest of the church, and
as the eschatological gift, with the purposes of God's coming new creation. Living as we are amidst a highly individualistic Western culture
that also imposes its values on the rest of the world, the Spirit experience challenges our self-made ghettos and inspires us to transcend
ourselves and reach out to others to receive and to give. Studying
pneumatologies of various persuasions—from the highly speculative
Hegelianism to mystical traditions of the Middle Ages to the charismatic enthusiasm of Montanism—not only humbles us with regard to
our limited yet authentic spirituality but also widens our horizons. In
a systematic survey, we never study history for its own sake but rather
to remind us of the fact that the place we are now has grown out of two
millennia of Christian reflection, based on the heritage of Israel's long
tradition.

Our survey of the emergence of the Spirit experience both in the biblical canon and in history revealed that from the beginning the approaches taken to the Spirit have been varied and often conflicting. The
very fact that even Scripture does not force a harmonizing between various approaches to pneumatology should alert us to the necessary pluralism of pneumatology; this is the thrust of Michael Welker's reflections on the Spirit. The ancient challenge of philosophy—One and yet

2. Ibid., 115.

Many—stands out in the doctrine and spirituality of the Spirit. The one Spirit of God opens himself into a myriad of experiences: the Eastern churches' vision of deification in the Spirit; the Pentecostal/Charismatic yearning for power in the Spirit; the Roman Catholic insistence on the infallibility of the church through the Spirit; the green pneumatologies' hope for the preservation of the earth by spiritual resources; the liberationists' dream of Spirit-wrought freedom; or the cry for equality of the womanist pneumatologies. Each of these, and many more, testify to the endless bounty and richness of the Spirit's agenda in God's creation.

Beholding what the Spirit is doing in the world sets us at the beginning of a path, a new path. New discoveries, new challenges, new potentialities await. It belongs to the nature of the Spirit, so Balthasar again reminds us, to bring forth new things, new insights, new life, because the very nature of the Spirit in his understanding points to the birth of new things. The love in which God is Father and the begotten is Son has two sides that resound in the distant echo of human love. Whereas father and son or mother and daughter love each other in the unity of their human nature, a man and a woman love one another in such a way that there arises from their union the unfathomable miracle of their common child. This child stands before her parents and all the world as evidence of the oneness of the two who gave her birth. The child bears the traits of both of them but in a way that represents a new, indivisible unity. Says Balthasar:

> As the unity of Father and Son, God is one single Spirit: i.e., the love that makes the Father a Father as the one who begets and the love that makes the Son a Son as the Word which expresses him are one single, concrete Spirit-being, and yet the divine Spirit as the "Third Person" comes from this fellowship as the miracle of eternal fruitfulness, not begotten by them both (as in the child by man and woman), but ineffably welling forth from the common "breath" *(pneuma)* of their mutual indwelling. Love in the absolute is the eternal miracle that remains a miracle to itself in all eternity, because it is logically incomprehensible that this ineffable element should continually come into being out of love, [and] that love should continually put forth fresh fulfillment between lovers.[3]

So the end of our survey concerning the Spirit of God is also a beginning for new discoveries. The most exciting thing about writing a text concerning pneumatology is that the very moment the book comes out, it already issues a call for a new text, a fresh interpretation of what the Spirit is doing.

3. Ibid., 106–7.

Bibliography

Biblical Studies

Barnett, Maurice. *The Living Flame: Being a Study of the Gift of the Spirit in the New Testament, with Special Reference to Prophecy, Glossolalia, and Perfection*. London: The Epworth Press, 1953.

Barrett, C. K. *The Holy Spirit and the Gospel Tradition*. London: SPCK, 1947.

Breck, John. *The Holy Spirit in Johannine Tradition*. Vol. 1, *The Origins of Johannine Pneumatology*. Crestwood, N.Y.: St. Vladimir's Seminary Press, 1991.

Del Colle, R. *Christ and the Spirit: Spirit Christology in Trinitarian Perspective*. Oxford: Oxford University Press, 1994. (Although this is a theological study, it also has a great deal of biblical material.)

Dunn, James D. G. *Baptism in the Holy Spirit*. London: SCM Press, 1970.

———. *Jesus and the Spirit*. London: SCM Press, 1975.

Ervin, Howard. *Conversion-Initiation and the Baptism in the Holy Spirit: An Engaging Critique of James D. G. Dunn's* Baptism in the Holy Spirit. Peabody, Mass.: Hendrickson, 1984.

Ewert, David. *The Holy Spirit in the New Testament*. Scottdale, Pa.: Herald, 1983.

Fee, Gordon. *God's Empowering Presence: The Holy Spirit in the Letters of Paul*. Peabody, Mass.: Hendrickson, 1994.

Gaffin, Richard B. *Perspectives on Pentecost: New Testament Teaching on the Gifts of the Holy Spirit*. Phillipsburg, N.J.: Presbyterian & Reformed, 1979.

Hamilton, Neil Q. *The Holy Spirit and Eschatology in Paul*. Edinburgh: Oliver & Boyd, 1957.

Hawthorne, Gerald F. *The Presence and the Power: The Significance of the Holy Spirit in the Life and Ministry of Jesus*. Dallas: Word, 1991.

Levison, John R. *The Spirit in First Century Judaism*. Leiden: E. J. Brill, 1997.

Martin, Ralph P. *The Spirit and the Congregation: Studies in 1 Corinthians 12–15*. Grand Rapids: Eerdmans, 1984.

Montague, George. *The Holy Spirit: Growth of a Biblical Tradition*. Peabody, Mass.: Hendrickson, 1994.

179

Penney, John M. *The Missionary Emphasis of Lukan Pneumatology*. Sheffield: Sheffield Academic Press, 1997.

Schatzmann, Siegfried. *A Pauline Theology of Charismata*. Peabody, Mass.: Hendrickson, 1987.

Schweizer, Eduard. *The Holy Spirit*. London: SCM Press, 1980.

Shelton, James B. *Mighty in Word and Deed*. Peabody, Mass.: Hendrickson, 1991.

Shepherd, William H. *The Narrative Function of the Holy Spirit as a Character in Luke-Acts*. Atlanta: Scholars Press, 1994.

Turner, Max. *Power from on High: The Spirit of Prophecy in Luke-Acts*. Sheffield: Sheffield Academic Press, 1996.

Historical Studies

Belval, Norman Joseph. *The Holy Spirit in St. Ambrose*. Rome: Officium Libri Catholici, 1971.

Burgess, Stanley M. *The Holy Spirit: Ancient Christian Traditions*. Peabody, Mass.: Hendrickson, 1984.

———. *The Holy Spirit: Eastern Christian Traditions*. Peabody, Mass.: Hendrickson, 1989.

———. *The Holy Spirit: Medieval Roman Catholic and Reformation Traditions*. Peabody, Mass.: Hendrickson, 1997.

Congar, Yves. *I Believe in the Holy Spirit*. 3 vols. New York: Crossroad Herder, 1997.

De Clerk, Peter, ed. *Calvin and the Holy Spirit: Papers and Responses Presented at the Sixth Colloquium on Calvin and Calvin Studies*. Grand Rapids: Calvin Studies Society, 1989.

Egert, Eugene. *The Holy Spirit in German Literature until the End of the Twelfth Century*. The Hague/Paris: Mouton, 1973.

McDonnell, Kilian, and George T. Montague. *Christian Initiation and Baptism in the Holy Spirit: Evidence from the First Eight Centuries*. Collegeville, Minn.: Liturgical Press, 1991.

Opsahl, Paul D., ed. *The Holy Spirit in the Life of the Church from Biblical Times to the Present*. Minneapolis: Augsburg, 1978.

Reid, H. M. B. *The Holy Spirit and the Mystics*. London: Hodder & Stoughton, 1925.

Stagg, Frank, E. Glenn Hinson, and Wayne E. Oates. *Glossolalia: Tongues Speaking in Biblical, Historical, and Psychological Perspective*. Nashville/New York: Abingdon Press, 1967.

Walsh, Christopher. *The Calabrian Abbot: Joachim of Fiore in the History of Western Thought*. New York: Macmillan, 1985.

Watkin-Jones, Howard. *The Holy Spirit from Arminius to Wesley*. London: Epworth, 1929.

———. *The Holy Spirit in the Medieval Church*. London: Epworth, 1922.

Williams, Charles. *The Descent of the Dove: A Short History of the Holy Spirit in the Church*. Grand Rapids: Eerdmans, 1939.

General Works on the Holy Spirit and Pneumatology

Balthasar, Hans Urs von. *Explorations in Theology*. Vol. 3, *Creator Spirit*. 1967. Reprint, San Francisco: Ignatius Press, 1993.

Barr, R., and Rena M. Yocum, eds. *The Church in the Movement of the Spirit*. Grand Rapids: Eerdmans, 1994.

Berkhof, Hendrikus. *The Doctrine of the Holy Spirit*. Atlanta: John Knox Press, 1964.

Bilaniuk, Petro B. T. *Theology and Economy of the Holy Spirit: An Eastern Approach*. Bangalore, India: Dharmaram Publications, 1980.

Boer, Harry R. *Pentecost and Missions*. Grand Rapids: Eerdmans, 1961.

Bruner, Dale. *A Theology of the Holy Spirit: The Pentecostal Experience and the New Testament Witness*. Grand Rapids: Eerdmans, 1970.

Bruner, Frederick D., and William Hordern. *The Holy Spirit: Shy Member of the Trinity*. Minneapolis: Augsburg, 1984.

Castro, Emilio, ed. *To the Wind of God's Spirit: Reflections on the Canberra Theme*. Geneva: World Council of Churches, 1990.

Coffey, David. *Grace: The Gift of the Holy Spirit*. Manly, Australia: Catholic Institute of Sydney, 1979.

Congar, Yves. *The Word and the Spirit*. London: Geoffrey Chapman, 1986.

Dewar, Lindsay. *The Holy Spirit and Modern Thought*. London: Mowbray, 1959.

Doctrine Commission of the Church of England. *We Believe in the Holy Spirit*. London: Church House, 1991.

Durrwell, F.-X. *Holy Spirit of God*. London: Geoffrey Chapman, 1986.

Fatula, Mary Ann. *The Holy Spirit: Unbounded Gift of Joy*. Collegeville, Minn.: Liturgical Press, 1998.

Gelpi, Donald L. *The Divine Mother: A Trinitarian Theology of the Holy Spirit*. Lanham, Md.: University Press of America, 1984.

Hazelton, Roger. *Ascending Flame, Descending Dove: An Essay on Creative Transcendence*. Philadelphia: Westminster, 1975.

Heron, Alasdair I. C. *The Holy Spirit*. Philadelphia: Westminster, 1983.

Hinze, B. E. "The Mission of the Holy Spirit in the Theology of Karl Rahner." Ph.D. diss., Marquette University, Milwaukee, Wisconsin, 1968.

Hodgson, Peter C. *Winds of the Spirit: A Constructive Christian Theology*. Louisville: Westminster John Knox, 1994.

Hunter, Harold D., and Peter D. Hocken, eds. *All Together in One Place: Theological Papers from the Brighton Conference on World Evangelization*. Sheffield: Sheffield Academic Press, 1993.

Jones, James W. *The Spirit and the World*. New York: Hawthorn Books, 1975.

Kärkkäinen, Veli-Matti. *Spiritus ubi vult spirat. Pneumatology in Roman Catholic-Pentecostal Dialogue 1972–1989*. Schriften der Luther-Agricola-Gesellschaft 42. Helsinki: Luther-Agricola Society, 1988.

Küng, Hans, and Jürgen Moltmann, eds. *Conflicts about the Holy Spirit*. New York: Seabury Press, 1979.

Kuyper, Abraham. *The Work of the Holy Spirit*. Grand Rapids: Eerdmans, 1973.

Lacey, Thomas Alexander. *The One Body and One Spirit: A Study in the Unity of the Church*. London: James Clarke, 1920.

Lampe, Geoffrey W. H. *God as Spirit*. Oxford: Clarendon Press, 1977.

Latourelle, Rene. *The Miracles of Jesus and the Theology of Miracles*. New York: Paulist Press, 1988.

Lawler, Michael G., and Thomas J. Shanahan. *Church: A Spirited Communion*. Collegeville, Minn.: Liturgical Press, 1995.

Maloney, George A. *The Spirit Broods over the World*. New York: Alba House, 1993.

McIntyre, John. *The Shape of Pneumatology*. Edinburgh: T & T Clark, 1997.

McKenna, John H. *Eucharist and Holy Spirit: The Eucharistic Epiclesis in the Twentieth Century (1900–1966)*. London: SPCK, 1975.

Mills, Edward. *The Holy Spirit: A Bibliography*. Peabody, Mass.: Hendrickson, 1988.

Moltmann, Jürgen. *The Church in the Power of the Spirit: A Contribution to Messianic Ecclesiology*. New York: Harper & Row, 1977.

———. *A New Theology of Creation and the Spirit of God.* San Francisco: Harper & Row, 1985.

———. *The Source of Life: The Holy Spirit and the Theology of Life.* Minneapolis: Fortress Press, 1997.

———. *The Spirit of Life: A Universal Affirmation.* Translated by Margaret Kohl. Minneapolis: Fortress Press, 1992.

Newbigin, James Edward Lesslie. *The Holy Spirit and the Church.* Madras: Christian Literature Society, 1972.

O'Carroll, Michael. *Veni Creator Spiritus: A Theological Encyclopedia of the Holy Spirit.* Collegeville, Minn.: Liturgical Press, 1990.

Olson, Alan. *Hegel and the Spirit: Philosophy as Pneumatology.* Princeton: Princeton University Press, 1992.

Pope John Paul II. *Celebrate 2000! Reflections on the Holy Spirit: Weekly Readings for 1998.* Selected and arranged by Paul Thigpar. Ann Arbor, Mich.: Servant Publications, 1997.

———. *On the Holy Spirit: An Encyclical Letter of the Supreme Pontiff, John Paul II.* Shebrooke, Quebec: Editions Paulines, 1986.

Prenter, Reginald. *Spiritus Creator: Studies in Luther's Theology.* Trans. John M. Jensen. Philadelphia: Muhlenberg, 1953.

Rahner, Karl. *The Dynamic Element in the Church.* New York: Herder & Herder, 1964.

———. *Experience of the Spirit: Source of Theology.* Theological Investigations 16. New York: Crossroad, 1981.

———. *Spirit in the World.* 1939. Reprint, New York: Herder & Herder, 1968.

Rayan, Samuel. *Breath of Life: The Holy Spirit, Heart of the Gospel.* London: Geoffrey Chapman, 1979.

Rosato, Philip J. *The Spirit as Lord: The Pneumatology of Karl Barth.* Edinburgh: T & T Clark, 1981.

Staniloae, Dimitru. "The Holy Spirit in Theology and Life of the Orthodox Church." *Sobornost* 7, no. 1 (1975): 4–21.

Stylianopolis, Theodore, and Mark Heim. *The Spirit of Truth: Ecumenical Perspectives on the Holy Spirit.* Brookline, N.Y.: Holy Cross Orthodox Press, 1986.

Taylor, John V. *The Go-Between God: The Holy Spirit and the Christian Mission.* London: SCM Press, 1972.

Thielicke, Helmut. *The Evangelical Faith.* Vol. 3, *The Holy Spirit, the Church, Eschatology.* Grand Rapids: Eerdmans, 1982.

Thomas, W. H. Griffith. *The Holy Spirit of God.* Grand Rapids: Eerdmans, 1973.

Tillich, Paul. "Life and the Spirit." In *Systematic Theology.* Vol. 3. Chicago: University of Chicago Press, 1963.

Tsirpanlis, Constantine N. *Introduction to Eastern Patristic Thought and Orthodox Theology.* Theology and Life Series 30. Collegeville, Minn.: Liturgical Press, 1991.

Vandervelde, George, ed. *The Holy Spirit: Renewing and Empowering Presence.* Winfield, B.C.: Wood Lake Books, 1988.

Van Dusen, Henry P. *Spirit, Father, and Son: Christian Faith in the Light of the Holy Spirit.* New York: Scribner's, 1958.

Vischer, Lukas, ed. *Spirit of God, Spirit of Christ: Ecumenical Reflections on the Filioque Controversy.* London: SPCK; Geneva: WCC, 1981.

Volf, Miroslav. *Work in the Spirit: Toward a Theology of Work.* New York/Oxford: Oxford University Press, 1991.

Welker, Michael. *God the Spirit.* Translated by John F. Hoffmeyer. Minneapolis: Fortress Press, 1994.

Specialized and Contextual Pneumatologies

Anderson, Allan H. *Moya: The Holy Spirit from an African Perspective.* Pretoria: University of South Africa, 1994. (African Pentecostal theology)

Ashby, Geoffrey. "The Spirit and Wisdom: Thoughts Arising from the Charismatic Movement in South Africa." *Sobornost* 7, no. 2 (1975): 89–98. (African theology)

Boff, Leonardo. *Church, Charism, and Power.* New York: Crossroad, 1985. (Latin American liberation theology)

Chung, H. K. "Welcome the Spirit; Hear the Cries: The Holy Spirit, Creation, and the Culture of Life." *Christianity and Crisis* 51 (1991): 220–23. (Asian feminist and ecological theology)

Comblin, Joseph. *The Holy Spirit and Liberation.* Maryknoll, N.Y.: Orbis, 1989. (liberation theology)

Griffin, David. "Holy Spirit: Compassion and Reverence for Being." In *Religious Experience and Process Theology: The Pastoral Implications of a Major Modern Movement.* New York: Paulist Press, 1976. (process theology)

Johnson, Elisabeth. *She Who Is: The Mystery of God in Feminist Theological Discourse.* New York: Crossroad, 1992. (feminist theology)

———. "Who is the Holy Spirit?" *Catholic Update* (June 1995): 1–4.

———. *Women, Earth, and Creator Spirit.* New York/Mahwah, N. J.: Paulist Press, 1993.

Jongeneel, Jan A. B. et al., eds. *Pentecost, Mission, and Ecumenism: Essays on Intercultural Theology.* Frankfurt am Main: Peter Lang, 1992. (intercultural, charismatic, ecumenical theology)

Ma, Wonsuk. "Toward an Asian Pentecostal Theology." *Asian Journal of Pentecostal Theology* 1 (1998): 15–41.

McFague, Sallie. "Holy Spirit." In *Dictionary of Feminist Theologies.* Edited by L. M. Russell and J. S. Clarkson. Louisville: Westminster John Knox Press, 1996. (feminist theology)

———. *Models of God: Theology for an Ecological, Nuclear Age.* Philadelphia: Fortress, 1987. (ecotheology/green theology)

Müller-Fahrenholz, Geiko. *God's Spirit: Transforming a World in Crisis.* New York: Continuum, 1995. (political theology)

Reynolds, Blair. *Toward a Process Pneumatology.* London: Associated University Presses, 1990. (process theology)

Wallace, Mark I. *Fragments of the Spirit: Nature, Violence, and the Renewal of Creation.* New York: Continuum, 1996. (ecotheology/green theology)

Pentecostal/Charismatic Theologies and Pneumatologies

Bittlinger, Arnold, ed. *The Church Is Charismatic: Renewal and Congregational Life.* Geneva: World Council of Churches, 1981.

Burgess, Stanley M., and Gary B. McGee, eds. *Dictionary of Pentecostal and Charismatic Movements.* Grand Rapids: Zondervan, 1988.

Christenson, Larry. *A Charismatic Approach to Social Action.* Minneapolis: Bethany House, 1974.

———, ed. *Welcome Holy Spirit: A Study of Charismatic Renewal in the Church.* Minneapolis: Augsburg, 1987.

Hamilton, Michael P., ed. *The Charismatic Movement.* Grand Rapids: Eerdmans, 1975.

Hocken, Peter. *Glory and Shame.* Guilford, Surrey, U.K.: Eagle, 1994.

———. *One Lord, One Spirit, One Body.* Gaithersburg, Md.: Word Among Us, 1987.

Hollenweger, Walter J. *Pentecostalism: Origins and Developments Worldwide.* Peabody, Mass.: Hendrickson, 1997.

Kraft, Charles. *Christianity with Power.* Ann Arbor, Mich.: Servant Publications, 1989.

Land, Steven J. *Pentecostal Spirituality: A Passion for the Kingdom.* Sheffield: Sheffield Academic Press, 1993.

Lederle, Henry I. *Treasures Old and New: Interpretation of "Spirit Baptism" in the Charismatic Renewal Movement.* Peabody, Mass.: Hendrickson, 1988.

McDonnell, Kilian. *Charismatic Renewal and Churches.* New York: Seabury Press, 1976.

———. *Charismatic Renewal and Ecumenism.* New York: Paulist Press, 1978.

———, ed. *The Holy Spirit and Power: The Catholic Charismatic Renewal.* Garden City, N.Y.: Doubleday, 1975.

———, ed. *Presence, Power, Praise: Documents on the Charismatic Renewal.* 3 vols. Collegeville, Minn.: Liturgical Press, 1980.

McDonnell, Kilian, and Arnold Bittlinger. *The Baptism in the Holy Spirit as an Ecumenical Problem.* Notre Dame: Charismatic Renewal Service, 1972.

McDonnell, Kilian, and George T. Montague. *Christian Initiation and Baptism in the Holy Spirit: Evidence from the First Eight Centuries.* Collegeville, Minn.: Liturgical Press, 1991.

Muhlen, Heribert. *A Charismatic Theology: Initiation in the Spirit.* London: Burns & Oates, 1978.

Ruthven, Jon. *On the Cessation of the Charismata: The Protestant Polemic on Postbiblical Miracles.* Sheffield: Sheffield Academic Press, 1993.

Smail, Thomas. *Reflected Glory: The Spirit in Christ and Christians.* Grand Rapids: Eerdmans, 1975.

Smail, Thomas, Andrew Walker, and Nigel Wright. *Charismatic Renewal: The Search for a Theology.* London: SPCK, 1993.

Spittler, Russell P., ed. *Perspectives on the New Pentecostalism.* Grand Rapids: Baker, 1976.

Stephanou, Eusebius. *The Charismatic Renewal in the Orthodox Church.* Fort Wayne, Ind.: Logos, 1976.

Suenens, Léon Joseph, and Dom Helder Camara. *Charismatic Renewal and Social Action: A Dialogue.* Malines Documents 3. Ann Arbor, Mich: Servant Publications, 1979.

Suurmond, Jean-Jacques. *Towards a Charismatic Theology.* Grand Rapids: Eerdmans, 1995.

White, John. *When the Spirit Comes in Power.* Downers Grove, Ill.: InterVarsity Press, 1985.

Williams, J. Rodman. *Renewal Theology: Systematic Theology from a Charismatic Perspective.* 3 vols. Grand Rapids: Zondervan, 1988–1992.

Wilson, Mark W., ed. *Spirit and Renewal: Essays in Honor of J. Rodman Williams.* Sheffield: Sheffield Academic Press, 1994.

Subject Index

action, 155
adoption, 86
"affective redemption," 151
African Instituted Churches (AIC), 148, 170
African pneumatologies, 148, 170–74
Albrecht, Daniel, 91
allegory, 151
Anabaptists, 55–57, 91
Anderson, Allan H., 172
animals, 27
anointing, 34, 71
anonymous Christians, 116–17
Anselm of Canterbury, 48
antinomians, 83
apocalyptic literature, 36
Apollonius of Ephesus, 41–42
Aquinas, Thomas, 19, 48, 97
Aristotle, 138, 164
asceticism, 70
Assemblies of God, 90
Athanasius, 12, 20, 43, 70, 121, 152
atonement, 153
Augustine, 16, 18, 38, 46–48, 49, 70, 80, 81, 82, 83, 152–53, 166, 176
Avircius Marcellus, 41n. 17
Azusa Street Mission, 87

Badcock, Gary, 63
Balthasar, Hans Urs von, 175, 177
baptism, 71, 97–98, 107, 132

formula, 44
in the Spirit, 32, 88, 93, 94–98
Baptism, Eucharist, and Ministry, 103
Barrett, David, 89n. 109
Barth, Karl, 13, 61, 63–64, 97, 117, 127, 135, 141
Basil, 12, 20, 43, 44, 69, 70, 71, 162
Benevolence, Spirit as, 82
Bennett, Dennis, 88
Bergson, Henri, 148
Berkhof, Henrikus, 17n. 23
Bermejo, Luis, 166
Bernard of Clairvaux, 51–52, 143
Bethel Bible School (Topeka, Kansas), 87
Bible
    authority of, 56
    inspiration of, 36
biblical theology of the Spirit, 21, 133
bifurcationalism, 150
biology, 119
bishops, 39–40
body, 28, 94, 128, 169
Bonaventure, 53–54
breath, 23, 82, 161
Burgess, Stanley, 45

Calvin, John, 153
Cappadocian fathers, 37, 44, 69, 152
categorical revelation, 113
Catherine of Siena, 54–55
Catholic base communities, 131, 155

185

Scripture Index